Analysis and Visualization of Citation Networks

Synthesis Lectures on Information Concepts, Retrieval, and Services

Editor
Gary Marchionini, *University of North Carolina, Chapel Hill*

Synthesis Lectures on Information Concepts, Retrieval, and Services publishes short books on topics pertaining to information science and applications of technology to information discovery, production, distribution, and management. Potential topics include: data models, indexing theory and algorithms, classification, information architecture, information economics, privacy and identity, scholarly communication, bibliometrics and webometrics, personal information management, human information behavior, digital libraries, archives and preservation, cultural informatics, information retrieval evaluation, data fusion, relevance feedback, recommendation systems, question answering, natural language processing for retrieval, text summarization, multimedia retrieval, multilingual retrieval, and exploratory search.

Analysis and Visualization of Citation Networks
Dangzhi Zhao and Andreas Strotmann

ISBN:978-3-031-01163-4   print
ISBN: 978-3-031-02291-3   ebook

DOI 10.1007/978-3-031-02291-3

A Publication in the Springer series
SYNTHESIS LECTURES ON INFORMATION CONCEPTS, RETRIEVAL, AND SERVICES #39
Series Editor: Gary Marchionini, University of North Carolina, Chapel Hill

Series ISSN   1947-945X Print   1947-9468 Electronic

Analysis and Visualization of Citation Networks

Dangzhi Zhao
School of Library and Information Studies, University of Alberta, Canada

Andreas Strotmann
ScienceXplore, Bad Schandau, Germany

SYNTHESIS LECTURES ON INFORMATION CONCEPTS, RETRIEVAL, AND SERVICES #39

ABSTRACT

Citation analysis—the exploration of reference patterns in the scholarly and scientific literature—has long been applied in a number of social sciences to study research impact, knowledge flows, and knowledge networks. It has important information science applications as well, particularly in knowledge representation and in information retrieval.

Recent years have seen a burgeoning interest in citation analysis to help address research, management, or information service issues such as university rankings, research evaluation, or knowledge domain visualization. This renewed and growing interest stems from significant improvements in the availability and accessibility of digital bibliographic data (both citation and full text) and of relevant computer technologies. The former provides large amounts of data and the latter the necessary tools for researchers to conduct new types of large-scale citation analysis, even without special access to special data collections. Exciting new developments are emerging this way in many aspects of citation analysis.

This book critically examines both theory and practical techniques of citation network analysis and visualization, one of the two main types of citation analysis (the other being evaluative citation analysis). To set the context for its main theme, the book begins with a discussion of the foundations of citation analysis in general, including an overview of what can and what cannot be done with citation analysis (Chapter 1). An in-depth examination of the generally accepted steps and procedures for citation network analysis follows, including the concepts and techniques that are associated with each step (Chapter 2). Individual issues that are particularly important in citation network analysis are then scrutinized, namely: field delineation and data sources for citation analysis (Chapter 3); disambiguation of names and references (Chapter 4); and visualization of citation networks (Chapter 5). Sufficient technical detail is provided in each chapter so the book can serve as a practical how-to guide to conducting citation network analysis and visualization studies.

While the discussion of most of the topics in this book applies to all types of citation analysis, the structure of the text and the details of procedures, examples, and tools covered here are geared to citation network analysis rather than evaluative citation analysis. This conscious choice was based on the authors' observation that, compared to evaluative citation analysis, citation network analysis has not been covered nearly as well by dedicated books, despite the fact that it has not been subject to nearly as much severe criticism and has been substantially enriched in recent years with new theory and techniques from research areas such as network science, social network analysis, or information visualization.

KEYWORDS

citation analysis, citation network analysis, citation data sources, disambiguation in citation analysis, visualization of citation networks, co-citation analysis, bibliographic coupling analysis, bibliometrics

Contents

Acknowledgment

The authors would like to thank Dr. Howard D. White for his encouragement, input, and feedback on our draft manuscript.

Dedications

Dangzhi Zhao would like to dedicate this book to her father who passed away when this book was under revision, to her mother, and to her family. She feels fortunate and grateful to have loving parents and family who provided compassion, care, and support during one of the most difficult times in her life so that she was able to continue writing this book.

Andreas Strotmann would like to dedicate the book to his mother who passed away before it started forming but always believed it would come one day.

CHAPTER 1

Foundations of Citation Analysis

1.1 INTRODUCTION

Citation analysis is a well-known technique that has long been applied in a variety of research fields to study, among others, knowledge flows, the diffusion of ideas, intellectual structures of science, relevance of information resources, and evaluation of researchers and research institutions. Among the research fields that have employed citation analysis methods, sociology, history of science, library and information science, management science, and research policy are the most prominent. Together with citation indexing and citation linking, citation analysis also provides the foundations for effective information retrieval that, applied to web links, was at the core of the success of Google's search engine.

Recent years have seen a burgeoning interest in citation analysis to help address various research, management, or information service issues such as university rankings, research evaluation, and knowledge domain visualization. This renewed interest is a result of the increasingly available digital citation data and computer power that have made large-scale citation analysis studies possible, and has resulted in many exciting new developments in data sources, as well as techniques and tools for citation data collection, analysis, and visualization.

This chapter introduces the concepts of citation and citation analysis, examines the assumptions underlying citation analysis, and provides an overview of what can be done with citation analysis (and why), as well as a discussion of strengths and weaknesses of citation analysis and cautions required when applying citation analysis. Based on this overview, the scope and structure of this book are then discussed at the end of this chapter.

1.2 WHAT IS CITATION ANALYSIS?

The reference list in a research paper is an essential part of the paper. By pointing to prior publications that have influenced the research reported in the current paper in one way or another, the references link the current paper to these prior publications and, by extension, to the global network of research publications. It is generally assumed that a citation represents the citing author's use of the cited work, and indicates an influence of the cited work on the author's new work, and as such a flow of knowledge from the cited to the citing works' authors. Citations also indicate relatedness (e.g., similar subject matter or methodological approach) between these two works.

Citation analysis deals with the study of these uses and relationships. Although individual uses and relationships can be useful to examine, citation analysis mostly provides macro perspectives through the use of large datasets, exploiting the consensus among a large number of citing authors regarding the influence of and the relationships between scholars and scholarly works.

Based on the basic assumption underlying citation analysis that references indicate usefulness or relatedness, a number of different types of applications of citation analysis have been developed and employed over the years in the study of science and scholarly communication. The basic assumption itself, however, has also been challenged in the literature. We will begin by discussing applications of citation analysis before moving on to examine criticisms and challenges.

Here we need to be careful about the terminology. It is common for the term *citation* to be used interchangeably for either "citation" or "reference," with the context providing the meaning. Similarly, the concept of how authors make references is called either *citing behavior* or *referencing behavior*. When article A makes a reference to article B, it is often said that A cites or references B, and B is cited by, receives a citation from, or is one of the "cited references" in A. In essence, a reference from article A to article B is a citation received by B from A.

Both the terms "citation" and "reference" are of course also used in other contexts that do not directly relate to citation analysis. In the field of library and information studies, for example, the term "reference librarians" refers to librarians who answer users' questions regarding the use of the library and library resources; similarly, citation data or databases may mean the same as bibliographic data or databases, which normally only include information about the citing documents such as title, author, abstract, etc., and may or may not include any information about their cited references at all.

1.3   WHAT CAN WE DO WITH CITATION ANALYSIS, AND WHY?

In general, citation analysis can effectively assist in the discovery of new knowledge, and in the management and use of existing knowledge resources (Garfield, 1979; Swanson, 1986; Small, 1999b; White et al., 2000). In particular, citation analysis can be used for:

1. assessing information resources and evaluating scholarly contributions,

2. mapping research fields to study their intellectual structures,

3. tracking knowledge flows and the diffusion of ideas,

4. studying users and uses of scholarly literature, and

5. assisting with information organization, representation, and retrieval.

All these applications of citation analysis rely on the consensus among a large number of citing authors regarding the influence of and relationships between scholars and scholarly works as recorded in the reference lists of these authors' publications. Some areas, however, e.g., applications 3, 4, and 5, also often involve the examination of individual reference links.

This section will review and discuss these applications of citation analysis, as well as some other uses of citation analysis in the study of science and scholarly communication, including patent citation analysis for the study of innovations and sociometric studies of science and scholarly communication.

1.3.1 ASSESSING INFORMATION RESOURCES AND EVALUATING SCHOLARLY CONTRIBUTIONS

It is assumed that the existence of a cited document in a reference list implies its use by the citing author when the citing document was written. And as Peritz (1992, p. 448) points out, since "it is generally accepted that the publication of research papers is part of the reward system in science and hence that citations are, in some sense, tokens of recognition," the number of citations a paper receives "can be used as a rough-and-ready indicator of its merit—granting, of course, variations in the citation's importance and the inevitable amount of error and noise." Similarly, and on a broader scale, the number of citations received by all publications in a journal or in a subject area, or by all publications written by a scholar or all scholars in a scientific institution or in a nation, roughly indicates the impact of the journal, the scientist, the scientific institute, etc. Therefore, citation analysis is considered a legitimate and meaningful research tool in the assessment of information resources and in the evaluation of scholarly contributions. This type of citation analysis is sometimes referred to as *evaluative citation analysis* (Borgman and Furner, 2002).

Although the assumptions underlying evaluative citation analysis noted above have been challenged since their introduction (which will be discussed later in this chapter), citation analysis has been widely used in research evaluation to inform decisions that may seriously affect individuals or institutions (Garfield, 1979; Meho and Sonnenward, 2000; Moed, 2010). For example, the Journal Impact Factor, which is essentially the average number of citations received by all articles published in a journal within a time period (e.g., 2 or 5 years), has been used by university librarians to make journal subscription decisions, and by university management to estimate the quality of journals in which professors publish for the evaluation of their research performance; and the citation impact of individual scholars has been used to inform decisions on their hiring, tenure, promotion, and research funding. Furthermore, most of the world university ranking systems that emerged in recent years and have had profound impact on universities (especially regarding recruitment), such as the Times Higher Education (THE) World University Rankings and the Academic Ranking of

World Universities (also known as the Shanghai Ranking), use citation analysis to measure research impact as one of the indicators for ranking (THE Methodology, 2013; Liu and Cheng, 2005).

It is therefore imperative to address the various issues involved in evaluative citation analysis that affect citation counts and, by extension, the fairness of citation-based research evaluation. Although counting citations or calculating impact indicators derived from citation counts (e.g., h-index) is relatively simple, addressing the complicating factors (such as field differences in publishing and citing behavior and problems of citation data sources in coverage and indexing) is not, and has therefore been a primary focus of research on evaluative citation analysis. For an in-depth examination of these issues, readers are referred to Moed (2010), who provides a comprehensive treatment of evaluative citation analysis. Discussions in some later chapters in this book will also shed light on some of these issues, such as data sources for citation analysis, research field delineation, and counting collaborative works in citation analysis.

1.3.2   MAPPING RESEARCH FIELDS

Mapping research fields through citation analysis can help with the organization of knowledge, and also allows researchers to examine the characteristics, structures, and evolution of research fields and scholarly communities.

As Cronin (1984, p. 25) so eloquently stated, "Citations are frozen footprints on the landscape of scholarly achievement." They represent the decisions made by citing authors regarding relatedness (e.g., with respect to similarities in the subject, topic, or methodology) of the documents they were writing (i.e., the citing documents) and the works they decided to reference in it (i.e., the cited documents). Therefore, by mapping the networks of literatures at some moment in time through an analysis of the relationships established by citations in scholarly publications that represent a scientific specialty and community, the structures and characteristics of such a specialty and community can be studied. By making comparisons between time periods, the historical development of the specialty and community can be modeled. In this book, we use the term "citation network analysis" to refer to this type of citation analysis.

In citation network analysis, a set of objects (documents, authors, journals, or groups of them) is selected to represent a research area, the strengths of the interrelationships (or levels of connectedness) between these objects are measured by various scores derived from citation counts, and structures and characteristics of the corresponding research fields and scholarly communities are then inferred from these relationships. To reveal the structures that underlie these relationships, multivariate statistical analyses are often applied using the citation scores as similarity measures. Since a spatial representation of information, as Small (1999b, p. 799) points out, can "facilitate our understanding of conceptual relationships and developments," network visualization tools are also frequently used to produce visual maps of these relationships. All these measures, analyses, and visualizations together will then inform interpretive descriptions and explanations of the observed structures and characteristics of the research fields and scholarly communities being studied, and assist in the examination of their evolution and "in the making of inductive predictions of future trends" when applied to a series of time periods (Borgman and Furner, 2002, p. 11).

Depending on the units of analysis (documents, or groups of them by authors, journals, research field, nation, etc.) and the thresholds of citation scores, both macro-structures—overall maps of the entire science endeavor with each node in the network representing a discipline—and micro-structures—structures of a single specialty with each node in the network representing a single document—of science can be mapped and studied, allowing the user to get overviews of research fields as well as to explore their underlying fine structures (Small, 1999b).

There are three types of commonly used citation-based measures of the strength of the interrelationship between two objects:

- *inter-citation counts:* the number of times two objects have cited each other

- *co-citation counts:* the number of documents that have cited two objects together, and

- *bibliographic coupling frequencies (BCFs):* the number of cited references that two objects have in common.

Analyses using these measures are correspondingly called *inter-citation analysis*, *co-citation analysis*, and *bibliographic coupling analysis*, respectively. Each type of analysis can employ any one of a number of different counting and weighing schemes. For example, the BCF of two articles can be counted simply as the number of items that appear in both articles' reference lists or their cited references can be weighted by how many times they are cited in the texts. Such counting and weighing schemes will be discussed in detail in Chapter 2.

Among the three types of analyses, co-citation analysis is the most commonly used technique. It is generally accepted that the co-citation concept was discovered independently by Small (1973) and Marshakova (1973), and that document co-citation analysis was introduced by Small (1973) and author co-citation analysis by White and Griffith (1981). Many co-citation analysis studies have been conducted since. They either refine the techniques (Small, 1974; Shaw, 1985; Zhao and Strotmann, 2008a), explore the application of co-citation analysis in studying various research areas and in answering various research questions (Small, 1977, 1981; White, 1983; McCain, 1984), or discuss limitations of the techniques (Sullivan et al., 1977; Hicks, 1987). Recent years have also seen studies of the application of advanced scientific visualization technology in co-citation mapping to dynamically present maps of science (see Small, 1999b and Boyack et al., 2005 for a good review). As a result, co-citation analysis has developed into a well-known literature-based technique for studying the intellectual structure of scholarly fields and the characteristics of scholarly communities.

The assumptions underlying citation network analysis are (1) when two documents cite each other often, are frequently cited together, or have many references in common, then this indicates that these two documents are related, that is, generally perceived to be similar in subject matter or methodological approach; and (2) the more frequently two documents cite each other, are co-cited, or the more references two documents have in common, the more closely they are related (Borgman, 1990; White, 1990). These assumptions are generally valid and have not been challenged much at all, unlike those for evaluative citation analysis, as even when parties who are affected by citation-based research evaluation do game the system by manipulating their reference lists in their favor, the less relevant citations they may add will still be related to the citing documents.

1.3.3   TRACKING KNOWLEDGE FLOWS AND THE DIFFUSION OF IDEAS

Knowledge flows and the diffusion of ideas can be traced through citations because a citation informs the reader of the citing author's use of the cited document that contains that knowledge and those ideas (Rogers and Cottrill, 1990). Of course, they can also be tracked through terminology, especially after the knowledge and ideas have been integrated into larger contexts.

Citations are considered concept symbols, in that a citation has a function in the text to link an idea or concept with the source of that idea or concept, i.e., the publication in which that idea or concept was addressed (Small, 1978, 1998; Small and Greenlee, 1980). By analyzing how the publication has been used in later documents, it is therefore possible to trace the spread of the ideas it contains across disciplinary boundaries as well as over time (McCain, 2011).

In order to do so, a single work or a small set of works "representing a coherent and clearly defined topic of interest, such as the original statement of a theory, description of a research methodology, or first articulation of an important concept or other significant contribution" (McCain, 2011) is first identified. All of the citations to this set of works are then collected, and their distribution by subject area as well as by time can then be studied.

This type of citation analysis has been carried out from the very start of citation analysis studies, but relatively more rarely than other types of citation analysis (McCain, 2011). Borgman (1990, p. 20) provides some examples of the ideas traced through citations including the "double helix" (Winstanley, 1976), Shannon's information theory (Dahling, 1962), and topics relevant to psychiatry originating in related fields (Davis, 1970). McCain (2011, p. 1413) reviews some more recent studies of this kind:

> … Oehler (1990) traced citations to a set of 29 articles in general equilibrium theory and noted the citation counts in non-social science journals (e.g., natural sciences, mathematics, statistics, and engineering.) O'Rand (1992) studied the diffusion of cooperative game theory and used the spread of citations to *The Theory of Games and Economic Behavior* (von Neumann and Morgenstern, 1944) across disciplinary boundaries to support discussion of

the development of various research schools in psychology, sociology, and political science. McCain and Salvucci (2006) examined the relative use of concepts in Brooks' *Mythical Man-Month* (Brooks, 1975) across five time periods and 15 subject areas ranging from the "home" discipline of software engineering to areas in the social science, humanities, and law. Sarafoglou and Paelinck (2008) used citation data to study the diffusion of the concept/field of "spatial econometrics" by means of, in part, the temporal and subject distribution of citations to the key book in the field—*Spatial Econometrics: Methods and Models* (Anselin, 1988). Garfield (1985) reported "over 80 specialties and disciplines" citing Price's *Little Science, Big Science* (Price, 1963). In a more theoretical vein, Van der Veer Martens and Goodrum (2006) discuss the use of citation content and context analysis along with other assessment approaches to model the diffusion of eight theories in the social sciences. They suggest a typology of citation function but do not consider citing subject breadth.

1.3.4   STUDYING USERS AND USES OF SCHOLARLY INFORMATION

The information behavior of scientists and engineers has been of great interest to LIS researchers, and interviews and surveys have comprised the primary sources of data for their studies (Brown and Ortega, 2005; Brown, 2007, 2010; Hemminger et al., 2007). Citation analysis can enhance results from these types of studies by providing a different perspective on people's information behavior gleaned from their citing behavior.

A citation represents a citing author's use of a cited document. An examination of all the references made by a group of authors can therefore reveal an important aspect of their information behavior, i.e., what scholarly information they have used in the development of their own scholarly publications. Details can be determined about how often information of different types (e.g., journals, books, e-resources), years, languages, countries, and subjects have been used by this group of authors, and how this group compares with other groups of people in terms of these uses.

For example, by comparing the types of references made by all students who have taken a certain course (e.g., bibliographical instruction or how to use an academic library) before and after they took the course, the effect of this course on students' information-seeking behavior can be measured (Brunvand and Pashkova-Balkenhol, 2008; Cooke and Rosenthal, 2011; Reinsfelder, 2012). Similarly, the differences in research by faculty and practitioners in a field can be studied by comparing what they cite and how they are cited. For example, Zhao (2009) compared the intellectual structure of LIS through an author co-citation analysis of research publications by LIS faculty and practitioners. Interestingly, and contrary to what one may have expected, the study found, among others, that LIS practitioners cite theories and foundations more than LIS faculty do. By extension, uses of scholarly information by users of a research library indicated by citations can be compared with the library's collections, and results can be used to measure the extent to which library collections meet the needs of its users (Kayongo and Helm, 2012).

Also by examining uses of scholarly information indicated by citations, the interactions and interdisciplinarity of disciplines, fields, journals, institutions, or authors' oeuvres can be assessed (Zitt and Bassecoulard, 2006; Bassecoulard et al., 2007). For example, Huang and Chang published two articles in 2012 that classified citations made in LIS journals during the period of 1978–2007 in terms of their disciplines in order to study the interdisciplinary characteristics of LIS (Chang and Huang, 2012; Huang and Chang, 2012). They found that LIS articles have cited documents from across 30 disciplines, and the degree of interdisciplinarity of LIS measured by a number of citation-based indicators was high. Clearly, this type of citation analysis is similar to but different from the study of knowledge flows as discussed in the previous section.

1.3.5 ASSISTING INFORMATION ORGANIZATION, REPRESENTATION, AND RETRIEVAL

It has been a tradition in scientific writing for writers to acknowledge each other by giving citations to related work. Citations represent the decisions made by citing authors regarding the relationships (e.g., similarity in the subject, topic, or methodology, etc.) between the documents they are writing (citing document) and the work they are about to cite (cited document). Following citation links has been proven to be a unique and effective way of finding related literature because the relevancy is judged by the authors of citing papers who are domain experts (rather than an indexer who is often a librarian by training), and documents can be located independent of language, keywords, and traditional knowledge classifications, which is of great value particularly for researchers in interdisciplinary fields. This way of organizing and retrieving information has been made easier and more efficient by creating "actionable" or "clickable" citation links that lead from references to the full text articles they represent, thanks to Web technologies and to collaborations among the various parties in the scholarly publishing enterprise, such as scientific publishers, libraries, and producers of bibliographical databases including citation databases. *CrossRef* and *OpenURL* were examples of such technology or collaboration (Hitchcock et al., 1997; Hitchcock et al., 2000; Van de Sompel and Beit-Arie, 2001).

Citation databases are bibliographical databases with citation indexes in addition to standard indexes such as authors, keywords, and subject headings. Citation indexes record and organize reference links in such a way as to allow easier and larger-scale navigation through scientific literature following citation links. With a citation index, it is possible to follow citation links both backward from current articles to older ones they cite (like following reference links at the end of an article) and forward from older articles to newer ones. Users can start with a seed paper, author, journal, or combination of these, and retrieve all publications written by them, cited by them, and/or citing them, which is a very effective method of information retrieval.

Citation databases also support easier and larger-scale collections of data for citation analysis. The results of citation analyses can in turn further assist information organization, representation, and retrieval.

For example, evaluative citation analysis results can help retrieve highly influential documents or publications by influential players (authors, institutes, countries, etc.), while citation network analysis results can facilitate an understanding of the structure of the research field and the relationships between concepts, documents, or authors. This understanding in turn helps users with query expansion and search refinement, as well as supports visual browsing interfaces to information retrieval systems (Chen, 1999; Chen et al., 1998a; Chen et al. 1998b; Ding et al., 2000; Lin et al., 2003; Strotmann and Zhao, 2008).

The two largest citation databases, the ISI databases by the Institute for Scientific Information (now part of Thomsen Reuters' Web of Science) and Scopus by Elsevier, have demonstrated the value of incorporating citation analysis results into information retrieval systems by providing impact indicators (e.g., citation counts, h-index, and journal impact factor) for articles, authors, and journals, calculated from evaluative citation analyses of data in the corresponding citation databases. Search results can be ranked by impact indicators, allowing users to focus on high impact sources. They also provide related documents based on bibliographic coupling analysis. The ISI databases also provide a visual representation of citation links both backward and forward, allowing users to follow these links to retrieve needed information.

Because citation analysis can identify key concepts, documents, authors, and their relationships, studies have also explored the use of citation analysis methods to supplement traditional manual methods of knowledge organization with automatic summarization, categorization, and thesaurus construction and maintenance (Chen et al., 2010; Fiszman et al., 2009; Sparck-Jones, 1999; Schneider and Borlund, 2004). As Birger Hjørland (2013, p.1) points out, "the main difference between traditional knowledge organization systems (KOSs) and KOSs based on citation analysis is that the first group represents intellectual KOSs, whereas the second represents social KOSs" as they are based on the collective views of a large number of citing authors regarding relationships between documents or their authors.

With the amount of available information increasing dramatically and sometimes chaotically, especially on the Web, it has been and will continue to be of great importance to explore appropriate ways of organizing and searching information there. Citation analysis principles provide unique and effective ways of enhancing information organization, representation, searching, and browsing. A good example for this is the success of the Google Web search engine which applies an algorithm that has close ties to citation analysis to focus on resources that are both high quality and relevant to users' information needs (Brin and Page, 1998).

1.3.6   OTHER APPLICATIONS

Over the years, citation analysis has been used widely and in innovative ways. Although most uses fall within the categories discussed above, some applications have distinct places in the study of science and scholarly communication. The following are two such examples.

Patent citation analysis

What makes patent citation analysis special in the area of citation analysis is not the types of analyses being performed but the data used, i.e., patent documents and their references.

Patents are a major representation of innovations in science and technology, and patent citation analysis is thus used to study innovation-related phenomena. Examples include the effect of a major innovative technology (as represented by a high-impact patent) on the science on which it draws or on the industry to which it belongs, as well as the networks of key players in its industry, including who has contributed to the technology and who is using it. Particularly when combining patent and science citation analyses, the interaction or relationship between science, technology, and innovations can be studied (Sternitzke, 2009; Érdi et al., 2013; Etzkowitz and Leydesdorff, 2000).

It is important to note, however, that the meaning of a patent citation differs considerably from that of a scholarly citation. While scholarly citation represents influence on a work, a patent citation represents prior art or prerequisite technology. In principle at least, anyone who licenses a patent will need to license the technologies in the cited patents as well. As this is likely to reduce the monetary value of the patent, inventors tend to try and avoid citing patents other than their own, and patent examiners play a crucial role in completing patent references. Clearly, it is important to include references provided by both the patent applicants and the examiners in patent citation analysis.

Unlike citation data for scholarly publications, patent citation data are publicly available and can be obtained from the websites and databases of patent offices such as the United States Patent and Trademark Office (http://patft.uspto.gov/netahtml/PTO/search-bool.html) and the European Patent Office (http://worldwide.espacenet.com). Retrieval and processing of patent citation data from these sites is considerably more complex than that of scholarly citation data from the standard citation indexes; however, commercial versions of patent databases and Google Scholar provide more usable access.

The value of citation analysis in sociometric studies of science and scholarly communication

Although the present book will not examine sociometric analyses, the value of citation analysis in sociometric studies of scholarly communication will be briefly discussed here to show the full power of citation analysis.

Sociometric studies of scholarly communication seek to reveal the structures of informal communication in specific scholarly communities by looking at interpersonal interactions among scholars regarding their research, emphasizing the social properties of scholarly communication (Lievrouw, 1990).

Citation analysis can aid sociometric studies in identifying scholarly communities or specialties (De May, 1982, p. 130), which is the first step in all sociometric studies of scholarly communication. Citation analysis can help with recognition of interesting points in the structure and process of scholarly communication that are worthy of further study by sociometric or other methods (Crane, 1972; Mullins, 1973; Mullins et al., 1977; Lievrouw et al., 1987). Furthermore, citation analysis can be used to validate the results from sociometric data, because people who respond to interviews or surveys in sociometric studies are usually a subset of people whose citation behaviors are studied by citation analysis (Borgman, 1990).

1.4   EVALUATION OF CITATION ANALYSIS

With the many problems in citation data, citation analysis is an imperfect yet very useful method for studying knowledge flows, the diffusion of ideas, social and intellectual structures of science, information resources, and research evaluation.

This section covers problems and criticisms that have been discussed over the years, reasons why citation analysis is a reliable and valid approach despite the problems and criticisms, and cautions that are required when citation analysis is applied.

1.4.1   VALIDITY AND RELIABILITY

As mentioned earlier, there are two basic assumptions underlying citation analysis: (1) A citation represents the citing author's use of the cited work. The more citations a document receives, the more influence it has had on research. Evaluative citation analysis examines the evaluation of scholars, journals, institutions, etc., based on this assumption. (2) A citation indicates some relationship between citing and cited works, i.e., a generally perceived similarity of subject matter or methodological approach. Two articles being cited together often or having many references in common indicates some relation between these two articles. The more frequently two documents are co-cited or the more references two documents have in common, the more closely they are assumed to be related. Citation network analysis examines structures of literatures and disciplines based on this assumption.

Other types of citation analysis are essentially variations of these two basic types of analysis. For example, citation counts have been used as an indicator of the extent of the diffusion of scientific discoveries, and citation links have been used for information representation and retrieval.

Most types of citation analysis are informed by Merton's normative view of science (Griffith, 1990; MacRoberts and MacRoberts, 1989; Edge, 1979; Cronin, 1984; Peritz, 1992), which sees science as a social activity governed by a set of norms. These norms include *universalism* (the impersonality of science), *communism* (scientific knowledge is treated as a common good communicated and distributed freely), *disinterestedness* ("science for science's sake" [Cronin, 1984, p. 17]), and *organized skepticism* (new knowledge claims are evaluated critically and objectively based on empirical or theoretical evidence (Merton, 1942)). Citation is considered to be a serious activity of science and therefore citation behavior is also governed by a set of norms and values. These norms and values require authors to cite the works that have influenced them in the development of current papers in order to give credit where credit is due. Although they may not always be clear why they cite certain works at certain times and how citations are related to the ideology of science—"the norms and values presupposed in the conduct of science" (Trancy, 1980, p. 191)—authors share "a tacit understanding of how and why they should acknowledge the works of others" (Cronin, 1984).

The normative view of science is compatible with the assumptions underlying citation analysis, and therefore makes it possible to conduct valid citation analysis.

However, it has been observed by many studies that scientists' behavior does not *always* adhere to the norms, and that, in terms of citation behavior, various reasons and motivations for citing do exist—some normative, some egotistical. A number of articles have reviewed these studies, including Bornmann and Daniel (2008), Cronin (1984), Liu (1993), Nicolaisen (2007), and White (2010a).

The observed departure of scientists' behavior from the norms and the existence of egotistical citations do not invalidate citation analysis for several reasons.

First, the failure of scientists to observe norms strictly does not necessarily mean a violation of norms. Norms are standards "that are not rigidly defined or precisely restricted to a single specific behavior. They are far too deeply embedded to be easily legislated into a code of ethics for science or to be taken out for daily discussion and assessment. Private and consensual discomfort is the usual response to violations of norms and is also important indicators of their presence" (Griffith, 1990, p. 35).

Second, most scholars do adhere to the norms, and citation analysis is based on the *collective* perceptions of citing authors. As Small (1976) observes, "the reasons and motivations for citing appear to be as subtle and as varied as scientific thought itself, but most references do establish valid conceptual links between scientific documents" (p. 67). Individual citations may be made for various reasons that do not conform to the norms ("egotistical citations" in Borgman and Furner's (2002) words), but the number of such citations is not likely to become large enough to influence conclusions of citation analysis because most subsequent writers do not recurrently see the same influence or relation implied by such citations (White, 1990). Therefore, the accrual of citations or co-citations indicates a consensus among a large number of citing authors regarding the influence of and the relationships between scholars and scholarly works. Citation analysis, which is concerned with "achieving a macro perspective on scholarly communication process through the use of voluminous datasets" (Borgman, 1990, p. 26), relies on this consensus to draw conclusions in evaluation of scholarly contributions and in mapping of intellectual structures, rendering the "psychological approach" (White, 1990) that is concerned with the motives and purposes of individual citations largely irrelevant.

Third, numerous validation studies of citation analysis provide evidence that the assumptions underlying citation analysis are statistically valid. There are many empirical studies that test and verify the validity of citation analysis by various methods. Garfield (1979, p. 241) mentions several validation studies of citation analysis as an evaluation tool in his book *Citation Indexing*, including Carter (1974), Bayer and Folger (1966), and Virgo (1977), that show the high correlations between citation counts and peer judgments, a widely accepted way of ranking scientific performance. White (1990, pp. 101–102) summarizes some validation studies of co-citation analysis including Mullins et al. (1977), Sullivan et al. (1980), and Sullivan et al. (1977), which established the usefulness of article co-citation mapping despite its limitations; and Keen (1987), Lenk (1983), McCain (1986), White and Griffith (1981), and White (1983), which validate results from author co-citation analysis using various validation approaches. McCain (1986) categorizes validation studies of co-citation results by validation methods used, showing that most studies demonstrate a high correlation between results from citation analysis and those from other sources, although in some cases a lack of correlation was observed. Borgman (1990) stresses the importance of comparing the research objectives or motives when comparing results from citation analysis and those based on other types of data such as sociometric data and interview data in validity studies. In many cases, the lack of correlation between the results is because they are measuring different domains of scholarly communication (formal vs. informal), or they are looking at the same phenomena at different levels (micro-level vs. macro-level, or "ground level" vs. "aerial view") or different time points (citation analyses reveal pictures of several years back due to the lag in publication, while interviews provide current pictures) (White, 1990, pp. 91, 100).

Citation analysis is not only valid but also has high reliability because the data can be collected unobtrusively from readily accessible published records of scholarly communication and thus can be easily replicated by others. According to Borgman (1990, p. 25), reliability problems "generally can be identified and corrected by careful researchers," although they do exist in individual data sources (Moed and Vriens, 1989; Rice et al., 1989).

1.4.2 CRITIQUES AND DEFENSE

Critiques of citation analysis (notably Edge, 1979; MacRoberts and MacRoberts, 1989) have focused on the assumptions underlying citation analysis, and on the sources of citation data

(Osareh, 1996). Defenses (notably Garfield, 1979; White, 1990) have focused on the irrelevance of the (individual-scale) psychological approach to (large-scale statistical) citation analysis and on the illogic of "quarrelling with imaginary opponents" (White, 1990, p. 91). The following is a brief discussion of these critiques and defenses. Detailed discussions can be found in the studies referenced above and in review articles on bibliometrics or citation analysis such as White and McCain (1989), White (2010a), and Nicolaisen (2007).

Critics of the assumptions either have mixed up the "aerial" and "ground-level" views of citations as discussed above, or are quarrelling with an imaginary opponent (White, 1990, p. 91). They claim that citation analysis researchers have made certain assumptions that are problematic, but in fact the assumptions are rarely found in citation analysis studies (Borgman, 1990; White, 1990). They question some other assumptions based on the existence of individual egotistical citations, missing the view that citation analysis is meant for large datasets and macro perspectives, where small numbers of individual misconduct are mere statistical noise to be filtered out by statistical means.

For example, although studies (e.g., Mullins et al., 1977; Small, 1977; McCain, 1986) show that personal communication ties often do exist among frequently co-cited authors and that the structure of the literature is congruent with the social structure of the field producing it, citation researchers do not take this as a given; instead, they only assume that the relationship is "generally perceived similarity of subject or methodological approach in published and cited works," and stress the independence of establishing social relationships that may exist among highly co-cited authors (White, 1990, p. 96). The only assumption underlying evaluative citation analysis that Garfield, the inventor of citation index and citation analysis, made in his monograph on citation indexing theory and application is that citation counts represent the perceived utility or impact of scientific work as determined by the corresponding scientific community (Garfield, 1979).

The problems with the sources of citation data include those that are characteristic of all sources of citation data and those introduced by using citation databases. Some of the former include the difficulties in counting citations caused by homonyms (two or more different individuals having the same name), allonyms (a single individual having more than one name), implicit citations, self-citations, and errors in citations. Some of the latter include the limited and biased coverage of citation databases and the problems caused by inadequate indexing of cited references (see Smith, 1981 and MacRoberts and MacRoberts, 1989, for detailed discussions of these problems).

As an imperfect method, citation analysis does suffer from the problems of sources of citation data. Even Garfield admits these problems while he refutes almost all the critiques of the validity of citation analysis in his systematic examination of citation analysis as an evaluation tool (Garfield, 1979). However, remedies often can be used to correct the data. For example, two solutions for distinguishing individuals in the case of homonyms are proposed by Garfield (1979, pp. 243–244): examining the titles of the journals in which the cited work and the citing work were published, and obtaining a complete bibliography of the individual being evaluated. Various other methods have also been suggested, such as using author affiliation information to reduce problems caused by homonyms and allonyms, and using multiple or alternative data sources to alleviate problems introduced by individual citation databases (Zhao and Logan, 2002; Zhao and Strotmann, 2014b). In fact, recent years have seen an increased interest in addressing problems in citation data with the advances in text processing and other technologies (e.g., Boyack et al., 2013; Ding et al., 2013; Hou et al., 2011; Jeong et al., 2014; Zhu et al., 2014). We therefore include separate chapters on citation data sources (Chapter 3) and on name disambiguation (Chapter 4).

In summary, regardless of the problems in citation data and the existence of egotistical citations, citation analysis has been demonstrated to be a unique and valid method for evaluating scholarly contributions and for studying intellectual structures. Garfield (1979, p. 250) considers citation analysis "a valid form of peer judgment that introduces a useful element of objectivity into the evaluation process and involves only a small fraction of the cost of surveying techniques." Arunachalam (1998, p. 142) stresses that "citation analysis is an imperfect tool but which one could still use with some caveats to arrive at reasonable conclusions of different levels of validity and acceptability." It is generally accepted that citation analysis is most useful when it is used in combination with other methods such as interviews, surveys, and sociometric studies, and for people who are knowledgeable in the fields being studied (Borgman, 1990; Garfield, 1979).

1.4.3   STRENGTHS, LIMITATIONS, AND SPECIAL CARE REQUIRED

Major strengths of citation analysis are its unobtrusiveness, objectivity, low cost, and reliability (Harter and Kim, 1996; Smith, 1981). As Smith (1981, pp. 84–85) explains:

> … citations are attractive subjects of study because they are both unobtrusive and readily available. Unlike data obtained by interview and questionnaire, citations are unobtrusive measures that do not require the cooperation of a respondent and that do not themselves contaminate the response (i.e., they are nonreactive). Citations are signposts left behind after information has been utilized and as such provide data by which one may build pictures of user behavior without ever confronting the user himself. Any set of documents containing reference lists can provide the raw material for citation analysis, and citation counts based on a given set of documents are precise and objective.

The limitations of citation analysis in the study of science and scholarly communication have been extensively discussed in the literature (e.g., Garfield, 1979; MacRoberts and MacRoberts, 1989; White, 1990; White and McCain, 1989), including the following:

1. Citation analysis results are potentially inaccurate and/or biased due to the problems of citation data and citation databases used as data sources.

2. Citation analysis has a strong dependence on subject experts—people who are knowledgeable in the fields being studied by citation analysis—in interpretations of results as well as in research field delineation.

3. Citation analysis results are only as good as the analyst's choice of authors or documents being analyzed as well as the analytical tools used.

4. Citation analysis results are never "up to the minute" because it takes time for the documents it analyzes to publish and the cited references they include are even older.

5. Writing, citing, and publishing behavior varies significantly with research fields and scholarly communities (e.g., mathematics vs. biomedicine), making cross-field comparisons difficult, especially in research evaluation.

6. Citation analysis is only applicable in the study of formal aspects of scholarly communication represented in research publications, and when inferring informal communication ties and social relationships from the formal communication structures revealed by citation analysis, other types of data are often required to confirm or further study the relationships inferred.

7. Citation counts and the scores derived from them measure the impact rather than the quality of research cited, making its usefulness in evaluation of scholarly contributions limited. While impact is closely related to quality, citation impact can be affected by many other factors. For example, review articles tend to have higher citation impact simply because their wider coverage makes them relevant to more articles than articles reporting individual studies; and research that is easy to understand and follow tends to be cited more than more difficult research simply because ease of comprehension is a major determinant of popularity.

It is important to take advantage of its strengths and to work around the limitations when designing a citation analysis study and when interpreting citation analysis results.

Problems of citation data and citation databases need to be addressed and alleviated as much as possible by, e.g., going beyond citation databases when collecting data and performing disambiguation in processing citation data. Subject experts should be consulted as much as possible throughout the process, especially for field delineation and interpretation of results. Field-normalized indicators should be devised and used when making comparisons across research (sub)fields (e.g., percentiles and citation counts normalized by field average), and research fields should be carefully delineated.

In fact, every step of citation analysis needs to be carefully designed and thought out, from field delineation, through selection of objects (e.g., authors, documents) being examined and of analytical tools used, to analyzing results and drawing conclusions (see Chapter 2 for details).

For example, when applying statistical procedures and visualization tools (e.g., MDS) to show high-dimensional relationships between objects in two or three dimensions, information is lost and pictures may be distorted; one needs to be careful to draw conclusions regarding the relationships between two objects based on their positions on a two-dimensional map because being close to each other may be an artifact of the tools and procedures. Only features that remain stable with different algorithms, procedures, or tools can be used to draw conclusions. For example, in a factor analysis of co-citation data with an oblique rotation, usually the layout of the visual representation of the structure matrix remains stable while that of the pattern matrix changes with each redrawing of the map using Pajek; the structure map was therefore used to study the interrelationships of authors and author groups, and the pattern matrix was only used to show the grouping of authors (Zhao and Strotmann, 2008a; 2008b; 2008c; 2014a).

Problematic assumptions and overgeneralization in conclusions should be avoided, such as attempts to equate citation impact to research quality, intellectual connections to social relationships, or *one view* gained from current data and methods to *the view* of the field being studied.

For example, citation analysis using data from the ISI databases cannot provide a fair comparison between North America and other parts of the world because of their biased coverage in the favor of English-speaking countries, thus the many criticisms of the *THE* university rankings in which the top-ranked universities have always been American or British (Rauhvargers, 2011; van Leeuwen et al., 2001); while the overall structure of a research field being citation analyzed remains robust, details do change depending on how the fields are delineated and how citations are counted, suggesting that citation analysis should only be used to obtain aerial views of research fields (Leydesdorff, 2008; Zhao, 2009).

Further understanding of above-mentioned approaches to working around limitations of citation analysis can be gained from discussions in later chapters on citation data sources, field delineation, disambiguation, citation counting of collaborated works, and visualization of citation networks.

1.5   RELATED FIELDS

Citation analysis is one of the two major parts of bibliometrics, defined by Fairthorne (1969, p. 319) as "the quantitative treatment of the properties of recorded discourse and behaviour appertaining to it" for the study of science and scholarly communication, with the other major part being publication analysis.

The term "bibliometrics" is used interchangeably with scientometrics and informetrics, but with slight difference in scope and focus. Webometrics (or Cybermetrics), which emerged with the Web in recent years, applies, often with modifications, citation analysis, and other well-established principles and techniques from bibliometrics to the study of the characteristics and link structures of the Web. For example, Ingwersen (1998) introduced Web Impact Factor as a criterion for the evaluation of websites just as the Journal Impact Factor has been used for the evaluation of journals; sitation analysis, coined by Rousseau (1997), is a Web-based counterpart of citation analysis, which considers hyperlinks to and from other websites as "bibliographical citations" in traditional citation analysis; classic bibliometric laws, such as Bradford's Law, Lotka's Law, and Zipf's Law, have also been tested on the Web (Cui, 1999; Egghe, 2000; Rousseau, 1997). White (2010b) provides a gloss on the differences among bibliometrics, scientometrics, informetrics, and webometrics.

Bibliometrics and Webometrics also interact with network science and Web science, which have emerged recently (Börner et al., 2008; Zhao and Strotmann, 2014a). Network science is a multi-disciplinary research field concerned with the analysis of all types of large and complex systems that can be modeled as networks. Citation analysis (especially citation network analysis) and Webometrics have been substantially influenced by, and also influenced, network science, as seen from leading researchers in these fields citing each other. The interdisciplinary field of Web Science aims to consolidate a wide range of research views of the Web—both as a communication technology and as a complex system of social and cognitive spaces which emerge from its ubiquitous presence. The study of the social Web is naturally part of Web Science, as well as of Webometrics.

Citation analysis is related to content analysis and discourse analysis through citation context analysis, which examines the context in which each citation is made in the text (White, 2010a; Zhang et al., 2013). Citation network analysis has applied techniques from social network analysis, as well as from co-word analysis and text mining. While some social network analysis techniques that have been applied in citation network analysis will be discussed in later chapters, readers are referred to other resources for a thorough treatment of social network analysis as applied to scholarly communication networks and to information science (e.g., Börner et al., 2008; Otte et al., 2002; White, 2011).

1.6   SCOPE, DELIMITATION, AND STRUCTURE OF THIS BOOK

The following chapters of this book will discuss citation analysis in the context of citation network analysis, which is one of the two main types of citation analysis (with the other being evaluative citation analysis). While the discussion of many topics (e.g., field delineation, citation data sources, name disambiguation, and collaboration in science) applies to all types of citation analysis, the structure and details (e.g., procedures, examples, and tools) are built around citation network analysis. In other words, topics specific to citation network analysis (e.g., visualization of citation networks) are covered in detail, but those specific to other types of citation analysis (e.g., research evaluation) are not.

This choice was based on the following considerations:

• Although evaluative citation analysis has attracted much of the attention and money, there have been many criticisms of this type of citation analysis, and many of the issues involved are difficult to address. Citation network analysis, on the other hand, has not been criticized much at all, and has started to gain increased attention in recent years as large-scale citation network analysis has become increasingly feasible, interesting, and important with the emerging disciplines of network science and Web science.

• Citation network analysis has been applying new techniques from several research areas such as network science, social network analysis, and information visualization. By contrast, evaluative citation analysis, which essentially ranks documents, authors, institutions, nations, etc., by their citation counts or scores derived from citation counts, is relatively easy to conduct, allowing less room for new techniques, which can be seen from the "h-bubble": the research community on evaluative citation analysis moved immediately and almost completely to a focus on the h-index once this "clever find" was made in 2005 as a simple way to measure individual scientists' lifetime achievements (Rousseau et al., 2013, p. 294; Zhao and Strotmann, 2014a). It appears that research in this area was waiting for breakthrough ideas on the one hand, and was feeling the pressures of a huge demand for practical tools for research evaluation on the other.

• There are already several well-perceived books dedicated to evaluative citation analysis (e.g., Andres, 2009; De Bellis, 2009; Garfield, 1979; Moed, 2010), but almost none to citation network analysis.

This book will first present the general steps and procedures of citation network analysis and the concepts and techniques associated with each step (Chapter 2), which will simultaneously provide an overview of the theoretical aspects of citation network analysis and also a practical how-to guide for conducting citation network analysis studies. This is followed by more detailed discussion of thoughts and ideas about important issues in citation analysis in general and in citation network analysis in particular, with a focus on those with which the authors have substantial personal experiences, including the following:

• field delineation and data sources for citation analysis (Chapter 3),

• disambiguation of names and references (Chapter 4), and

• visualization of citation networks (Chapter 5).

There are two types of access to citation databases as data sources for citation analysis: the regular one via the search interfaces (e.g., Web of Science and Scopus) provided by these companies (e.g., Thomson Reuters, Elsevier) to retrieve and download datasets from these citation databases, and a very expensive special direct access to all the database files provided by the citation database providers for data-mining purposes. The former is usually through a subscription to these databases with a more or less standard license agreement that prohibits mass downloads and imposes other limits on their use, while the latter can only be accessed through a negotiated purchase contract. Discussions of citation databases in this book are based on the experience of the authors with the "normal" type of access to citation databases, and therefore discussions related to access (e.g., indexing and search facilities, downloading options) may or may not apply to the special type of access.

In addition, as is well understood, citation databases can serve as both information retrieval systems and citation analysis tools. Discussions in this book on citation databases are in the context of citation databases as data sources for citation analysis, although these discussions may also have implications for the enhancement of their retrieval functions.

Finally, the term "ISI databases" was chosen in this book to refer to the oldest and most dominant citation databases, which were created by the Institute for Scientific Information (ISI) in the 1960s, and include three databases: Science Citation Index, Social Science Citation Index, and Arts and Humanities Citation Index. These databases have now become part of the core collection of Thomson Reuters' Web of Science, which also includes a few other citation databases (e.g., book and conference citation indexes) that have not reached the same level of quality as the ISI databases to be used much for citation analysis purposes. In addition to the core collection, Web of Science also includes a number of other bibliographic databases such as MEDLINE that do not have citation indexes and therefore cannot be used for citation analysis purposes. To avoid confusion, the term "Web of Science" is only used in this book when more than the ISI databases are concerned and discussed or when the context clarifies the meaning.

CHAPTER 2

Conducting Citation Network Analysis: Steps, Concepts, Techniques, and Tools

A citation indicates that the cited document is related to the citing document in some way (e.g., similarity in the subject, topic, or methodology) perceived by the citing author. The collective view of a large number of citing authors regarding the relationships between documents represented by citations, that is the *citation networks*, can therefore be analyzed to study the intellectual structures of research fields, and to inform knowledge organization and information retrieval. By making comparisons between time periods, the historical development of research fields can be studied, and knowledge organization systems (e.g., thesauri) can be updated. These are concerns of citation network analysis (Borgman and Furner, 2002).

A fairly consistent sequence of steps has been developed for conducting citation analysis network analysis (McCain, 1990b; Zhao, 2003). In a nutshell, a set of objects (documents, authors, journals, or groups of them) representing a research area is selected, the strengths of their interrelationships (or levels of connectedness) are measured by various scores derived from citation counts, and the structures and characteristics of the corresponding research fields are then inferred from these relationships. In order to reveal the underlying structures of these relationships, multivariate statistical analyses are often applied using the citation scores as similarity measures, and network visualization tools are used to produce visual maps of these relationships.

Specifically, citation network analysis studies follow six steps:

1. Delineation of the research field being studied: collecting a complete and clean set of scholarly publications produced in this field,

2. Selection of core sets of objects representing this research community,

3. Measures of connectedness between objects in the core sets,

4. Multivariate statistical analysis,

5. Network analysis and visualization, and

6. Interpretation of results and validation.

This chapter discusses in detail these steps and associated concepts, techniques, and tools, and concludes with an actual citation network analysis study that demonstrates how to follow these steps and how to use some of the techniques discussed. This chapter thus both provides a theoretical understanding of citation network analysis and serves as a practical how-to guide for conducting citation network analysis studies.

2.1   FIELD DELINEATION: COLLECTING SCHOLARLY PUBLICATIONS PRODUCED IN A RESEARCH FIELD OR BY A SCHOLARLY COMMUNITY

A citation network analysis study is usually concerned with structures and characteristics of a certain research field or scholarly community during a certain time period. Depending on the research problems being investigated, the time period can range from a single year to all years during which the research field has existed. Similarly, research fields or scholarly communities can be defined in different ways and the size can vary from all of science to a single small specialty (Small, 1999a). Examples include a nation (e.g., Spain), a discipline (e.g., Information Science), a university department (e.g., the physics department of the University of Alberta), research output from tri-council grants in Canada (i.e., research funded by grants from the three Canadian national research granting agencies), a journal (e.g., *Journal of Documentation*), a specialty (e.g., knowledge management research, or all researchers who have studied the game theory), or a group of these (e.g., G20 countries, or top N journals in field x).

The first step in a citation analysis study, therefore, is to collect a set of citing papers (along with their reference lists) to represent a defined research field or scholarly community within a specified time period (which is called the *citation window*). The subsequent analyses are then based on these citing authors' collective view of the intellectual relationships in their research field as recorded in the reference lists of their publications. Clearly, these are views of the insiders, i.e., researchers in the research field being studied.

Of course, while insiders' views are often the most relevant and desired, especially with respect to the study of intellectual structures of research fields using citation network analysis, studies do not need to be limited to these views when it comes to the evaluation of research impact that can go beyond the research field being studied. In that case, the collective view of all scholars who have cited works in the research field being studied are used to study the field, which means that it would still be necessary to collect a set of papers representing the research field being studied. These papers would then serve as cited papers rather than citing papers in the subsequent analyses.

The ideal situation would thus be to include all publications produced in this research field being studied within the time period concerned. As long as relatively robust techniques are to be employed in the subsequent analyses, the practical approach, however, is to sample a subset of these publications to represent this research field. How to ensure that the sample well represents the scholarly community being studied, at least for the purpose of addressing the research problems under investigation, is itself an unsolved research problem in citation analysis—the "field delineation" problem.

A commonly used approach is to search a citation database such as the ISI databases or Scopus and use the search results to represent the research field being studied. Search results from a citation database normally include detailed information about each of the citing papers, basic information about the cited references, and, most importantly for citation analysis, citation links, i.e., information about which papers cited which other papers. Combinations of citation databases and standard bibliographical databases to overcome some of the limitations of citation databases for field delineation purposes have also been used for citation analysis.

The retrieval strategies for collecting data for citation analysis are dictated by the citation databases used, and are mostly limited to searching for a set of keywords, or a set of names (e.g., journals, authors, institutions, or countries), or a combination of the two.

For example, if the scholarly community being studied is the Information Science research field, we can identify a set of core journals in this field, search each of the journal names in the ISI databases or Scopus, and use the search results as the dataset, i.e., all articles published in these journals (White and McCain, 1998; Zhao and Strotmann, 2008a; 2008b; 2014a). If a comparison of the physics department between two universities in terms of their research profiles is to be carried out, one approach to collecting the citation data is to first identify the names of the faculty members in these two departments, and then search these names in the ISI databases or Scopus as "author name." The search results, i.e., all publications in the ISI databases or in Scopus that are written by all faculty members in these two departments, then become the dataset for citation analysis. If the diffusion of ideas is to be studied, a dataset needed for the study can be achieved by searching the "cited reference" field in the ISI databases or Scopus for a single or a small set of articles in which the ideas were first presented.

Care is required to ensure that the search results are as complete and as clean as possible, meaning that all relevant *but only* relevant documents are retrieved. For example, it is a well-known problem in citation analysis that authors may publish under different names (e.g., maiden and married names) or different authors may have the same names. This problem often needs to be addressed in citation analysis studies, at least to some extent and for highly cited authors that one wishes to examine more closely. That means that articles retrieved from searching an author name that are written by other authors with the same name should be identified and removed, and that all names under which an author has published should be searched and results added to the dataset.

The "field delineation" problem, as well as commonly used citation databases for and approaches to field delineation will be discussed in detail in Chapter 3. Name disambiguation will be further examined in Chapter 4.

As a final note here, another method is in principle possible for field delineation using major citation databases (Boyack and Klavans, 2011a; Boyack et al., 2005): all records in the ISI databases or Scopus within a citation window (e.g., 3-year) are first clustered into research fields and specialties and their relationships mapped out based on bibliometric measures of the relatedness between the records (e.g., bibliographic coupling frequency, discussed in detail later in this chapter); the cluster(s) corresponding to the research field to be delineated can then be picked out and used for further study. An advantage of this method could be that one can delineate both the field itself and its immediate vicinity in the science landscape, to allow the study of both the internal structure of the field and its connections to closely related fields. Needless to say, this method is available only to the few people in the world that have access to such a dataset and to the computational power for processing such large datasets.

2.2   SELECTING CORE SETS OF OBJECTS FOR THE STUDY

The dataset collected from the previous step can then be processed to either calculate the network features and create visualizations directly from the entire dataset, or extract small sets of core objects to examine further and more closely, depending on the size of the dataset and the research questions being addressed.

The advances in computer power and in technologies for network analysis have made network analysis on large datasets possible as well as interesting. For example, Boyack et al. (2005) analyzed the citation networks of the entire ISI databases within selected citation windows, and produced a map of the entire research enterprise. The same research team then went on to evaluate the structure of the chemistry research field over a period of thirty years using computational scientometrics (Boyack et al., 2009).

However, those large-scale network analyses are still beyond the capacity of regular social science researchers, either to conduct them or to make sense of their results, and are limited in terms of the types of research questions that can be addressed using citation analysis methods. Therefore, this section will focus on studies that examine smaller significant sub-networks of the dataset collected at the previous step, i.e., citation networks of core objects (documents, authors, journals, etc.). The features of the entire network can only be inferred from these sub-networks. It is therefore very important to select core objects properly.

2.2.1   SELECTION CRITERIA

Core objects should be representative, although they may not be "wholly definitive," of the research field being studied (White and McCain, 1998, p. 332), with respect to the research questions being addressed. For example, highly influential ones (e.g., top-ranked documents or authors by their citation impact) would be a good option for "core objects" when a study is concerned with the structure of its knowledge base or of the intellectual influences on it, but might not necessarily be representative if a study is concerned with the structure of current research activities of a research field due to the fact that some, if not many, of these highly influential objects (e.g., a deceased author) may no longer be active.

For studying current research activities of a research field or its research front, it has been suggested that strongly *and* frequently coupled documents comprise "core documents" of a research field (Glänzel and Czerwon, 1996) and that both an author's productivity (as measured by her number of publications) and her connectivity with the field (as indicated by her average level of bibliographic coupling frequency) should be considered for author-based studies (Zhao and Strotmann, 2008b).

For studying intellectual influences on a research field or its knowledge base, a set of core influential objects can be selected in various ways (McCain, 1990b). Citedness being above some threshold (determined differently for each analysis) is considered a good method and has been used by many studies (e.g., Zhao and Strotmann, 2008a; 2008b; 2008c; 2011b, 2014a). In addition, other measures of citation impact (e.g., h-index), field expert recommendations, or any references that can help identify the significance of the objects, such as Who's Who, can all be used for this purpose. For example, if one wants to do an author-based analysis in the Information Science research field, one could select a set of X authors who have been cited most often in this field during the past Y years. One could also use Who's Who in information science to select the core authors, or/and ask a number of experts in the Information Science research field to provide a list of the most influential authors from their perspectives. One would then compare the lists and make the final selection of the authors to be used in the citation network analysis study.

It is important to keep in mind that the most highly cited objects tend to represent only the most active and prolific areas within the field. They will represent a range of research areas within a field only if each area has a number of exceptionally highly cited representative documents or researchers within it. In highly interdisciplinary research fields, subfields may have wildly different citation characteristics, and there may be significant research areas within the field that will not be represented at all by highly cited documents or authors of the whole field. In the stem cell field, for example, only biomedical researchers were found among the most highly cited, and social scientists (e.g., those addressing the ethics of stem cell research or therapy) are entirely absent there despite the existence of a strong research community in that area (Bubela et al., 2010).

It is therefore important to keep in mind that citation network analysis will always provide a (not the) bird's eye view of a field's intellectual structure. Against this background, it becomes an interesting research question to find the best ways to choose core objects to represent the entire research field when its intellectual structure is to be studied, especially when the field is highly diverse. McCain (1990b) recommends the use of a variety of sources for author selection, but it is also interesting to find out how to improve citedness-based author selection. This may require something like field normalization in citation-based research evaluation but at a finer level of granularity, i.e., specialty normalization within a field (Bornmann, 2010). Addressing this question could improve not only co-citation mapping but also citation ranking in research evaluation because specialty normalization takes into account differences within a field and is perhaps more fair, especially given the broad field categorizations provided in citation databases (i.e., the ISI databases and Scopus) that have been used in field normalization. Leydesdorff and Bornmann (2011) recently proposed a simple approximate citation count normalization method based on Small and Sweeney's (1985, p. 393) "fractional citation counting" that does not rely on assigning objects to fields but rather directly smoothes out citation style differences between citing publications. With this counting method, a paper citing 5 references would contribute 20 to the citation count of each of the 5 cited references, and a biomedical paper citing 100 would contribute 1 to the citation count of each of the 100 cited references. Insofar as these differences are due to cultural differences between fields or between specialties within fields, his method serves as an approximate field or specialty normalization of citation counts.

2.2.2   NUMBER OF OBJECTS

There are no strict rules regarding the number of core objects to select (McCain, 1990a). Because the more objects are analyzed the better a research field may be represented, the goal is to use as large a number as possible within the constraints of the research questions being addressed, the type of objects being analyzed, the capacity of the analytical tools used, and the clarity of the visual maps of the resulting citation networks, among other considerations.

For example, in author-based citation network analysis, the number of authors included in a study ranges from below 50 to 200 with most recent studies being 120 or above (White and McCain, 1998; Zhao and Strotmann, 2008a; 2008b; 2008c; 2011b, 2014a). The smaller number of authors in earlier studies had much to do with the maximum number of variables that the Multi-dimensional Scaling (MDS) routine in the SPSS Statistics software package was able to process, as studies back then relied on MDS to create visual representations of author co-citation networks. The fact that a smaller number of authors were sufficient for author co-citation analysis (ACA) studies was also due to the type of objects that ACA deals with: authors instead of documents, as discussed below.

2.2.3   TYPES OF OBJECTS

Many types of objects can be used in citation network analysis, such as documents, authors, journals, institutions, nations, and subject categories. The most frequently studied objects are documents, authors, and journals. These three differ in several ways, which should be taken into account in research design.

Granularity

A research paper usually reports a single study that is usually narrow in scope and can be quite focused and specific in the natural sciences. Review papers are of course different in this regard, and should therefore be excluded from citation network studies that use documents as the unit of analysis, although they have been included in many citation analysis studies.

An author represents a school of thought as seen from all publications written by this author, i.e., the author's oeuvre. Because of the nature of research, most authors stay within a single specialty or a small number of closely related specialties over their careers as researchers. An author's oeuvre therefore normally represents a coherent school of thought belonging to a single research area, although the topics that the author covers can vary from very focused to wide-ranging.

The scope of a journal, on the other hand, can range from a single small specialty (e.g., *Journal of Contemporary Ethnography*) to the entire discipline (e.g., JASIST, JDoc) or even the whole scope of science (e.g., *Science, Nature, Proceedings of the National Academy of Sciences*). Some may therefore find it hard to conceive what a journal represents or what the connotation is when mapping research fields using journals as the units of citation analysis. In other words, the ambiguity in meaning is much higher with journals than with documents or authors.

Coverage of the field

Because of the difference in granularity, the portion of the field being studied that is covered by the same number of objects analyzed increases from document to author to journal. In other words, to characterize an entire field, far fewer author names are needed than the number of documents, and citation windows can be smaller as author citation counts are usually higher than document citation counts, which improves statistical quality. Journals are normally only useful for studying the structure of the entire science or very large disciplines (Boyack and Klavans, 2011b; Leydesdorff, 2008; Leydesdorff and Rafols, 2009).

Data collection and processing

Clearer visual maps of citation networks can be expected from author-based analyses because of the smaller number of objects required and larger counts of citations compared to document-based analyses, and due to the lower ambiguity in meaning compared to journal-based analyses.

Citedness-based selection of core objects for the study is much easier with document-based than author-based analyses because documents in the search results from citation databases can be ranked directly by their citation counts, but authors' citation counts have to be obtained by searching for individual authors one by one. As for journal-based analyses, because of the small number of journals indexed in citation databases compared to documents or authors, all journals are often included in the mapping, leaving further selection unnecessary.

Although data collection for author-based analyses is easier than document-based in the sense that the names of prominent authors are the only things needed, author name disambiguation is normally necessary and requires additional information similar to that for document-based studies (e.g., journal, page, publication year). Journal-based analyses are similar to author-based in this regard, but the name ambiguity problem is less severe.

Potential for studying social relationships

The "use of authors as the unit of analysis opens the possibility of exploring questions concerning both perceived cognitive structure and perceived social structure of science" (White, 1990). This potential has yet to be well studied, however. At the least, the people who conduct research can be studied when authors are used as the unit of analysis in addition to their research itself, which can be studied by any unit of analysis. For example, Zhao and Strotmann (2008b) characterized research profiles of authors who were both highly influential and highly active in Information Science 1996–2005 by comparing their citation identity (i.e., how they cite) and citation image (how they have been cited). They found that some authors published in several specialties but were only recognized in a single specialty, some others were very focused in publishing but were influential in more than one specialty, and still others became icons of a specialty as they both published in and strongly influenced research in this single specialty.

2.2.4   CITATION COUNTING

As mentioned earlier, citation counts have to be obtained by searching for individual authors one by one.

Citedness-based selection of core objects normally requires computer processing of bibliographical records downloaded from citation databases, i.e, counting citations to all objects that appear in the dataset and ranking them by their citation counts. This requirement is for both authors and documents but not for journals. Although retrieved documents from citation databases can be ranked directly by their citation counts readily available there, these documents do not include those that are highly cited but not indexed as "source papers" in the databases (e.g., books). Book and conference citation indexes can mitigate but are currently unlikely to solve this problem completely. So, if one needs to make sure that all highly cited documents are included in citation analysis, counting citations from downloaded records is necessary.

Of course, other measures of citation impact (e.g., h-index) may replace citation counts, but they normally require more, not less, processing, and therefore there have to be good reasons for choosing these measures over citation counts for impact-based selection of core objects for citation network analysis.

Counting citations and ranking objects for the selection of core objects should take into account some important issues in citation network analysis, including field normalization, disambiguation, and how to treat multi-author publications in order to take into account collaborations in scholarly communication. Disambiguation applies in fact to all citation analyses while the issue of multi-author publications clearly only applies to author-based or affiliation-based analyses. When a citation analysis study is concerned with more than one research field, field normalization is often necessary. These issues will be discussed in detail in later chapters, but the basic ideas and concepts relevant to the selection of core objects are summarized below.

Disambiguation

Disambiguation deals with the problems in citation data that are caused both by homonyms (e.g., different authors with the same name), and by allonyms, a term introduced by Howard White (White, 2001; 2010a) to cover the confusion of variant names of the same authors, journals, research institutions, countries, individual articles and books, and so on. For example, the names of the two Howard D. Whites who currently publish research (one in information science and the other in medicine) are homonyms that must be disambiguated in citation analysis so that the two authors' citation counts can be *separated*; "Jones KS" and "Sparckjones K" are allonyms for Karen Sparck Jones, and "J Doc" and "J Document" are allonyms for the *Journal of Documentation* in data downloaded from the ISI databases. Citation counts for allonyms need to be *combined*.

Homonyms and allonyms are common in citation data for various legitimate reasons (e.g., translations, transliterations, or renamings), but also because errors or inconsistencies occur frequently in making references and in indexing them. Disambiguation is important for representing an object's true impact on research. It can affect the ranks of objects (more significantly so for some objects than others, of course) and thus the resulting core objects selected for further study. Derek de Solla Price is a good example. This highly influential scholar in Science History and Information Science has received a large number of citations under several forms of his name, including Derek John de Solla Price, Derek deSolla Price, Derek John Price, and D. De Solla-Price, among others. He might not make it to the core without proper disambiguation even though he clearly belongs there.

Treatment of multi-author publications

How to treat multi-author publications in order to take into account collaboration in scholarly communication has been discussed thoroughly in the literature for research evaluation (Endersby, 1996; Lange, 2001; Smart and Bayer, 1986; Zhao, 2006b) and also explored recently for citation network analysis (Zhao and Strotmann, 2008c; 2011a). First-author, all-author, and last-author counting have been suggested and compared. Whenever a research paper with N authors in the by-line is cited, the first and the last of these N authors receives one more citation with first- and last-author citation counting respectively, and each of the N authors receives one more citation with complete all-author counting or 1/N more citation with fractional all-author counting.

It has been found that these different counting methods often result in different ranks for authors, more for some than others. This has important implications for research evaluation, especially given the fact that first-author citation counting has traditionally been the norm, partly because the ISI databases only index the first of all authors of each cited reference. As an extreme example, if only the first authors of cited papers are counted, as is traditionally the case, it can happen that even a Nobel Laureate will be missed completely, as in the case of Shinya Yamanaka (Medicine 2012), whose ground-breaking publications all listed him as last author (Zhao and Strotmann, 2011a; 2011b). Had the Nobel Prize Committee relied on traditional citation-based author ranking (which it of course doesn't), the prize would have gone to someone else.

For citation network analysis, however, it has been found that the overall intellectual structure of a research field revealed remains more or less the same regardless of how citations and measures of connectedness are counted, while the details of the structure (e.g., the specific set of small specialties identified) do change with counting method. These changes result mainly from different authors being selected for the networks due to different counting methods. In the just-mentioned case of Shinya Yamanaka, for example, the first-author-only co-citation network still identified the specialty associated with his ground-breaking work, but marked by name of the Ph.D. student whom Yamanaka had hired to work out his breakthrough ideas and whose name was therefore, according to life science traditions, listed as the first author on those crucial publications (Zhao and Strotmann, 2011a; 2011b).

In fact, each method of treating multi-author publications has different connotations (Zhao and Strotmann, 2011a) and may thus be more appropriate for certain research questions being addressed: all-author counting identifies researchers with high overall impact; first-author counting tends to identify researchers who have conducted highly influential studies and to emphasize a researcher's unique areas of study and most influential contributions; and last-author counting appears to successfully aggregate a researcher's contributions as head of a lab in a field where the tradition of listing the lab head last in the by-line is pervasive, but with an emphasis on the individual's unique contributions as head of the lab rather than on his or her full oeuvre. Last-author counting thus tends to identify established researchers in such fields who are successful in securing research funding and attracting outstanding researchers to their labs, as was the case with Shinya Yamanaka.

Field normalization

When a citation analysis study is concerned with more than one research field, field normalization is also an important issue. Field normalization adjusts citation counts by the size, citation patterns, etc., of the research field, so that scholars with similar levels of research impact in their respective fields have similar normalized citation scores. For example, a mathematician with a citation count of 50 and a researcher in medicine with a citation count of 5,000 may be ranked close to each other by field normalized citation scores because these two very different citation counts may well represent the same level of influence due to the differences between these two fields.

Traditionally in research evaluation, field normalization is done at the level of the categorization of research fields in the ISI databases. But for diverse research fields such as information science, differences between specialties within the field may be large enough to warrant normalization at specialty level. The simple first-order approach to specialty normalization that Leydesdorff and Bornmann (2011) have been advocating as mentioned earlier might come in handy in this context, and might actually be superior to the traditional real field normalization.

Field normalization is always a requirement for evaluative citation analysis, but may or may not be desired for citation network analysis depending again on the research questions being addressed. The size of a research (sub)field and the amount of knowledge flow within it are often among the characteristics that are examined and compared between research fields in citation network analysis studies. Field normalization would not be appropriate for these types of studies as it smoothes out the differences among research fields in size and knowledge flow as indicated by citations.

2.3   MEASURING THE CONNECTEDNESS BETWEEN CORE OBJECTS SELECTED

Once core objects have been selected, measures of how closely pairs of core objects are related from the point of view of citers are then calculated, and results are normally put into a matrix with rows or columns or both being the core objects. This matrix represents the citation network of these core objects, and will be processed and examined further at later steps.

The key to this step is to select a method for measuring the connectedness between objects and to actually calculate the measures. A few commonly used methods are discussed here.

2.3.1   CITATION COUNT

The most direct and simple measure is the citation count. A matrix of citation counts (i.e., a citation matrix) is a matrix with the core objects as rows/columns, all documents that have cited (or been cited by) these objects as columns/rows, and citation counts as cell values. For example,

Table 2.1 below lists three articles and their reference lists, and Table 2.2 and 2.3 show the citation matrix when the three citing articles (Table 2.2) or the cited authors (Table 2.3) are the objects to be studied in a citation network analysis, assuming that they are among the core objects selected.

Table 2.1: Three articles and their reference lists		
Article 1	**Article 2**	**Article 3**
Andy. (2000). J1	Andy (2000). J1	Andy. (2000). J1
Andy (2002). J2	Andy (2005). J2	Andy (2003). J2
Bailey (1998). J1	Bailey (1998). J1	Bailey (1998). J1
Bailey (2000). J3	Bailey (2000). J3	Bailey (2000). J5
Candy (2008). J1	Candy (2010). J4	Cindy (2008). J3
Daisy (2009). J2	Daisy (2009). J2	Daisy (2010). J4

Table 2.2: Three citing articles as the objects to be studied			
Cited Articles	**CitingArticle1**	**CitingArticle2**	**CitingArticle3**
Andy (2000). J1	1	1	1
Andy (2002). J2	1	0	0
Andy (2003). J2	0	0	1
Andy (2005). J2	0	1	0
Bailey (1998). J1	1	1	1
Bailey (2000). J3	1	1	0
Bailey (2000). J5	0	0	1
Candy (2008). J1	1	0	0
Candy (2010). J4	0	1	0
Cindy (2008). J3	0	0	1
Daisy (2009). J2	1	1	0
Daisy (2010). J4	0	0	1

Table 2.3: Three citing authors as the objects to be studied					
	Andy	**Bailey**	**Candy**	**Cindy**	**Daisy**
CitingArticle1	2	2	1	0	1
CitingArticle2	2	2	1	0	1
CitingArticle3	2	2	0	1	1

In a citation matrix, the objects to be examined can be either citing objects (if the research front is being studied) or cited objects (if the knowledge base is being examined), depending on the research questions being addressed. The citing and cited objects can be the same type of objects (e.g., both being articles as in Table 2.2) or different types (e.g., author by article as in Table 2.3). The rows/columns of the matrix other than the objects to be examined can be limited to the objects to be examined (i.e., a square matrix), or include more or even all objects that have cited or been cited by the objects to be examined (i.e., a rectangular matrix). A citation matrix with the same set of objects (e.g., authors) as both rows and columns is an *inter-citation matrix*. Inter-citation happens when a member of a bounded group cites works by another member of the same group (White et al., 2004), and inter-citation analysis can help with the study of the intellectual interaction among members of a group (e.g., a physics department or a scholarly association). Clearly, inter-citation only applies to the types of objects that may cite each other, which include authors, journals, or their aggregates (e.g., a country), but not documents because normally only newer articles cite older ones but not the other way around.

Although document citation counts may simply indicate citation links between documents, author or journal aggregated citation counts (as in Table 2.3) can serve as measures of the level of connectedness between the citing and cited objects, and can therefore be analyzed and visualized directly (following the rest of the steps in this chapter), precisely as inter-citation analysis does. Using citation counts directly as a measure of relatedness, however, has been found to be less optimal for citation network analysis of science compared to relatedness measures derived from them. This is partly because a citation matrix is normally very large and sparse, which does not help produce informative and meaningful results using the multivariate analysis procedures and visualization methods that are normally applied to citation network analysis. The two matrices in Tables 2.2 and 2.3, for example, would be in reality much larger and sparser, as many more citing or cited articles are actually involved and the overlap between reference lists is much smaller. This is even more true when examining objects as cited rather than as citing objects because citations tend to follow power law-like distributions and a small number of highly cited objects (e.g., authors) are normally cited by an extremely large number of documents.

Two methods for measuring the connectedness between objects derived from a citation matrix have been found to work well for citation network analysis of science, and have thus been used for most studies to date: co-citation count and bibliographic coupling frequency (BCF), which are discussed below.

2.3.2   CO-CITATION COUNT

Co-citation analysis is the most commonly used citation network analysis technique. It is generally accepted that the co-citation concept was discovered independently by Small (1973) and Marshakova (1973), and that document co-citation analysis was introduced by Small (1973), author co-citation analysis by White and Griffith (1981), and journal co-citation analysis by McCain (1991).

Two objects are considered *co-cited* when they appear in the same reference list. The number of documents whose reference lists contain both of the objects is the co-citation count of these two objects. This assumes that the authors of an article perceive two objects as being related to the same general subject matter or methodological approach when they include both objects in the reference list of their article, and that the more articles which do the same the more closely the two objects are related in some way.

For example, for the data in Table 2.2, the document co-citation count is 3 between Andy (2000) and Bailey (1998) because both appeared in all three articles' reference lists, and 1 (article 1) between Andy (2002) and Bailey (1998). The author co-citation count is 3 between Andy and Bailey and between Andy and Daisy, 2 (articles 1 and 2) between Andy and Candy, and 1 (article 3) between Andy and Cindy. The journal co-citation count is 3 between J1 and J2 and between J1 and J3, 2 (articles 2 and 3) between J1 and J4, and 1 (article 3) between J1 and J5. These co-citation counts can be easily derived from the citation matrices in Tables 2.2 and 2.3.

Variations of co-citation counts come from two main sources:

1. Consideration of factors affecting co-citation counts as relatedness measure.

    One of these factors is how often an object has been cited in each of the citing articles. As shown in the example above, each citing article gets one vote in co-citation counting that determines the relatedness between cited objects and it does not matter how many times these objects are cited in this article. The same author or journal, for example, often appears multiple times in a reference list as several articles written by the same author or published in the same journal may be cited in the same document (e.g., authors Andy and Bailey and journals J1 and J2 above). Similarly, the same document may be cited in the text multiple times even though each cited document can only appear once in the reference list. Although one may expect that Andy is more closely related to Bailey than, say, to Daisy as Daisy only appears once and the other two authors appear multiple times in each of the three citing articles, traditional co-citation counting method gives the two pairs the same count (3) as all three citing articles include both in their reference lists. It may be worth studying whether co-citation counts between two objects should be weighted by the number of times they are cited in the texts as well as in the reference lists to be more precise in measuring their relatedness.

    In addition to frequency-weighted co-citation counting, location-weighted counting weighs co-citations by the locations where documents are cited in the text. For example, two documents that appear in the same in-text citation (e.g., in the same set of parentheses in APA) would be expected to be more closely related than two that are cited in the same sentence, or in the same paragraph. Co-citation counts that take into account the relative in-text location of citations have been found to help produce clearer pictures of the intellectual structures of the research fields (Boyack et al., 2013). However, a drawback of this variation or refinement is that it requires access to the full-text citing articles in addition to the citation databases. More research is clearly necessary to investigate whether the benefit would be worth the extra cost.

Another factor affecting co-citation counts as relatedness measure is size-related. Two objects may be more closely related if they are co-cited whenever they are cited than two objects that are only co-cited in 10% of the cases when they are cited, even if the former number is smaller than the latter. For example, two highly influential documents (X and Y) in a research field are each cited 500 times, and co-cited 10 times. Another two documents (A and B) also have a co-citation count of 10 but are each cited 10 times total. That means that 100% of articles that have used A and B perceive them as being related to the same topic while only 5% of those that have used X and Y consider them being related. This percentage may be a better indicator for connectedness than raw co-citation counts.

This idea was suggested and tested very early in citation network analysis history by Henry Small, who used co-citation counts of two documents divided by the sum of the citation counts of these two documents as a way to normalize the co-citation counts by size before performing cluster analysis of the co-citation matrix (Small, 1973). Although author or journal co-citation counts may be even more subject to the size factor than document co-citation count, this variation of co-citation count, i.e., co-citation count normalized by citation count, has unfortunately not been used much by other researchers.

2. Various possible ways of counting author co-citations in the case of documents with multiple authors.

Ever since its introduction by White and Griffith (1981), author co-citation analysis (ACA) has been a primary research tool for the study of the intellectual structure of research fields. ACA defines two authors as co-cited when at least one document from each author's oeuvre occurs in the same reference list, and their co-citation count as the number of different publications that co-cite them in this sense. Classic ACA defines an author's oeuvre as all the works with the author as the first author (McCain, 1990b), and thus only uses information on the first author of a publication when calculating author co-citation counts. This is called *first-author co-citation counts*.

For example, for the data in Table 2.1, the first-author co-citation count is 3 between Andy and Daisy or between Andy and Bailey because all three citing articles include both names in their references, 2 (articles 1 and 2) between Andy and Candy, and 1 (article 3) between Andy and Cindy.

This definition stems to a considerable degree from the relative ease with which these counts can be retrieved directly from the main data source for ACA studies, the ISI databases, which only indexes the first authors in cited references. The only way to find the full set of authors of a cited document in these citation indexes is by matching the reference code to a corresponding source paper—an operation that is laborious and error-prone, and only possible if the cited reference refers to a document that also happens to have been indexed as a source paper (citing paper). As a result, it has been practically impossible to go beyond first-author co-citation counting using the ISI databases.

With alternatives to the ISI databases becoming available (e.g., Scopus), it has become possible to perform all-author co-citation analysis studies, i.e., studies that rely on a dataset that includes all authors of all cited references. As a result, the concept of author co-citation count has been extended from first-author to all-author based counting, and several possible definitions of all-author co-citation count have been identified (Rousseau and Zuccala, 2004; Zhao, 2005b; 2006a; Zhao and Strotmann, 2007; 2008c; 2011a).

Inclusive all-author co-citation derives from classic first-author co-citation by simply redefining an author's oeuvre as everything that lists the author as *one of* its authors rather than as its *first* author, and by retaining the definition of co-citedness between two authors as the number of papers that reference both authors' oeuvres. This definition therefore *includes* cited co-authorship in co-citation, because two authors are also considered co-cited when a paper they co-authored is cited.

Exclusive all-author co-citation excludes pure cited co-authorship from inclusive all-author co-citation by re-defining co-citedness between two authors as the number of papers that contain *distinct* references to both authors' oeuvres, i.e., references to these authors' oeuvres that do not both refer to the same document co-authored by these two authors.

Note that inclusive and exclusive author co-citation counts are identical when calculated for distinct authors who both only ever wrote single-authored papers. Same-author co-citation counts (i.e., an author's co-citation count with herself), however, will differ: inclusive counts would result in an author's number of citations, while exclusive counts strictly count the number of times that that author is co-cited with him- or herself. The latter therefore provides a meaningful diagonal even for a first-author co-citation matrix.

Last-author co-citation counting has also been introduced to account for the special role that the last author in the by-line plays in some research field such as biomedicine: the head of a research laboratory is traditionally listed as the last author of most if not all publications produced at that lab (Sonnenwald, 2008). As mentioned earlier, for example, one of the winners of the 2012 Nobel Prize for Medicine, Shinya Yamanaka, was listed as the last author on the high-impact publications that won him the prize.

Last-author co-citation counting is very similar to first-author counting except that an author's oeuvre is defined as all the works with the author as the last (instead of first) author.

All in all, exclusive all-author co-citation counting appears to be the most appropriate among the three methods (i.e., first-, last-, and all-author counting), although different types of counting do appear to carry different meanings, with each representing and eliciting slightly different aspects of the intellectual structure of the field. Any of the counting methods appear useful in ACA studies that aim to obtain a broad overview of the major overall intellectual structure of a research field, but they should be used with great caution for drawing conclusions about detailed structures and unclear or peripheral specialties. Such caution is especially necessary for ACAs that select a set of representative authors to analyze based on citedness measures, but may be less so when authors are selected in other, more directly relevant ways (e.g., Who's who) and ACA is only used to map out the interrelationships between these authors.

Although it appears to be the most appropriate among the three, all-author citation and co-citation counting are much more complex and expensive to perform than first-author (and perhaps also last-author) counting because of the limited support from current citation databases. First-author counting is directly supported by data from both the ISI databases and Scopus, and last-author counting (or an almost-all-author analysis in many research fields) is possible directly with Scopus data, which readily provides the names of the first seven and the last authors of cited references (even for those with large numbers of authors). All-author counting, however, requires the combination of existing citation and other bibliographic databases in a complex multi-step process just to collect and clean the necessary data. On the other hand, automatic author name disambiguation can be much easier in an all-author (or nearly all-author) setting as some successful methods rely quite heavily on the availability of all authors of each cited reference and full author names (rather than just the last name plus initial combinations) for many, if not all, of the cited references (Strotmann et al., 2009b).

Collecting author co-citation counts (or co-citation counts of other types of objects, e.g., documents or journals) is normally only practical by running computer programs on downloaded records from the ISI databases or Scopus. Unfortunately, publicly available, relatively easy-to-use computer programs for processing and visualizing citation data (e.g., CiteSpace, VOSviewer) do not output co-citation counts even though they produce the counts internally as an intermediate step.

2.3.3   BIBLIOGRAPHIC COUPLING FREQUENCY (BCF)

The concept of bibliographic coupling is even older than that of co-citation. Two documents are considered bibliographically coupled if they contain the same items in their reference lists, and the number of items that their reference lists share is the BCF of these two documents. The higher the BCF, the more closely related two documents are considered to be (Kessler, 1963).

For example, in Table 2.1, the BCF between articles 1 and 3 (or that between 2 and 3) is 2 as they share two cited references, Andy (2000). J1 and Bailey (1998). J1, while the BCF between articles 1 and 2 is 4. This indicates that article 1 is more closely related to article 2 than to article 3.

Using BCF to measure the relatedness between documents, it is the *citing* articles or their authors or journals that are being mapped, instead of *cited* articles or their authors or journals as in co-citation analysis. As a result, BCF allows the study of the recent research activities (or the research front) of a research field, whereas co-citation analysis examines the past intellectual influences on the field or the knowledge base of the field (Cornelius et al., 2006; Persson, 1994). Together, bibliographic coupling analysis and co-citation analysis may reveal a more complete picture of a research field and may support the study of the development trajectory that a research field is on (Zhao and Strotmann, 2008b; 2014a).

BCF was introduced mainly for the purpose of information retrieval (Kessler, 1963), and has rarely been applied to research evaluation or knowledge network analysis, despite its promises there as an indicator of relatedness between documents. This may in part be due to the difficulty of retrieving BCFs directly from the citation databases that citation analysis studies were heavily relying on (i.e., the ISI databases). Recent years, however, have seen a resurgence in knowledge network analysis studies based on BCF measures at all levels: *document* (e.g., Jarneving, 2005; 2007), *journal* (e.g., Boyack, et al., 2007), and *author* (e.g., Zhao and Strotmann, 2008b; 2014a).

Variations of BCF are also mainly from the two sources discussed above for co-citation counts: how to weigh citations and how to treat multi-author publications. In addition, how to accumulate BCF for authors (i.e., how to calculate author-aggregated BCF) may result in various BCF counts.

As the BCF between two documents is defined as the number of references that these two documents share, the BCF between two authors can be defined as the number of references these two authors' oeuvres share. On the one hand, this could be understood to mean the extent to which the individual publications in the two authors' oeuvres share references, and the BCF between these two authors could thus be calculated by accumulating these document BCFs. On the other hand, we could more simply treat an author's complete oeuvre as if it were a single publication, and calculate the BCF between two authors as the overlap between the sets of references of their respective oeuvres. This can be combined with frequency-based weighting mechanisms, which may result in even more refined counts (Zhao and Strotmann, 2008b). For example, a document that is cited by

N documents in author A's oeuvre and by M documents in author B's oeuvre can be defined to contribute min(N, M) (i.e., the smaller of N and M) to the BCF of authors A and B, as in (Zhao and Strotmann, 2008b). Mathematically, this corresponds to calculating the intersection of multisets, not sets, of references. Research is required to explore other variations and to compare their effects on the mapping of science.

2.3.4 OTHER SIMILARITY INDICATORS DERIVED FROM CITATION COUNTS

Both co-citation count and BCF can be easily derived from a raw citation matrix. In the example above (Table 2.2), if articles 1, 2, and 3 are the objects to be mapped, the BCFs between them can be calculated as the scalar product of the two corresponding vectors. For example, BCF (articles 1 and 3) = V1(1,1,1,1,1,1,0,0,0,0,0,0) x V2(1,0,1,0,0,0,0,0,1,1,1,1) = 2. Similarly, if the cited documents are the objects to be mapped, their co-citation counts can be calculated in the same way. For example, the co-citation count between Andy (2000) J1 and Daisy (2009) J3 is 2 (= (1,1,1) x (1,1,0)).

Co-citation count, BCF, and their variations can in fact be considered examples of researcher-defined relatedness measures, except that they have been well established and widely accepted. In other words, they are special cases of researcher-defined relatedness measures between objects linked by citations. In principle, other relatedness measures could also be defined and derived from the citation matrix by the researcher or by applying a commonly used statistical similarity measures (e.g., Pearson's r, Cosine). The Cosine similarity measure between articles 1 and 3 in the Table 2.2, for example, is 1/3, calculated using scalar products of citation vectors. However, further research is required to test how these measures would work in citation network analysis.

2.4 STATISTICAL ANALYSIS OF CITATION NETWORKS

Matrices of connectedness measures discussed above (i.e., citation matrix, co-citation matrix, and BCF matrix) represent citation networks of objects selected for studying. They can be analyzed using a combination of techniques and procedures in statistical analysis, network analysis, and information visualization. In this section, statistical analysis procedures often applied in citation network analysis are discussed along with issues involved. The section following discusses network analysis and visualization, as some statistical analysis results (e.g., factor matrices from factor analysis) can be considered as networks as well.

2.4.1   COMMONLY USED STATISTICAL ANALYSIS METHODS

The most frequently used statistical analyses in citation network analysis are factor analysis, cluster analysis, and multidimensional scaling (MDS). All three are interdependence techniques, which means that they examine the entire set of interdependent relationships and make no distinction between dependent and independent variables. There exist various statistical software packages such as SPSS or R that contain routines for cluster analysis, factor analysis, and MDS.

Cluster analysis, or clustering, classifies a set of objects into two or more mutually exclusive groups (called clusters) so that the degree of association is strong between members of the same cluster and weak between members of different clusters. *Factor analysis* identifies a smaller number of factors underlying a large number of variables, and determines variables' factor scores. Factor scores indicate the level of association between observed variables and identified underlying factors, which helps with putting variables into categories and selecting those that are representative of the categories.

Clearly, both cluster analysis and factor analysis allow us to gain insight into groupings, and helps us put objects into groups. The difference is that clusters as groups are mutually exclusive while factors as groups can overlap, which means that each object can be put into only one group in cluster analysis, but may have membership in more than one group in factor analysis, with different levels of association with different groups indicated by factor loadings. Applying these concepts to citation analysis, a document (or group of them by authors, journals, etc.) may only belong to a single group (i.e., specialty) with cluster analysis, but can have membership in more than one specialty with factor analysis, with membership strength in each specialty indicated by its factor loadings. Factor analysis, therefore, appears to fit citation data better as an author or a journal can easily belong to two or more specialties, and even a document with a narrow scope may influence research in more than one specialty and thus be perceived by citers to belong to two or more specialties. Cluster analysis applied to citation data focuses on the primary membership of each object, and can be faster and thus used to classify large number of objects. Almost all attempts of visualizing the entire scholarly enterprise based on citation links, for example, use cluster analysis (Boyack et al., 2009; Boyack et al., 2005; Small, 1999b). Hierarchical clustering methods also provide details about the clustering process (i.e., which objects merges into which cluster at which point) that can in principle be useful for the mapping of science studies.

MDS maps interrelationships in N dimensions to lower (usually two or three) dimensions so that the interrelationships among objects can be visually represented and explored. Another chief goal of MDS is to interpret (and in particular, to label) the two or three axes on which objects are scaled (White and McCain, 1998). Although natural grouping may be visible on an MDS map, MDS is often used along with cluster analysis in citation analysis so that objects plotted on a two-dimensional map using the coordinates produced by MDS can be marked explicitly into groups corresponding to the clusters from cluster analysis.

More recently, Latent Dirichlet Allocation (LDA) has been promoted as an alternative to cluster analysis in bibliometric studies (Porter et al., 2013). LDA is closely related to factor analysis in that it determines to what degree an object belongs to a topic (the LDA term for factors or clusters). At the same time, LDA algorithms are similar in speed to clustering algorithms, thus promising an ideal compromise between cluster and factor analysis methods in bibliometrics. However, LDA as such is originally a full-text analysis method and requires adaptation to work for citation data. In the case where author names are extracted as words from full texts, one can see how such an adaptation might work in practice (Strotmann and Bleier, 2013).

2.4.2   FACTOR ANALYSIS IN AUTHOR CO-CITATION ANALYSIS (ACA)

When applying these multivariate statistical analysis methods in citation network analysis studies, a number of methodological decisions need to be made. Different decisions may well produce different results (Leydesdorff and Vaughan, 2006), and it is therefore important to understand the options that are available, the different results that may be obtained using different techniques, and when and why certain techniques may be more appropriate than others. This is illustrated here by factor analysis in author co-citation analysis.

Factor analysis (FA) has been used in ACA from the very beginning (White and Griffith, 1981). Its goal, as mentioned earlier, is to seek a small number of meaningful underlying factors that explain the relationships among a larger number of objects, and it is used in ACA to reveal specialty structures of research fields and authors' memberships in one or more such specialties. FA applied in ACA has been shown to provide clear and revealing results as to the nature of a discipline (White and McCain, 1998).

In addition to the specialty structure of a research field that other multivariate analysis techniques (such as cluster analysis and MDS) can also identify, FA can assign individual authors to more than one specialty, can indicate the level of association between authors and the specialties to which they belong, and can provide measures of "the degree of relationship between specialties" (White and Griffith, 1982, p. 260).

A researcher faces a number of methodological decisions when applying FA in ACA, including the type of data to input for the FA routine, the method for extracting factors, the number of factors to extract, which factor rotation method to apply, and which factor loadings to consider meaningful for interpreting factors.

An examination of previous ACA studies shows some common practices in the application of FA techniques in ACA: (a) principal component analysis has been the major method used for extracting factors; (b) Kaiser's rule of "eigenvalue greater than one" has been the main technique for deciding the number of factors to select; (c) raw co-citation frequency matrices have been used as input data for the factor analysis procedure; (d) both orthogonal and oblique rotations have been applied in ACA to facilitate the interpretation of results; and (e) various thresholds of factor loadings have been reported for interpretation, ranging from 0.3 to 0.5.

However, studies appear to be largely silent on why a particular technique was chosen instead of other techniques of the same type, nor do they compare ACA results obtained using different techniques (e.g., oblique versus orthogonal rotation) on identical data sets to help researchers choose among them. Zhao and Strotmann (2008a), however, examined the rotation methods of FA in ACA where confusion exists in the literature.

There are two types of rotation methods in FA: orthogonal and oblique. Theoretically, an orthogonal rotation assumes that resulting factors are not correlated and works best for revealing independent dimensions of the underlying structure being studied. An oblique rotation, by contrast, is not restricted to keeping the extracted factors independent of each other and therefore works better at separating out factors when it can be expected theoretically that the resulting factors would in reality be correlated (Hair et al., 1998).

In the case of ACA, large factors are interpreted as specialties within a research field, and the correlation between factors can therefore be expected to be fairly high. Indeed, high correlations between factors were found in different fields, with the highest correlation between two factors reported in a given study ranging from 0.39 to 0.65 (McCain, 1990a; White and Griffith, 1982; Zhao, 2006a). An oblique rotation, therefore, appears theoretically more appropriate for ACA. As an additional advantage, an oblique rotation produces some additional information which can be useful for ACA, including (a) a component correlation matrix which indicates the degree of correlation between resulting factors (McCain, 1990a; White and Griffith, 1982), (b) a pattern matrix in which factor loadings represent the unique contribution of individual authors (variables) to specialties (factors), and (c) a structure matrix where loadings are "simple correlations between variables and factors" and are determined both by an author's unique contribution to each factor and by the correlation among factors (Hair et al., 1998, p. 113). An orthogonal rotation only produces one component matrix that is subsequently used for interpretation.

In practice, however, both oblique and orthogonal rotation methods have been used in ACA studies, even by the same authors, and both types of studies have demonstrated how useful and informative the factor-analytic approach is to ACA. For example, McCain (1990a) and White and Griffith (1982) applied an oblique rotation method and discussed its advantage of providing measures on the interrelationships between factors. Later studies by these authors, however, switched to an orthogonal rotation instead, without discussing why they made this choice. And yet the orthogonal rotation in that study still produced clear and revealing results as to the nature of the Information Science field (White and McCain, 1998).

2.4.3 INPUT DATA TO STATISTICAL PROCEDURES

Traditionally in citation network analyses such as ACA, a symmetric co-citation or BCF matrix has been used as input for the multivariate analysis routines discussed above. This requires some data preparation and has also raised some questions.

Manual examination and editing of input data

When the relatedness measures (e.g., co-citation counts, BCFs) are entered into a matrix, some rows and columns may contain too many zero cells, which means that the authors corresponding to those rows and columns were not related with many other authors based on citation links, and therefore may not be good representatives of the field being studied by citation network analysis. Such objects and their corresponding rows and columns in the relatedness matrix need then to be deleted according to some ad hoc criteria (McCain, 1990b), such as more than 5% zero value cells. As a result, in case some objects would end up being deleted in this way, it is usually a good idea to build a relatedness matrix for more objects than the number of objects to be eventually mapped.

Because of the ambiguity problem with citation data and the difficulty in disambiguation mentioned earlier in Section 2.2.4, it is quite possible that multiple object names exist in the co-citation or BCF matrix that represent the same object (e.g., two variations of the same author name). Manual examination is often required to identify these cases and to merge these objects by adding up their numbers. With the sample data above, if it turned out that Candy and Cindy are two names for the same person, the two columns corresponding to these names should then be merged to become a single column CandyCindy (1,1,1). If the relatedness matrix is a symmetric matrix of co-citation or BCF counts, the same would need to be done to corresponding rows as well.

Diagonal values

Another technical detail that needs to be determined in the case of a symmetric matrix of co-citation counts or BCFs is what to put in the main diagonal cells.

Conceptually, a diagonal value is the co-citation count or BCF of an object with itself, which corresponds to the number of citations the corresponding object has received or the number of cited references it has made in the case of document co-citation and BCF of all types of objects (document, author, journal, etc.). The problem here is that these diagonal values can be much, much larger than any values in the off-diagonal cells, which can be a problem for statistical analyses, thus requiring them to be scaled down somehow (Kreuzman, 2001; White and McCain, 1998; McCain, 1990b). Because of this problem, and as these diagonal values cannot be given the same interpretation as off-diagonal values, they are often replaced by values calculated from corresponding off-diagonal values. Some studies, for example, take the average of the sum of the three highest off-diagonal values for each object (Culnan et al., 1990; White and Griffith, 1981) while others simply leave the diagonal empty and let the statistical procedures treat them as missing values and replace them with means (McCain, 1990b; Zhao and Strotmann, 2008a; 2008b).

In the case of co-citation analysis of objects other than documents (e.g., authors, journals), the co-citation count of an object with itself can be calculated as the number of articles that have cited at least two different documents produced by the corresponding object. For example, the co-citation count of an author with herself is the number of articles that cite at least two different publications written by this author. As mentioned earlier in Section 2.3.2, these diagonal values are consistent with off-diagonal values in both meaning and scale when exclusive co-citation counting is used. These theoretically ideal diagonal values also have been found to produce better results in the practice of mapping of science (Zhao and Strotmann, 2008c).

For example, in Table 2.2, the co-citation count of Daisy with herself is zero and that for Andy is 3, as all three articles cited two different articles by Andy.

Concerns about using symmetric co-citation or BCF matrices

Most statistical analysis methods have requirements for data to be statistically analyzed, some stricter than others, such as distribution and variable-case ratio. Violating these requirements normally means invalid results, and data that meet these requirements are normally more desirable. For example, averages (or means) as predictors of "typical" behavior requires data with a normal distribution but citation data often follow highly skewed power law distributions. When comparing research impact between different parties (e.g., authors, universities) using citation data, it is therefore generally accepted by now that percentile should be used rather than average or mean citation counts, which used to be the primary indicator for this purpose.

In citation network analysis (e.g., ACA), however, there is an interesting phenomenon: the requirements of statistical procedures may be violated, sometimes seriously, and yet the results of the co-citation analysis are meaningful and either more informative than or comparable with those from data that do conform to the requirements. This phenomenon has already been seen in the previous section on factor analysis in ACA; it is seen here with respect to input data, and it will also be seen in the next section regarding statistical similarity measures.

Data in a symmetric co-citation matrix as input (i.e., co-citation counts) are treated by the multivariate analysis routines (e.g., factor analysis and MDS) as raw observations, from which statistical similarity or distance measures (e.g., Pearson's r correlation coefficients) are calculated and used in subsequent processing. Considering that co-citation counts or BCFs can in fact be considered researcher-defined similarity measures calculated from raw citation counts, as mentioned earlier in Section 2.3.4, questions have been raised about whether this way of data handling is statistically appropriate, as it appears to calculate similarity or distance measures from another similarity measure (i.e., co-citation counts or BCFs) for multivariate statistical analysis, and about whether it would therefore be better to use either co-citation counts as similarity measures directly or citation matrix as input data for statistical analysis routines instead (Schneider et al., 2009).

Furthermore, with a symmetric co-citation or BCF matrix as input data, the number of variables (i.e., authors being analyzed) and the number of cases or observations (i.e., authors co-cited or coupled with authors being analyzed) are the same, which violates a requirement of factor analysis clearly stated in many statistics textbooks: the number of cases should be a large multiple of the number of variables in order for factor analysis to work.

Studies have explored these questions by comparing MDS mapping results between symmetric co-citation matrix and asymmetrical citation matrix as input data for MDS (e.g., Leydesdorff and Vaughan, 2006; Schneider et al., 2009), or by using more cases (i.e., co-cited authors) than variables (i.e., authors being analyzed) in factor analysis of author co-citation data and comparing the results with those from a symmetric co-citation matrix (Zhao and Strotmann, 2008c). These studies appear to have essentially concluded that symmetric co-citation matrix works better than (or at least as well as) asymmetric citation matrix in citation mapping practice, despite the fact that the asymmetric citation matrix is more appropriate theoretically.

The robust results from factor analysis of a symmetric co-citation or BCF matrix are theoretically quite unexpected, but it is also true that they are a baffling practical reality as the citation analysis literature has amply demonstrated over decades. This mathematical conundrum may intrigue professional statisticians to refine their statistical procedures in the future. It appears that a citation matrix is very sparse while a matrix of co-citation counts or BCFs is much denser, and that using a matrix of co-citation counts or BCFs instead of a raw citation matrix as input data to these multivariate analysis procedures serves as a way of applying smoothing or folding operations to datasets prior to a statistical analysis. Unlike values in raw document by document or document by author citation matrices, those in the derived co-citation or BCF matrices exhibit the typical power-law-like distribution of values that is the hallmark of bibliometrics, which translates into highly amplified signals for the statistical methods to latch on to.

It must be noted, however, that the resultant statistical model applies to the summarized data rather than the underlying "raw" data, i.e., it is a model of how authors are co-cited rather than how they are cited. As summary data, the results are highly likely to exhibit much higher model fits. Note also that there is nothing "unorthodox" about data smoothing or folding operations, which are done regularly in statistics. Physicists use folding operations like the Fourier transform, and computer vision researchers, sombrero hat smoothing, to get their noisy data into an appropriate shape for analysis.

Nevertheless, it may be advisable to include more authors as cases than as variables to account for a variable-case ratio recommendation to some extent (Hair et al., 1998). For example, Zhao and Strotmann (2011a) chose only the top 200 authors in each of the three 300x300 co-citation matrices as variables in their factor analysis, resulting in an effective matrix of 200 variables (cited authors) by 300 cases (co-cited authors) of author co-citation count observations.

2.4.4   DETERMINING SIMILARITY MEASURES

Raw connectedness measures (e.g., co-citation counts) can be very misleading if compared directly. Thus, a matrix of raw connectedness measures are normally converted to a matrix of some kind of statistical similarity measures such as the Pearson's r correlation coefficient or the Cosine similarity. This conversion appears to have a number of advantages because the result is a normalized measure that takes into account the objects' entire co-citation or BCF records rather than their individual co-citation counts or BCFs, that is, their co-citations with all other objects (Kreuzman, 2001).

The multivariate analysis methods used in citation network analysis (i.e., cluster analysis, factor analysis, and MDS) as implemented in SPSS perform this conversion as an integral part of the routines. Some routines (e.g., MDS) can also take a matrix of pre-calculated similarity or distance measures and do the rest of the analysis directly from it (Leydesdorff and Vaughan, 2006), which supports the case when a certain type of similarity or distance measure is desired but is not one of the options integrated in the multivariate analysis routines.

Which similarity measure should be used to process citation data has been debated among the experts of co-citation analysis. It appears that although mathematically speaking, cosine similarity has more desirable properties than Pearson's r, which is an integral part of the Factor Analysis routine in SPSS and has been used frequently in author co-citation analysis studies, differences in the co-citation analysis results they produce are not substantial (Ahlgren et al., 2003; 2004a; 2004b; Bensman, 2004; White, 2003a; 2004a).

This outcome of the debate is another example that illustrates the interesting phenomenon in co-citation analysis (and probably in citation network analysis in general) just discussed above: citation analysis practice produces meaningful and informative results even when statistics theory says that there are problems with those methods employed.

2.5   NETWORK ANALYSIS AND VISUALIZATION

Although it has had a long history, the mapping and visualization of knowledge networks of various kinds (e.g., citation-based networks) has attracted great interest in recent years both within and outside of the Library and Information Science/Studies (LIS) field. This is probably due to a number of factors. Written knowledge has become widely available in digitized forms in recent years with the explosive development of the World Wide Web and its plethora of online databases, which provides huge amounts and large varieties of data for this type of study. Moreover, increased computing power has enabled routine analysis and visualization of such vast networks of information for social science researchers (Shiffrin and Börner, 2004; Zhao and Strotmann, 2008a; 2008b; 2008c).

There are three main components of network analysis and visualization: (a) the objects of analysis, (b) the relationships between these objects, and (c) the mapping or visualization tools. The former two components correspond to nodes and edges of a network, and the latter to methods for representing the resulting network in two- or three-dimensional space for simple, intuitive viewing or interactive exploration. Network properties such as centrality can also be calculated to measure the characteristics of the network and the participating objects.

Traditionally, as discussed earlier, individual articles or patents, authors' oeuvres, and scholarly journals have been used as objects of analysis, citation counts or scores derived from them such as co-citation counts and BCFs as measures of relatedness between these objects, and multidimensional scaling (MDS) as a mapping tool. The traditional MDS plots of objects as early examples of of citation network visualizations are often marked into groups that correspond to clusters resultant from cluster analysis (Small, 1977; White and Griffith, 1981).

All have recently been adapted to the Web environment (e.g., websites viewed as journals and hyperlinks as citation links), giving rise to Webometrics (Thelwall et al., 2005). New types of objects and relationships (e.g., genes and DNA sequences) have appeared in recent studies (Barabási et al., 2011; Hu et al., 2013); so have new mapping methods such as Pathfinder networks, self-organizing maps, and Crossmaps for visualizing complex relationships between different entities (Börner et al., 2004; Boyack et al., 2007; Boyack et al., 2005; Chen, 2006; Henzinger and Lawrence, 2004; Morris and Yen, 2004; Van Eck et al., 2005; White et al., 2004; Wilkinson and Huberman, 2004; Zhao and Strotmann, 2008a, 2008b). A number of software packages have also been developed either specifically for visualizing citation networks (e.g., CiteSpace, VOSViewer, Sci^2) or for general network analysis and visualization. Some of the latter (e.g., Pajek, UCINet) have been applied to citation data. All these software packages are freely available on the Web (except for UCINet which is a low-priced social network analysis package).

Two of the citation network analysis and visualization techniques found in recent studies are especially easy to understand and apply, and provide very informative results. They are therefore highlighted below. A more detailed discussion of these and other methods and of citation network analysis and visualization in general is provided in Chapter 5.

In recent years, social network analysis (SNA) methods and tools have been applied to citation networks (e.g., Leydesdorff, 2007; Wagner and Leydesdorff, 2005). SNA provides both a visual and a mathematical analysis of relationships between people and groups. In addition to visual representations of relationships, centrality measures of nodes in SNA provide insight into the various roles and groupings in a network: who are the connectors, mavens, leaders, bridges, and isolates; where are the clusters and who is in them; who is in the core of the network, and who is on the periphery? For example, degree centrality, which is the number of direct connections a node has, measures a node's local connectivity, and identifies connectors or hubs in a network, whereas betweenness centrality, which is the number of shortest paths from all nodes to all others that pass through a node, measures load placed on a node and indicates global importance: a node with high betweenness has great influence over what flows in the network.

Zhao and Strotmann (2008a) introduced a method for visualizing factor analysis results in ACA, but the method can also be used to visualize networks that are similar to a factor matrix as shown in Hu et al. (2013). The central purpose of this technique is to directly visualize the factor analysis results as a bipartite network of authors and factors (i.e., specialties) linked to each other according to the loadings of authors on the factors. This visualization allows us to see factor structures in a condensed visual way to help with comprehending and interpreting the results.

This technique has recently been improved by combining citation impact and the informative features of both the pattern and structure matrices from factor analysis with an oblique rotation, into one map (Zhao and Strotmann, 2014a). The resultant visualization is a single uncluttered map with a stable layout that visualizes more clearly the level of impact of each author (author node size), the prominence of each specialty (factor node size), the interrelationships between specialties and authors (map layout and node positions), and the memberships of authors in specialties (connecting lines).

Chapter 5 discusses this technique further and provides details about the steps for creating visualizations using this technique.

Of course, other biblometric networks that do not rely on citation links (e.g., co-author networks, co-word networks) can also apply many of these methods and tools in similar ways, but they are not discussed explicitly in this book. Nor is the visualization of citation trails over time (e.g., Bagatelj, 2003; Garfield et al., 2002), as citation trails hardly ever contain cycles and are of a somewhat different nature than the cyclic citation networks that are the focus of this book.

2.6   INTERPRETATION AND VALIDATION

Visualization along with multivariate statistical analyses such as factor analysis, cluster analysis, and MDS makes it much easier to identify relationships among objects. Large numbers of object relationships are first converted to relationships among factors or clusters (which are significantly fewer), as well as relationships between objects and these groups, then presented visually. An interpretation can then be attempted based on this visualization, which "relies on discovering what the author clusters, factors, and map dimensions represent in terms of scholarly contributions, institutional or geographic ties, intellectual associations, and the like" (McCain, 1990b, p. 441). Although citation analysis relies heavily on subject experts in the interpretation of results, one of the central advantages of citation analysis in the study of the intellectual structures of research fields is its ability to allow a careful non-expert to gain a basic understanding. Of course, domain experts may be able to make more out of citation analysis results than non-experts (White, 1990).

Results from different types of statistical analyses and visualization may require different interpretations, but there are some common points to explicate (White, 1990; Zhao and Strotmann, 2008a; 2008b; 2011a; 2014a).

Specialties or schools of thought

Large and clear groups of objects (e.g., clusters or factors) are interpreted as specialties or schools of thought in a research field. The term "specialty" is used here in the colloquial sense of an area of study (large or small), rather than in the very restrictive technical sense of a minimal cohesive research community as in Morris and van der Veer Martens (2009).

The size of a specialty is the number of objects belonging to it, and is interpreted as indicating the relative significance of the specialty in the research field. In the case of factor analysis results, the size of a specialty is measured by the number of objects that have primary loadings on the corresponding factor, and the clarity or distinctiveness of a specialty is indicated by the highest loading on the corresponding factor.

Naming of groups of objects is based on examination of documents or oeuvres of authors in the groups with the goal to identify common themes in the topics of the documents. In other words, a core literature for each factor or cluster is examined, and its common theme identified and interpreted as a research focus of the corresponding specialty. In the case of factor analysis, factor loadings can help focus the examination on objects that are most representative of each specialty, i.e., on objects with high loadings. For a factor that comprises a small number of objects, all of which have low loadings on that factor, however, this method will produce very small or even empty sets of core documents. These factors are often difficult to interpret with confidence because of the limited information available for examination, and can thus be labeled as Undefined.

The examination of core documents for each group of objects can be done either manually or automatically (by computer programs) or, in most cases, a combination of the two: computer programs can be developed to extract the most relevant information about the objects in each group so that the manual examination can be more focused and less time consuming. For example, for an ACA using factor analysis, a computer program can select authors with factor loadings above x in each factor as the most representative authors for that specialty, and documents written by these authors that have been cited more than y times as the most representative works of these authors. The manual examination can then focus on these documents. This basic algorithm of course can be refined in various ways, and the values of x and y should be determined by the actual data. Zhao and Strotmann (2011b), for example, took the top 10 authors in each factor and the top 10 documents by these authors ranked by their co-citation counts.

Most often, the common theme of a factor (or cluster) emerges from the publications themselves. Almost all factors can be easily labeled from phrases that appear repeatedly in the titles of these publications, either literally or in the form of cognates or closely related phrases (e.g., heart, cardiac, myocardial, etc.), because a very high percentage of highly cited papers in a set exhibits such a common phrasing. Human judgment is involved in this process mainly when making sense of these themes, in a similar manner as a physicist interprets data from a physics experiment. Sometimes, factor analysis produces two or more factors that are closely correlated to each other statistically. In these cases, which can be interpreted as a super-area composed of highly interconnected sub-areas, labels may initially be identical for all interconnected factors, and only a subsequent closer look will then identify their distinguishing features to finalize the labeling.

This "subjective" method for labeling factors appears to be quite effective compared to "objective" algorithmic labeling from text analysis in that it provides labels that are as meaningful, but appropriately more general (Chen et al., 2010).

Relationships among specialties

Labeling of groups of objects and thus interpreting them as cores areas of the research field being studied makes up only one part of the bird's eye view of the intellectual structure of a field revealed by citation network analysis. The other important aspect of this view comes from the interrelationships between the research areas in the field, which can be identified from the relationships among groups of objects, including connections and central or peripheral positions within the field.

Interrelationships among factors from a factor analysis are indicated by correlations of factors resulting from an oblique rotation, and those among clusters from a cluster analysis by the similarity measures at which clusters are merged. Interrelationships among groups of objects in a visualization of citation networks can be identified from the positions of the groups relative to each other and to the map as a whole. The closer two groups are placed on the map the more closely they are perceived to be related. Groups that are centrally located are related to many specialties within the research field, whereas those on the periphery are related to few specialties. Groups that are located between two other groups may play a bridging role between the two specialties.

For example, as mentioned in Section 2.4.2, the layout of the Zhao and Strotmann (2008a) visualization of the structure matrix from a factor analysis with an oblique rotation tends to be quite stable in terms of relative positions of factors on the map, and can therefore serve as indication for the interrelationships between specialties or research areas within the field. Close proximity of two factor nodes tends to indicate that the two corresponding specialties are closely related. Similarly, a factor node that is surrounded by many other factor nodes represents a specialty that is connected to many other specialties, whereas a factor node on the edge represents a research area that is relatively separate from the rest of the field.

Objects' membership in specialties

An object (e.g., an author) being placed in a group by a clustering algorithm or having loadings on one or more factors is interpreted as the object's membership in the corresponding specialty or specialties.

With factor analysis, objects' loadings on factors indicate the degree of relatedness of objects with specialties, with larger loadings representing closer ties. The number of factors an object loads on indicates the breadth of the object's scholarly contributions or research impact. Objects that load solely and highly on a single factor are considered focused: their research clearly concentrates on a single specialty and possibly even defines it. Objects that load on multiple factors are interpreted as connecting objects, and their research bridges several specialties. White and Griffith (1982) provides a perfect example of this with what they term "crystalized" vs. "pervasive" authors. Robert K. Merton is a pervasive or connecting author because he loads across several factors in specialties of science and technology studies, while Karl Popper is a crystalized or focused author because he loads solely on the "philosophy" factor.

Within the maps of the Zhao and Strotmann visualization, of which Figure 2.1 in next section is an example, a line connecting a square object node with a circular factor node indicates that the corresponding object is related to the corresponding specialty, with dark and thick lines representing close ties and a circular node with dark and thick lines connecting to it representing a clear and distinct specialty. Yellow object nodes represent focus objects, and object nodes of other colors represent connecting objects (with green for objects that are related to two specialties, red for three, blue for four, and other colors for more than four specialties). Two specialties that are connected by many "green" object nodes are interpreted as two subareas of a larger research area within the field that comprises them, because many objects load on both of these subareas, but not on others.

Objects' central or peripheral positions within specialties or the field

For certain types of visualizations, the locations of individual objects within groups and on the entire map may also be meaningful. Objects' central or peripheral positions in the visualization correspond to objects' central or peripheral positions within the specialties or within the field. MDS maps, for example, have been used this way by the inventors of ACA (e.g., White and Mc-Cain, 1998). These authors also interpreted (and/or labeled) the two or three axes on which items are scaled, which is one of the chief goals of MDS.

Clearly, the main source of information for interpretation is rooted in the documents most relevant to each specialty. From these documents and their groupings and relationships revealed by statistical analyses and visualization, some important aspects of the intellectual structures of research fields can be gleaned, such as the nature and size of major specialties that comprise a research field, the relationships between these specialties and between core objects (e.g., documents, authors, and journals) and specialties, and the characteristics of core objects' research activities or impact. These aspects of intellectual structures can be compared between time periods to show the development of research fields over time and to draw the trajectory of this development (McCain, 1990b; White and McCain, 1998; White, 1990).

As mentioned earlier, anyone could in principle gain a rough idea about the intellectual structure of a research field and its evolution and trends from the groupings and relationships of core objects in the field revealed by statistical analysis and visualization. However, subject experts, i.e., people with knowledge about the research field being studied or the knowledge domain being analyzed, would be able to make better sense of relevant information and to see important points about the field that people without this knowledge may simply miss. It is therefore important that the citation analyst either has the knowledge herself or has access to a group of subject experts who are willing to be interviewed.

Subject experts are also sources for the validation of citation analysis results. There are a number of ways of validating citation analysis results (Garfield, 1979; McCain, 1986; White, 1990). The basic idea is to compare results from citation analysis with judgments of subject experts obtained through interviews, surveys, or existing writings such as textbooks, reviews, and historical documents.

For both interpretation and validation, construction of object profiles can be of great help. An *object profile* is referred to here as a concise description of the characteristics of an object. In the case of author co-citation analysis, for example, an object profile could be a description of an author's research interest and publication records, and of the social or any other ties that this author has with other authors being studied.

Object profiles can not only give valuable clues as to the meanings of the clusters and factors of objects identified, but also aid in interviews with subject experts. Subject experts may not know in detail what other authors in their field are doing, and may need to access the authors' publications or other information in order to provide their assessments of the interrelationships. Object profiles provide subject experts with the information needed in a concise format.

These profiles can be produced by the researcher by going through the publications and authors' homepages, or may be generated automatically by computer programs from titles, abstracts, or even the full text of the articles based on word frequency analyses or other more sophisticated text mining techniques.

2.7   AN EXAMPLE: MAPPING INFORMATION SCIENCE 2006–2010: AN AUTHOR BIBLIOGRAPHIC COUPLING ANALYSIS

This example is adapted from Zhao and Strotmann (2014a) to demonstrate how an actual study is conducted by following the steps presented in this chapter:

1. Delineation of the research field being studied

2. Selection of core sets of objects representing this research field

3. Measures of connectedness between objects in the core sets

4. Multivariate statistical analysis

5. Network analysis and visualization

6. Interpretation of results.

The goal of this study was to identify the structure of the research front of Information Science (IS) 2006–2010. Therefore, author bibliographic coupling analysis (ABCA) was chosen for this study as it directly examines the active researchers in the field, rather than ACA's focus on highly cited authors in current research.

2.7.1 DELINEATION OF THE INFORMATION SCIENCE RESEARCH FIELD

This study used the core journal-based field delineation mentioned earlier in this chapter and further discussed later in Chapter 3. Following previous studies (White and McCain, 1998; Zhao and Strotmann, 2008a, 2008b), the IS research field was defined by all publications in 11 core IS journals (Table 2.4) during the years 2006–2010 retrieved from the ISI databases. White and McCain (1998) explained why this field delineation method is justified.

We chose "Full Record + Cited Refs" as the record format and saved the file in CSV format, resulting in 4,422 records of source papers that included 110,785 references altogether, i.e., an average of 25 references per source paper. These 4,422 IS publications are considered representative of the IS research field 2006–2010, and the collective view of the authors of these publications as citers (represented in the 110,785 references) was used to study the intellectual structure of the IS field.

Table 2.4: Journals used to define information science*

Information science

- *Annual Review of Information Science and Technology*
- Information Processing and Management
- *Journal of the American Society for Information Science and Technology*
- *Journal of Documentation*
- *Journal of Information Science*
- Library and Information Science Research
- Scientometrics

Library automation

- Electronic Library
- Information Technology and Libraries
- Library Resources and Technical Services
- Program—Automated Library and Information Systems

*Taken from White, H.D., and McCain, K.W. (1998). Visualizing a discipline: An author cocitation analysis of information science. *Journal of the American Society for Information Science*, 49, p. 330, with two updates: (a) removed Proceedings of the American Society for Information Science and Technology which is no longer indexed in the ISI databases; and (b) used the journals' current titles.

2.7.2   SELECTION OF CORE AUTHORS TO REPRESENT THE RESEARCH FRONT OF IS 2006–2010

This study used a combination of an author's productivity and connectivity within the field as the criterion for selecting core authors, as discussed earlier in this chapter and later in Chapter 3.

Specifically, authors were first ranked by their productivity; the first-ranked 500 authors were then re-ranked by their average BCF, and the first-ranked 300 authors out of these 500 authors were selected as core authors to represent the research front of the IS field. An author's productivity was indicated by the total number of publications written by this author in the 4,422 citing documents described above. As in Zhao and Strotmann (2008b), a document that is cited by N documents in author A's oeuvre and by M documents in author B's oeuvre would contribute $min(N, M)$ (i.e., the smaller of N and M) to the BCF of authors A and B, where an author's oeuvre is the complete set of documents written by that author as the first author (McCain, 1990b), and an author's average BCF is the sum of this author's BCFs with all the other authors in the dataset, divided by the total number of authors in the dataset less one. In this particular case, an author's average BCF is the sum of this author's BCFs with the other 500 authors divided by 499.

2.7.3   MEASUREMENT OF THE CONNECTEDNESS BETWEEN CORE AUTHORS

First-author BCFs were used to measure the connectedness between these 300 core authors. Using the method for calculating BCFs described above in Section 2.3.3, we developed a Python program to process the records downloaded from the ISI databases, determine authors' BCFs, and record them in a matrix. The diagonal of this matrix was left empty. Appendix 2.7.3 (http://tinyurl.com/Appendix2-7-3) is part of the resultant matrix of BCFs.

This matrix was then manually examined, and author names that were known to likely each represent multiple individuals, such as Liu Y, Kim H, Kim S, Lee S, Liu X, and Li X, were removed from the study, as suggested by Strotmann and Zhao (2012). The result was a 251 x 251 BCF matrix.

2.7.4   FACTOR ANALYSIS

This matrix was read into SPSS (version 21), and the first-ranked 150 authors of the matrix were analyzed as variables using SPSS's Factor Analysis routine to explore the underlying structure of the interrelationships between the selected authors. Because of the increase in the number of publications that define the field, a larger number of authors was used here (i.e., 150) than the 120 authors used in previous studies of the same field, in order to represent the IS field as well as before. Also, a higher case-to-variable ratio (2:1) was used here than in previous studies (most of which used symmetric matrices).

The diagonal values were treated as missing values and replaced by the mean in the Factor Analysis routine. Factors were extracted by Principal Component Analysis (PCA), and the number of factors extracted was determined based on an examination of the Scree plot; total variance explained; communalities, i.e., how well a variable (in this case, an author's oeuvre) is explained by the factor model; and correlation residuals, i.e., the differences between observed correlations and correlations implied by the factor model (Hair, et al., 1998). In this way, a 16-factor model was produced, which had a good model fit: it explained 83.7% of the total variance, had about 98.7% of the communalities above 0.6, and the differences between observed and implied correlations were smaller than 0.05 for the most part (close to 100%).

An oblique rotation (SPSS Direct OBLIMIN) was applied to this factor model, and produced a pattern matrix and a structure matrix as part of the output. In both matrices only loadings above 0.3 were considered substantial and thus retained. Appendix 2.7.4 (http://tinyurl.com/Appendix2-7-4) shows the pattern matrix presented in a table following the example of White and McCain (1998).

The pattern matrix tends to be very sparse after low loadings (in this case, those smaller than 0.3) are removed, as a loading here represents an author's unique contribution to a specialty and authors tend to be quite focused in their research. The structure matrix, on the other hand, is often quite dense and authors tend to load moderately or strongly on several specialties in this matrix because loadings here represent a combination of correlations between specialties and authors' unique contributions to specialties, and specialties within a research field are fundamentally interlinked. For example, CroninB has loadings greater than 0.3 in seven factors in the structure matrix, but in none of the factors in the pattern matrix in this present study. He appears to have cited from such a wide range of literature that he does not get placed strongly as a member in any one of the specialties in the IS field, but he cites enough papers that others cite in seven specialties to underscore the correlations between these specialties.

Both the pattern and structure matrices thus provide important information about the structure of the field: the pattern matrix shows the memberships of authors *within* specialties, while the structure matrix indicates the interrelationships between specialties.

2.7.5   VISUALIZATION OF FACTOR STRUCTURES

The pattern and structure matrices were visualized in a single two-dimensional map following the steps explained in detail in Section 5.4.6 of Chapter 5. This visualization shows the factor structure in a more condensed visual format but preserves all the relevant information that is contained in large tables such as those published in White and McCain (1989) and Zhao and Strotmann (2008a). The resultant map combines the informative features of both pattern and structure matrices and other important information (citation counts), and improves the visualization technique introduced in Zhao and Strotmann (2008a). The central idea of this technique, as mentioned earlier, is to directly visualize the factor analysis results as a bipartite network of authors and factors (specialties) linked to each other according to the loadings of authors on the factors.

For a combined visual representation of the structure, the densely connected structure matrix was used to automatically position the factor and author nodes in relation to each other in order to obtain a stable (and therefore potentially meaningful) layout of the visual map, and the sparse pattern matrix was used to draw lines connecting author and factor nodes in order to clearly show authors' memberships in specialties. The width of a line that connects an author with a factor is proportional to the loading of this author on this factor in the pattern matrix, as is its grayscale value, with wider and darker lines signifying higher loadings (and thus stronger memberships). It was found useful to retain the structure matrix links as a muted background to the main visualization, especially in the case where the pattern matrix network disintegrated into several disconnected components.

Authors are represented by square nodes and factors by circular nodes in these maps. The color of an author node represents the number of specialties to which this author belongs (i.e., how many factors this author loads on in the pattern matrix), with yellow, green, red, and blue indicating one, two, three, and four specialties respectively. The color of a factor node is not meaningful for the purpose of representing features of intellectual structures.

The size of an author node corresponded to the total citation count of the author (instead of the author's loadings), and the size of a factor node was determined by the sum of the citation counts of all authors who load sufficiently on its factor (i.e., with a value of 0.3 or higher in the pattern matrix in this case), weighted by their loadings. For example, if an author has a citation count of 100 and loads 0.8 on a factor, this author adds 100 x 0.8 = 80 to the sum representing this factor's approximate total citation count. The weighting takes into account that an author may contribute to several specialties, but only the part of the author's oeuvre that corresponds to this specialty should be counted. As a result, node sizes show the relative prominence of authors and specialties measured by citation counts, an obviously important feature of the intellectual structure of a research field.

Combining the informative features of both the pattern and structure matrices as well as citation impact into one map, the resultant visualization is a single uncluttered map with a stable layout. The map shows more clearly the level of impact of each author (author node size), the prominence of each specialty (factor node size), the interrelationships between specialties and authors (map layout and node positions), and the memberships of authors in specialties (connecting lines).

Unfortunately, node colors of these figures may not be available in print, and a few author names may be difficult to read in crowded areas. For detailed examination of the maps, readers are referred to the online copy of this book, which includes high-resolution full-color versions of all figures.

2.7.6   INTERPRETATION OF RESULTS

Results were interpreted by following the guidelines discussed earlier in this chapter.

Figure 2.1 is the visualization of the 16-factor model (after an oblique rotation) extracted from the BCF matrix, showing the structure of the research front of IS 2006–2010. Table 2.5 provides the factors' labels, sizes, and distinctiveness (i.e., highest loading). A factor is labeled as undefined (UD) if all loadings in this factor are lower than 0.7 or there are fewer than 3 primary loadings, although an attempt may still be made at interpreting it.

In Table 2.5, the size of a factor is the number of authors who load primarily on this factor in the pattern matrix, and this number divided by the total number of authors analyzed estimates the relative size (%Size) of the factor. The size of a factor node (circle) in Figure 2.1, however, is the weighted sum of the citation counts of all authors in this factor. Both sizes indicate the relative prominence of a specialty, one by the number of authors working on the specialty and the other by these authors' collective citation impact.

Figure 2.1 shows that the two-camp structure of the IS field that was observed in several previous studies is still clearly visible in the research front of IS 2006–2010, with strong and dense connections within each camp but weak and sparse ones between camps. The Knowledge domain analysis (KDA) camp (top left) is concerned with quantitative studies of science and technology, and the Information retrieval (IR) camp (bottom right) focuses on information representation, retrieval, users, and use.

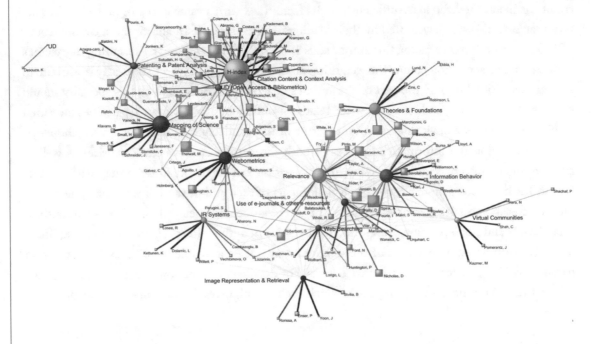

Figure 2.1: Structure of the research front of IS 2006–2010 as seen from ABCA (Zhao and Strotmann, 2014a).

Table 2.5: 16-factor results from ABCA of IS 2006–2010 (Zhao and Strotmann, 2014a)

Label	Size	%Size	HighestLoading
H-index (Bibliometric Distr.; Research Evaluation)	25	16.7	1.024
Information Behavior	16	10.7	0.914
Mapping of Science	15	10.0	0.886
Webometrics	14	9.3	0.897
Relevance	11	7.3	0.736
IR systems	9	6.0	0.914
IS Theories and Foundations	9	6.0	0.869
UD (Open Access and Bibliometrics)	8	5.3	0.600

Journal Editors	8	5.3	0.963
Virtual Communities	6	4.0	0.877
Citation Content and Context Analysis	6	4.0	0.837
Web Searching	6	4.0	0.778
Use of e-journals and other e-resources	6	4.0	0.777
Patenting and Patent Analysis	6	4.0	0.744
Image Representation and Retrieval	4	2.6	0.894
UD	1	0.7	0.511

The KDA camp is dominated by research on the h-index (in the context of Bibliometric distributions and of Research evaluation), followed by research on Mapping of science and Webometrics, and completed by three small areas of research: Patenting and patent analysis, Citation content and context analysis, and an area that cannot be defined clearly. The latter two small research areas are closely related to research on h-index related topics as seen from their close locations in Figure 2.1. The undefined area appears to be concerned with Open Access and Bibliometrics, such as the impact of open access resources and bibliometric studies using open access data sources (e.g., arxiv. org).

Research on the h-index is also by far the most prominent area of research in the entire field of IS 2006–2010. It appears that this "clever find" (Rousseau et al., 2013, p. 294) made by J. E. Hirsch in 2005 for measuring individuals' lifetime achievements (Hirsch, 2005) quickly generated a huge amount of attention from IS researchers, including some highly influential authors (large square nodes in Figure 2.1) in the areas of research evaluation and bibliometric distributions (e.g., EggheL, GlanzelW). Research has attempted to evaluate its effectiveness as an indicator for research evaluation, to improve on it by proposing various alternatives such as g-index and r-index, and to extend its use beyond just measuring individuals to measuring other types of objects such as journals and institutions.

In the IR camp, research on information behavior, especially on information seeking in various contexts and everyday information seeking, attracted the largest number of researchers. The citation impact of this area, however, is lower (as indicated by its smaller size in Figure 2.1) than that of the Relevance area that has almost 50% fewer researchers. In other words, as shown clearly in Figure 2.1, IS researchers with high citation impact (large square nodes in Figure 2.1) were not working primarily on information behavior, but on relevance and theoretical foundations in 2006–2010. Interestingly, the only exception was Spink, whose citation impact was the highest in the IR camp. Similarly, there were a good number of researchers (9) working in the IR systems specialty, but they all appear to have low citation impact in IS. This specialty, therefore, appears much smaller in Figure 2.1 than the IS Theories and Foundations specialty that has the same number of researchers.

Small areas of study in the IR camp included Virtual communities, Web searching, Use of e-journals and other e-resources, and Image representation and retrieval. Research on virtual communities appears to be only related to information seeking, searching, and use (i.e., soft IR) as seen from the links in Figure 2.1, but research on image representation and retrieval appears to have connections to both soft IR and hard IR (i.e., IR systems).

It is interesting to observe that the IR systems specialty has moved far away from the rest of the IR camp toward the KDA camp, actually bridging the two camps. Research on IS theories and foundations, on the other hand, appear to be located largely in the IR camp although it would be expected to integrate the entire IS field.

As seen clearly in Figure 2.1, all 150 core authors studied here have strong memberships (i.e., loadings greater than 0.3) in only one or two research areas (corresponding to yellow and green square nodes in Figure 2.1 respectively), except BrownC (red square) who belongs to three and CroninB (turquoise square) who appears to strongly focus on none.

Among the authors who have multiple memberships, almost all belong to only one of the two camps, with only nine exceptions: AhlgrenP, OppenheimC, PintoM, GalvezC, Lewandowski-kiD, PeruginiS, FryJ, DavisP, and BrownC. Most of these nine authors connect the Webometrics and Open Access and Bibliometrics specialties in the KDA camp with the IR systems and Use of e-journals and other e-resources specialties in the IR camp. It thus appears that the two camps are connected largely through Web-related topics.

It is interesting to observe that as an active researcher, Howard White has been placed in the Relevance specialty during 2006–2010, even though he has always been (and still is in this period) recognized by ACA as a leading author in the Mapping of science specialty for his pioneering and continuous work on ACA. This placement actually makes sense considering his actual publications during this time period, most of which study relevance theory as a central concept unifying Bibliometrics and IR.

It appears that ABCA has worked quite well capturing and showing characteristics of authors' research contributions and of the research front in IS 2006–2010, and better than ACA recognizing authors' contributions in different areas during different time periods.

CHAPTER 3

Field Delineation and Data Sources for Citation Analysis

As discussed in Chapter 2, a citation network analysis study is usually concerned with structures and characteristics of a certain scholarly community or research field during a certain time period. The first step in a citation network analysis study is therefore to collect a set of citing papers (along with their reference lists) to represent a defined scholarly community or research field within a specified time period (which is called a *citation window*). The subsequent analyses are based on these citing authors' collective view of the intellectual relationships in their scholarly community or research field as recorded in the reference lists of their publications.

The ideal situation would thus be to include all publications produced in this community within the time period concerned. The practical approach, however, is to sample a subset of these publications to represent this community. How to ensure that the sample well represents the research field being studied, at least for the purpose of addressing the research problems under investigation, is itself an unsolved research problem in citation analysis: the field delineation problem.

Field delineation has always been an integral part of bibliometric studies, and indeed has been recognized as a fundamental and largely unsolved problem in the bibliometrics literature (van Raan, 1996; Zitt, 2006). It has recently become a research area of its own because traditional field delineation methods appear to have reached their limits when dealing with highly interdisciplinary fields such as nanotechnology (Bassecoulard et al., 2007) or stem cell research (Zhao and Strotmann, 2011a; 2011b), which have recently become foci of science and technology policy research.

In this chapter, we will first discuss commonly used approaches to field delineation and examine how much of a difference field delineation makes in the study of intellectual structures of research fields. We will then discuss the pros and cons of commonly used citation databases (i.e., the ISI databases and Scopus) for field delineation, and how to combine subject databases with these citation databases for improved field delineation.

3.1 COMMONLY USED APPROACHES TO FIELD DELINEATION

As mentioned above, the purpose of field delineation in citation analysis is to collect a clean and complete set of citing papers (along with their reference lists) to represent the research field being studied during a specified time period, i.e., a dataset that includes all articles in a field but no articles on topics outside this field.

Field delineation can be done through subject (e.g., keyword), journal, or author and affiliation searches in a citation database (e.g., the ISI databases, Scopus). These searches can also be conducted in subject bibliographic databases (e.g., PubMed) to overcome limitations of citation databases in indexing and search facilities, but the search results must then be mapped back to a citation database in order to obtain information on cited references and citation links.

A time period or citation window (e.g., years 2006–2010) is often specified in these searches, and its length can vary depending on the objectives of the citation analysis study and the research field being studied. For the study of the evolution of a research field over time, for example, five and eight years have respectively been used for recent and early years of the relatively small Information Science field, compared to two years for the large and fast-developing stem cell research field (White and McCain, 1998; Strotmann et al., 2013; Zhao and Strotmann, 2008b; 2014a).

In addition, it is often necessary to limit these searches to certain types of documents, such as research articles or reviews. While both of these types of documents are often included in citation analysis studies, they are quite different in nature, scope, and citing behavior. It is therefore recommended in this book that only research articles be used to delineate research fields in citation analysis.

For the study of a single research field or a few fields, the Web interface of a citation database can be used for these searches. For the study of the entire research enterprise or a large number of disciplines, purchase of datasets from citation databases is often necessary. This type of citation analysis requires large datasets, but these databases normally prohibit automatic downloading of search results and make manual downloading of large datasets very difficult and time consuming, as discussed later in this chapter in detail.

When publications in the research field being studied are concentrated in a small number of journals, a set of core journals can be used to define this field and the dataset for this study would consist of all articles published in these core journals. Field delineation by core journals applies to traditional well-defined research fields (e.g., mathematics and psychology). Journals grouped into the subject areas in the ISI databases are often taken as core journals in the corresponding research fields. For example, studies have used all journals in the ISI subject area "Information Science and Library Science" to define the field of Library and Information Science (Ardanuy, 2012; Larivière et al., 2012; Levitt and Thelwall, 2009a; 2009b; Levitt et al., 2011; Tseng and Tsay, 2013), or a set of 12 journals hand-picked from these journals to define the Information Science field (White and McCain, 1998; Zhao and Strotmann, 2008a; 2008b; 2014a).

In contrast, when publications in the research field being studied spread over a large number of journals and across several disciplines that do not have a clear core, subject search becomes necessary. Field delineation by subject searching applies mostly to research topics that are relevant to and therefore studied in multiple research (sub)fields or for emerging research areas that do not yet have their own journals. For example, knowledge management or information retrieval is studied in business (e.g., organizational policy, management information systems), computer science, and LIS; research on stem cells is relevant to almost all biomedical research fields as well as some social sciences (e.g., ethics); and the fields of nanoscience and nanotechnology are embedded in many sciences, including physics, chemistry, and engineering, and researched from both industry and government perspectives (Zitt and Bassecoulard, 2006). These indeterminate research fields are typical examples of fields which have been delineated through subject searches (Ding, 1998; Gu, 2004; Ponzi, 2002; Zhao and Strotmann, 2011a; 2011b; Zitt and Bassecoulard, 2006).

For the study of author groups by department, institution, country, author, or affiliation, searches for the corresponding names can be used to collect data. For example, to compare two departments, two universities, or two countries, their names can be searched in the author affiliation index field, and the retrieved records can then be used as the dataset for the study; to compare two small units (such as departments of sociology in two different universities), a dataset for the study can also be retrieved by compiling a complete list of authors who are affiliated with the departments being studied and then searching for the names of these authors in the author index field. Of course, an even more complete list of publications by these authors may be obtained in other ways (e.g., from their CVs or institutional records), but these publications must then be mapped back to a citation database such as the ISI databases to obtain information on cited references and citation links.

In general, mapping a set of bibliographic records back to a citation database for citation links allows field delineation in citation analysis to overcome the limitations of citation databases in indexing and search facilities and in options for downloading. Subject bibliographic databases (e.g., MEDLINE) tend to have better indexes and search facilities, and field delineation using these databases can therefore be cleaner and more complete. For example, MEDLINE supports Medical Subject Headings (MeSH) and other types of searching which are specific to and very effective in biomedical research fields. These specialized searches are not always supported in citation databases that cover all research fields and only provide search facilities that apply to most of these fields. Scopus, for example, does not support MeSH term searching, although it includes the entire MEDLINE database that does provide such support. Field delineation by combining subject databases with citation databases have additional benefits, which will be discussed in more detail in Section 3.6.

3.2   EFFECTS OF FIELD DELINEATION ON CITATION NETWORK ANALYSIS

The commonly used approaches to field delineation discussed above have worked well for citation analysis studies of many research fields when well thought out (e.g., search strategy) and executed, but may not work well for some research fields. Examples include large research fields for which the limits put on the maximum number of records available for download (e.g., in Scopus) can be difficult to overcome and emerging, interdisciplinary, or multidisciplinary research fields in which research articles are published in an extremely wide range of journals and for which subject headings (or widely accepted keywords) have yet to be added to index these articles.

Researchers therefore have developed sophisticated algorithmic procedures to overcome these difficulties. Zitt and Bassecoulard (2006), for example, combined citation analysis, keyword search, and document clustering techniques to delineate the nanosciences literature using the ISI databases.

While it would be nice for all bibliometric studies to have a well-delineated field, and doing so might be essential for certain types of studies (e.g., research on policy issues), questions exist regarding how much a complete and clean dataset matters to typical evaluative and relational bibliometric studies such as ranking authors and co-citation mapping of a research field, and whether it is worth the significant extra costs to achieve a complete and clean dataset.

Further exploration of these questions is motivated by past studies that explored how much modified and sophisticated citation indicators improve upon simple citation counts for evaluation of impact, and those that compared author rankings using different citation databases (Cronin and Meho, 2006; Fiorenzo et al., 2013; Henzinger et al., 2010; Meho and Spurgin, 2005; Meho and Yang, 2007). These studies found that simple citation counts often work very well, and that author rankings based on different citation indicators or using different data sources are highly correlated, although ranks of some individual authors may vary substantially.

Zhao (2009) explored these questions through a case study of the LIS field on the differences in the intellectual structure shown in maps produced from an author co-citation analysis (ACA) of articles in two different but overlapping sets of core LIS journals. These two sets of core journals each consisted of 18 journals corresponding to the LIS faculty- and practitioner-valued publishing venues, respectively, and two-thirds of the journals in the two sets overlapped.

This case study found that major specialties identified from ACA based on these two sets of journals and the interrelationships between specialties in the mainstream LIS were identical for most specialties. However, substantial differences existed in the sizes of many specialties and in the connections between mainstream LIS and its extensions. For example, Children's information behavior is a distinct specialty in the LIS faculty dataset, but does not emerge as a separate specialty in the LIS practitioners dataset. Furthermore, in the LIS practitioners dataset the general Information behavior specialty is much larger, whereas the Scientometrics and IR systems specialties are much smaller than in the other dataset.

It was concluded in this case study that field delineation is not important to ACA studies of research fields only if the emphasis of a study is on a rough overall structure of the mainstream of a research field, and that studies that aim to go into great detail or which try to shed light on subtle research policy issues need to pay serious attention to the way that they delineate their fields.

Although it was not examined in this or in other studies explicitly, we can reasonably assume that the effect of field delineation on bibliographic coupling analysis is even stronger than on co-citation analysis. Co-citation analysis examines a set of highly cited objects in the field being studied, and reveals the structure of the field's knowledge base. Bibliographic coupling analysis, on the other hand, examines directly the active research or researchers in the field and thus provides a view of the structure of the field's research front (Cornelius et al., 2006; Persson, 1994; Zhao and Strotmann, 2014a). The nature of these two aspects of intellectual structures of research fields differs in that the knowledge base tends to have a relatively stable core while the research front can be diverse and quite dynamic. It is therefore even more important to have a clear field delineation in bibliographic coupling analysis studies.

3.3   REQUIREMENTS FOR DATA SOURCES FOR CITATION ANALYSIS

Clearly, field delineation affects the results of citation network analysis, and requires careful consideration when a citation analysis study is designed.

As mentioned earlier, the goal of field delineation is to collect a clean and complete set of citing documents (along with their reference lists) to represent a research field within a specified time period, at least for the purpose of addressing the research problems under investigation. The practical approach to field delineation has been to use the results retrieved from a citation database with an international or national coverage (e.g., the ISI databases, Scopus, Chinese Science Citation Database) because these databases record citation links that are required for any types of citation analysis.

The ISI databases have been the dominant citation database as most citation analysis studies to date have relied on this database to collect citation data. These studies include large-scale international or national research evaluation exercises such as university rankings (including the Times Higher Education World University Rankings and Leiden Rankings), trends in national publication output, and international collaboration within research fields (THE Methodology, 2013; Data Collection, 2013; Moed, 2010). Scopus is very similar to the ISI databases and now catching up in many aspects of a citation database and has surpassed the ISI databases in some areas (see details in a Section 3.5).

Problems with the ISI databases and Scopus as discussed later in this chapter, however, have led to researchers seeking alternative data sources for citation analysis. In early years, some researchers constructed their own citation databases for the study of small research fields (Chen and Carr, 1999; Eom and Farris, 1996). Citation data on the Web (e.g., CiteSeer, Google Scholar) have also been explored as data sources for citation analysis (Leydesdorff and Vaughan, 2006; Meho and Yang, 2007; Zhao, 2005a; 2006a). Recent years have seen studies that combine citation databases with subject bibliographic databases to take advantage of their respective features in order to improve datasets collected for citation analysis of large multidisciplinary and highly collaborative research fields (Strotmann et al., 2010; Zhao and Strotmann, 2011a; 2011b). It has also been proposed to use full-text research publications for the delineation of some research fields that are not covered well by citation databases, along with in-text citation data for the actual evaluative and relational analyses (Zhao and Strotmann, 2014b). Another good approach might be to supplement results retrieved from a citation database with additional publications (which are then indexed by researchers in the same format as the downloaded records) in order to reach the desired level of completeness for the study at hand.

All these different types of data sources for citation analysis, especially the two main citation databases, will be examined in the following sections with a focus on three aspects that are especially important for citation analysis: coverage, indexes and search facilities, and download options for people who work with the user interfaces provided by these databases.

Coverage

The coverage of a citation database is a key factor for determining how good the citation database is as a data source for citation analysis studies. As discussed in the previous section, field delineation relies on citation databases and affects the results of citation analysis. A better coverage of the research fields being studied leads to higher confidence in the results of citation analysis studies.

For example, the most commonly used citation databases (i.e., the ISI databases and Scopus) do not cover some of the research fields in the social sciences and humanities sufficiently, and therefore cannot be used as good data sources for the study of these research fields (Moed, 2010); on the other hand, citation data sources on the Web cover all research fields, but none systematically, and have thus not been used alone in citation analysis studies.

For longitudinal studies (especially studies concerned with growth), a stable coverage is also important so that differences in results of citation analysis of different time periods reflect the changes in the research fields being studied over time rather than changes in coverage of the databases used. For this reason, Scopus has not been used in citation analysis studies as much as the ISI databases despite the fact that Scopus has better coverage for many research fields and provides more information on cited references.

Indexes and search facilities

A citation database can only demonstrate its good coverage of a research field through good search facilities which maximize the number of documents retrieved from the citation database that are relevant for the citation analysis at hand, and minimize the number of irrelevant documents (i.e., noise) retrieved. This is essentially the fundamental problem in information retrieval (IR), i.e., how to retrieve the information needed and only the information needed (Saracevic, 1975).

As is well understood in IR, good search facilities require the support of quality indexes. The quality of indexing is indicated by whether all the information important for citation analysis is indexed and made searchable, how consistent indexing terms are used, and whether well-recognized controlled vocabularies (e.g., MeSH) are used and how well they are used.

Proper use of controlled vocabularies may improve both recall and precision of searches (Gross and Taylor, 2005; Rowley, 1994). For consistency, normalization and disambiguation should be performed in indexes of names (e.g., of journals, authors, institutions, departments, countries) and cited references so that all publications associated with an author (or journal, etc.) or citing a reference could be retrieved no matter which form of the author's name or of the cited reference is used for the searches. Information important for citation analysis includes, for example, authors' affiliations and complete information on cited references. Authors' affiliations should be indexed in the form of separated fields for department, institution, and country so that institutions and countries can be studied in citation analysis. The title, full journal name, and all authors (not just the first author) of each cited reference should be indexed so that cited references can be searched through these fields, authors' contributions as co-authors can be counted in citation analysis, and the interpretation of results is possible based directly on information provided for cited references (instead of having to link back to corresponding source articles).

Both the ISI databases and Scopus, for example, have an excellent coverage of the biomedical research fields, but do not support searching by MeSH terms. Instead, a search for a term always retrieves all publications that are indexed under that term as keywords or MeSH terms or other descriptors, which can result in a high level of noise for some terms (e.g., the term "stem cells"). Each cited reference is indexed in the ISI databases as a short string, which includes the first author, the abbreviation of journal name, and the publication year and page numbers. As a result, it is very difficult with the ISI databases to search cited references, or to conduct all-author-based citation analysis, or to interpret results of citation network analysis as there are no titles of cited references to inform the interpretation.

Download options

For the purpose of field delineation, a good data source for citation analysis should also support the systematic download of all search results in a standardized format that is easy to process by computer programs. Downloading analytical results produced by citation databases should be made possible as well, which can ease certain evaluative citation analyses.

With the ISI databases, for example, all search results can be downloaded, no matter how large the retrieved dataset is, although only 5,000 records can be added to the Marked List at a time and only 500 records of the Marked List can be downloaded at a time. With Scopus, however, only the first 2,000 records in the retrieved dataset can be downloaded, and workarounds are therefore required when the dataset required for a citation analysis study is large. All cited references of a citing document are indexed as a single field in both the ISI databases and Scopus. It is therefore required to parse this long string into individual cited references and then each cited reference into separate fields such as authors, title, journal, and year, which, unfortunately, is an error-prone process.

A better data format for output would be an XML document with individual references and these individual fields clearly marked up. Even better would be to link cited references to the corresponding citing documents if available in the same citation database, and to download these citing documents automatically when the cited references are downloaded because citing documents are represented much better in these databases than cited references are, with more complete information (e.g., keywords, author affiliation) and separate fields marked up. Readers who are not familiar with XML can try a search in PubMed, download the retrieved data in the XML format, and take a look at how information is represented there in order to understand why XML is a more desired format for data processing in citation analysis (and in other bibliometric studies, in fact). Appendix 3.3 provides an example of a PubMed record in XML format.

3.4   THE ISI DATABASES

Most citation analysis studies to date have used the ISI databases as data sources. The ISI databases have significantly contributed to the advance of citation analysis theory and methodology, but have also drawn considerable criticism and limited the further development of citation analysis theory and methods (Borgman, 1990; Edge, 1979; Egghe and Rousseau, 1990; Garfield, 1979; Lindsey, 1980; Long et al., 1980; MacRoberts and MacRoberts, 1989; McCain, 1988; Osareh, 1996; Smith, 1981; Stokes and Hartley, 1989; White, 1990).

In this section, advantages of and problems with the ISI citation databases for citation analysis will be discussed, followed by a brief description of how to use these databases in Web of Science for field delineation. Moed (2010) provides a detailed analysis of the ISI databases in terms of their basic principles and coverage as well as the implications of using these data sources for citation analysis in research evaluation.

3.4.1   ADVANTAGES OF USING THE ISI DATABASES FOR CITATION ANALYSIS STUDIES

The ISI citation indexes are comprised of three parts: the Science Citation Index (SCI), the Social Science Citation Index, and the Arts and Humanities Citation Index. As mentioned above, these databases have been the dominant data sources for citation analysis studies since the 1960s, when SCI was created, and continue to do so now even with strong competition from Scopus. Clearly, these databases have their own advantages.

Multidisciplinary stable coverage over a long history

First and foremost is the ISI databases' coverage of all disciplines over a long time period, allowing the study of an entire scholarly enterprise over long periods of development as well as comparisons between different parts of this enterprise (e.g., between countries or across disciplines). The Science Citation Index (SCI), for example, covers journals dating back to the year 1900. Citations can be traced from the present all the way back to the early dates of all disciplines or even to the origins of some research fields. In contrast, Scopus covers most disciplines only from the year 1996 onward and the arts and humanities from the year 2002 on; however, it includes all of Medline, which started in the 1960s and covers biomedical and life sciences journal articles back to the year 1946.

Well understood and widely accepted

Because of its long history and its dominant position in citation analysis, the ISI databases are well understood in terms of both their problems and positive features. Various workarounds and remedies have also been explored and proposed. Results based on these databases are therefore widely accepted with a full understanding of their problems.

Highly selective coverage

The ISI databases operate on the principle of Garfield's Law of Concentration, "which states that the tail of the literature of one discipline consists, in a large part, of the cores of the literature of other disciplines. So large is the overlap between disciplines, in fact, that the core literature for all scientific disciplines involves a group of no more than 1,000 journals, and may involve as few as 500" (Garfield, 1979, p. 23). Thomson Reuters claims that what is covered in the ISI databases represent the "best" and most important part of the literature, which is selected by the Thomson Reuters editors who have educational backgrounds relevant to their areas of responsibility and are also experts in the literature of their fields (Testa, 2012; MacRoberts and MacRoberts, 1989). This highly selective coverage is considered a desirable feature for citation analysis, especially evaluative citation analysis studies. Being indexed by the ISI databases has itself become an indication of prestige and quality, not to mention being cited by these indexed articles.

Consistent indexing policy

Indexing of the information important for citation analysis has been largely stable in the ISI databases over the years, making it easy to maintain computer programs for the processing and analysis of data downloaded from these databases. The changes they have been making over the years are mostly compatible, i.e., if you wrote your software well, it can still read the new data.

Support for downloading large datasets

As mentioned above, the ISI databases support systematical downloading of large sets of search results, 500 records at a time, whereas only the first 2,000 records of the search results from Scopus can be downloaded when cited references are included, all at once.

Cited reference search

In addition to regular searches for source papers by subject, author, etc., it is possible to search cited references directly by author and journal abbreviation. Although many problems exist with this search facility as discussed below, cited reference search has made it possible to collect co-citation counts of authors and journals directly from these databases, and to conduct co-citation analysis studies without sophisticated computer programing skills for data processing (White and McCain, 1998; Zhao and Strotmann, 2008b). This option also makes it possible to use the snowball technique for field delineation, i.e., starting from a small set of known highly cited documents or authors and retrieve all documents that have cited these documents, and so forth until reaching the desired size of dataset.

Journal Citation Report (JCR)

JCR provides annual analyses of journals covered in the ISI databases by various indicators, including the highly influential Journal Impact Factor (JIF) which measures the citation impact of the "average article" in a journal in a given time period. A journal's JIF in year N is defined as B/A where A is the total number of "citable" articles published in this journal in years N–1 and N–2 and B is the total number of citations these articles received from all articles published in year N in all journals indexed in the ISI databases. JIF has been widely used in research evaluation as an indicator of the quality of research publications, especially when the citation counts of these publications are not available, although this use has been strongly criticized by the research communities. For example, newly published articles assessed with the recent JIF of the journals where they were published have been routinely used in university professors' annual performance evaluations. JCR has also been used directly as a data source for journal citation analysis (Leydesdorff, 2006; Zhang et al., 2011).

3.4.2   PROBLEMS

Limited and biased coverage

One of the major criticisms of the ISI databases is their limited and biased coverage.

As discussed above, the ISI databases are highly selective in their inclusion of sources, which means that what is included in these databases is not a random sample but a selected group. This may cause validity problems in citation analysis studies because citation analysis essentially builds on statistical techniques that may require random samples (MacRoberts and MacRoberts, 1989). Perhaps more importantly, it has been found that the ISI databases' coverage of publications in some research fields, especially in the social sciences and humanities, is so poor that they are not considered as adequate data sources for citation analysis studies of these fields at all. Moed (2010) provides a detailed analysis of which fields are covered well and which inadequately.

In addition, the ISI databases only cover articles in journals, which ISI claims are the most important part of the literature because the journal has historically served as the primary scholarly communication channel. However, this may not be true in the humanities (and even in some fields in the natural and social sciences) where documents other than journals are considered more important. For example, books are extremely important in the humanities and some social sciences, as are conference papers for the computer science fields. To address this "journal only" coverage problem, Thomson Reuters has recently added citation indexes for conference proceedings as well as for books and book chapters. However, studies are required to evaluate how well these indexes cover the various research fields.

The ISI databases also have a bias in coverage toward publications in English-speaking countries (Moed, 2010; van Leeuwen et al., 2001), which have made comparisons between countries difficult and unfair in citation analysis when using these databases as data sources. This bias has been a major source of criticisms of the THE World University Rankings, which uses the ISI databases as the data source for calculating citation indicators and is dominated by universities in English-speaking countries in their lists of top 100 universities (Liu and Cheng, 2005; Rauhvargers, 2011).

Inadequate indexing of cited references

The ISI databases provide very limited information about each cited reference, as seen from Table 3.1 which shows the first few cited references from a source article downloaded from these databases along with the corresponding items from the reference list of this article itself. Essentially, only the surname and first initials of the first author, publication year, ISI abbreviation of the name of the journal where the article was published (or ISI abbreviated title in the case of a book), volume number, and the start page number of the article, are provided. For cited references that are also indexed in the ISI databases as source article, an identification number may also be provided, but this is not done consistently, as shown by cited references 7 and 8 that are both indexed as source articles but only one is linked to a DOI.

Table 3.1: ISI cited references and corresponding documents they refer to
Cited references from ISI databases
1. BATES MJ, 1989, ONLINE REV, V13, P407, DOI 10.1108/eb024320
2. BELKIN NJ, 1982, J DOC, V38, P61, DOI 10.1108/eb026722
3. BLAIR DC, 1990, LANGUAGE REPRESENTAE
4. BONZI S, 1991, SCIENTOMETRICS, V21, P245, DOI 10.1007/BF02017571
5. Borgman C.L., 1990, SCHOLARLY COMMUNICAT, P10
6. BOYCE B, 1982, INFORM PROCESS MANAG, V18, P105, DOI 10.1016/0306-4573(82)90033-4
7. BROOKS TA, 1986, J AM SOC INFORM SCI, V37, P34
8. COOPER WS, 1973, J AM SOC INFORM SCI, V24, P87, DOI 10.1002/asi.4630240204
Corresponding items from the reference list in the citing article
1. Bates, M. J. (1989). The design of browsing and berry-picking techniques for the online search interface. Online Review, 13, 407–424.
2. Belkin, N. J., Oddy, R. N., and Brooks, H. M. (1982). ASK for Information Retrieval: Part I. Background and Theory. Part II. Results of a Design Study. *Journal of Documentation*, 38, 61–71, 145–164.
3. Blair, D. C. (1990). Language and representation in information retrieval Amsterdam: Elsevier.
4. Bonzi, S., and Snyder, H. W. (1991). Motivations for citation: A comparison of self citation and citation to others. Scientometrics, 21, 245–254.
5. Borgman, C. L. (1990). Editor's Introduction. In C. L.Borgman (Ed.), Scholarly communication and bibliometrics (pp. 10–27). Newbury Park, CA: Sage Publications.
6. Boyce, B. (1982). Beyond topicality: A two stage view of relevance and the retrieval process. Information Processing and Management, 18, 105–109.
7. Brooks, T. A. (1986). Evidence of complex titer motivations. *Journal of the American Society for Information Science*, 37, 34–36.
8. Cooper, W. S. (1973). On selecting a measure of retrieval effectiveness. *Journal of the American Society for Information Science*, 24, 87–100.

The inadequate indexing of cited references makes the ISI databases very difficult to use for the interpretation of citation network analysis results and for studies involving more than the first author of each cited references.

As discussed in Chapter 2 (Section 2.6), the main source of information for interpretation of citation network analysis results is rooted in the documents associated with the objects being studied (e.g., documents, authors, journals). As cited references in downloaded records from the ISI databases do not include titles or full journal names of the cited documents to inform the interpretation, titles of the huge number of cited references normally involved in a co-citation analysis essentially have to be located as source papers through searches in the ISI databases or in other bibliographic databases. Such searches can be very time-consuming and difficult because queries created from these cited references are limited to the terse information available there and additional options such as keyword search are not possible. In addition, the ISI abbreviations of journal names available for these searches may not always be recognized, especially in other bibliographic databases, certainly not the abbreviated book titles. Although DOIs can be searched in the DOI field in the ISI databases to retrieve the full records of the corresponding source articles, DOIs are currently only provided for some of the cited references as shown by examples in Table 3.1 above. Even after DOIs were added to all cited references that are also indexed as source articles in the ISI databases, not all cited references can be matched back to the source articles as the ISI databases will never index all of the cited references as their source papers with Garfield's Law of Concentration as their operational principle (Bensman, 2001; Zhao and Logan, 2002). Disregarding references to non-ISI source papers makes the data incomplete and may invalidate the subsequent analysis, at least for research fields that are not covered well by these databases (Moed, 2010, Chapter 10).

While the first author in the by-line may represent the person with the most significant contribution to the paper in many fields, alphabetic ordering of authors is a common practice in other fields (Endersby, 1996; Lindsey, 1980; Rudd, 1977; Zhao and Logan, 2002; Zhao, 2005a). Similarly, depending on the research field, the last author in the by-line may either represent the person with the least contribution or the team lead whose contribution is unique and important (Sonnenwald, 2008; Zhao and Strotmann, 2011a; 2011b). How to distribute citation weight to authors in different positions in the by-lines of cited references should therefore be well considered in citation analysis studies. However, beyond simply counting the first authors, any thoughtful treatment of this issue would be very difficult, if not impossible, with the cited references in the ISI databases. Relying on matching cited references back to source articles cannot solve this problem completely as discussed above, at least for research fields that are not covered well there. Another approach to all-author counting using the ISI databases was suggested by Garfield, the inventor of these databases, who recommended that a complete list of publications authored or co-authored by each of the scholars being evaluated be compiled and citations to these publications obtained from the ISI databases and then used in evaluation (Garfield, 1979). This approach can in principle be used in all research fields and has in fact been used in real-life evaluations (Moed, 2010). However, it is only feasible for the evaluation of a known group of scholars, and becomes hopeless in answering such questions as "who are the most influential players in this particular research field as seen from citations?"

Errors and inconsistency in cited references

Last but not least, the accuracy of citation and co-citation counts using the ISI databases is questionable as both homonyms and allonyms are common in ISI data, which can be seen from the results of a cited reference search by author name (e.g., Zhao, DZ). References to books are particularly prone to this problem, as they frequently include the cited page number, and citations to different pages in different editions of the same book are considered citations to a different source in the ISI databases. For example, the oeuvre of Jürgen Habermas, sociologist and philosopher, was cited in more than 10,000 different forms according to the ISI databases, even though authoritative bibliographies tend to list about 100 of his works.

3.4.3   HOW TO DELINEATE A RESEARCH FIELD USING THE ISI DATABASES

The ISI databases are commercial and for profit, and citation analysis using these databases requires subscription to or purchase of these databases, which is quite expensive.

As discussed earlier, for the study of an entire research enterprise or a large number of disciplines, purchase of entire databases during certain time periods is often necessary. This type of citation analysis requires large datasets, which can be time-consuming to download from the ISI databases as it prohibits automatic downloading and only allows manual downloading of 500 records at a time.

For the study of a single research field or a small number of fields, the Web interface of the ISI databases that is available to users with a subscription can be used for all of the commonly used approaches to field delineation discussed earlier.

For journal-based field delineation, the journals listed in JCR of the ISI databases can serve as a starting point for selecting a set of core journals. Some journals can, and often should, be removed from the list based on the objectives of the study at hand. The journals in JCR's "Information Science and Library Science" category, for example, includes many journals in the area of management information systems which is normally considered as a research area in business rather than LIS. These journals should be removed from the list and the remaining journals can then be used to define the LIS research field. The names of these journals can be searched in the ISI databases in the Publication Name field, one at a time or all at once connected by the Boolean OR operator.

To download the search results, retrieved records need to be first added to the Marked List, and then downloaded from there. As only a maximum of 5,000 records can be added to the Marked List at a time, downloading search results of over 5,000 records needs to be completed in stages.

Click on the Add to Marked List button on the top of the main section on the search results page, and a popup window appears. In this window, specify the records to be added to the Marked List by filling in the Records and To boxes accordingly (i.e., 1 and 5,000 for the first time, and 5,001 and 10,000 for the second time, and so forth), and click on the Add button (Figure 3.1). You are now back to the search results page with the number of records you provided showing next to the Add to Marked List button. On the very top of the search result page, click on the Marked List link. On the next page, you will be able to choose which records and content to download and in which format. Choose records 1 to 500 in Step 1 (for the first time, and then 501 to 1,000 for the second time, and so forth), and make sure to check the Cited References box as part of the content to download in Step 2. In the Send to drop down list in Step 3, choose the Other File Formats option (Figure 3.2). In the popup window that appears, choose the Plain Text or a Tab-delimited option in the drop down list and then click on the Send button. The specified records will be saved in a file named savedrecs.txt in the download folder on your computer. To download the next set of up to 5,000 records of the search results, first clear the Marked List by clicking on the corresponding orange button on the top right of the Marked List page, and then go back to the search results page by clicking on the Exit Marked List link on the top left (Figure 3.2).

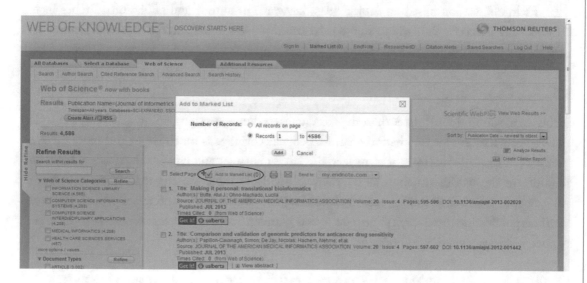

Figure 3.1: Downloading records from the ISI databases—Step 1: add to marked list.

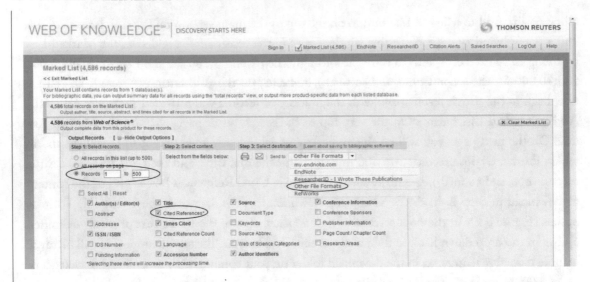

Figure 3.2: Downloading records from the ISI databases—Step 1: Download from marked list, 500 records at a time.

Field delineation based on subject (e.g., keyword) or author and affiliation searches in the ISI databases proceeds similarly to the journal-based process above, except that search terms will need to be searched in the corresponding fields (i.e., Topic, Author, and Address or Organization).

3.5   SCOPUS

Scopus came around much later than the ISI databases, but is catching up quickly both as an IR tool and as a data source for citation analysis. Scopus's coverage is much larger and more diverse than that of the ISI databases; it is, in fact, the largest abstract and citation database of research literature in the world, although its coverage is decidedly more current than historical. As of 2012, Scopus boasted 49 million records, including over five million conference papers, 100% of Medline publications, and 19,500 peer-reviewed journals. It has also made an effort to increase its book coverage, with 75,000 titles as of 2013 (Scopus, 2013).

3.5.1   PROS AND CONS AS A DATA SOURCE FOR CITATION ANALYSIS

Scopus has both advantages and disadvantages compared to the ISI databases as a data source for citation analysis.

More information on cited references

The chief advantage of Scopus over the ISI databases is that much more information about cited references is available from its downloaded records. In contrast to the terse information indexed in the ISI databases as discussed earlier, Scopus provides the full title, the full name of the journal, and names of the first seven authors and of the last author for each cited reference, which informs the interpretation of citation network analysis results very well and supports all-author citation analysis for most research fields, with the exception of those highly collaborative fields (such as high energy physics and some biomedical fields) in which publications with more than eight authors are quite common.

Better search facilities

Scopus also has better search facilities in general and a better Advanced Search facility in particular than the ISI databases.

Scopus incorporates the use of seven different controlled vocabularies (including MeSH, GEOBASE Subject Index, and Ei thesaurus) in 80% of its titles, leading to better search results within certain scientific fields (SciVerse, 2012), whereas controlled vocabulary is not used in the ISI databases core collection (i.e., the ISI databases). Scopus also stands out for supporting more precise proximity searches: the "precedes by" and "within" operators allow for more relevant results than the ISI databases' "near" operator. Particularly useful for delineating a research field in citation analysis studies (discussed in greater detail in the next section) are the refining options for search results in Scopus, which allow either limiting to or excluding results by year, author name, subject, affiliation, country, and more, whereas only limiting is possible in the ISI databases. Of particular note are the options for searching the first author, chemical name, or the American Chemical Society CAS registry number, which are not supported in the ISI databases.

Advanced Search is used for batch matching bibliographic records obtained from subject databases (or elsewhere such as authors' CVs) to Scopus (or the ISI databases) in order to obtain citation links, as discussed in the next section. The ISI databases limit the number of search terms per query to 500 in its Advanced Search, whereas there is no such limit in Scopus. As matching search strategies are complex and require many search terms for each document (see examples in the next section for details), searching for the same number of documents in Scopus would require only a fraction of the number of queries needed to issue in the ISI databases, were it possible in the ISI databases at all, because each query can search for many more documents in Scopus without the limit on the number of search terms.

Comparable support for downloading search results

Scopus and the ISI databases are comparable in terms of ease of downloading search results. Scopus supports the download of the first 2,000 records of search results, all at once, compared to all records but 500 at a time in the ISI databases. Using the ISI databases, field delineation can be achieved through a single search, but the downloading of search results has to be done 500 records at a time. Using Scopus, field delineation requires a series of searches that each result in a dataset smaller than 2,000 records and each of such small datasets can be downloaded all at once. It is normally quite easy to design these small searches. For example, if 5,000 records are retrieved from a search for the term "knowledge management" limited to five years, three or four searches for the same term can be carried out instead, each limited to one or two years; similarly, if a search for a set of 12 core journals returns 10,000 records, two or three journals can be searched at a time to keep each set of search results within the 2,000 limit. If a search cannot be broken into a series of smaller searches by year or journal, the "include" or "exclude" option for refining searches in Scopus can be used to break the search results into two subsets, which works for search results with 4,000 records or fewer. For larger sets of search results that cannot be broken down into smaller searches, downloading becomes difficult with Scopus, but is still done the same way as all other searches in the ISI databases. The next section provides one way to solve this problem with Scopus.

Problems in coverage and indexing

The biggest problems with Scopus are its relatively short-term and unstable coverage (which makes longitudinal studies difficult) and its insufficient coverage of research fields in the social sciences and humanities. Scopus is relatively new (launched in November 2004), and has been changing rapidly since then in all aspects, including coverage and indexing. Scopus originally covered most research fields from 1996 and on, but has been adding older records as part of their archive project, and now includes the complete abstracts of several major publishers (including Springer, the American Chemical Society, and Oxford University Press), with records going back as far as 1823 (SciVerse, 2012). Scopus's coverage of research fields and of journals expands regularly, and it now covers 19,500 journals (which is 60% more than the ISI databases). Many of these journals are published in non-English speaking countries such as China, and non-English titles are included so long as an English abstract is provided. As of 2012, Scopus claimed 21% of its titles were non-English, and more than half were from regions other than North America (SciVerse, 2012).

As a result, Scopus has a wider and less selective coverage of many research fields, and is less biased against non-English speaking countries, although it has been found to have a coverage bias toward European countries (Meester, 2013). In principle, the more covered a research field is by a citation database, the better it is represented by data from this database. However, as these citation databases do not randomly sample documents to cover, studies are required to determine whether Scopus's less selective coverage is a positive or negative feature as people have become accustomed to the highly selective coverage by the ISI databases. In some research fields, it may be fair to consider citation analysis using the ISI databases as based on the collective view of an elite group in the research field being studied, and it is still not clear how Scopus has expanded this view and what views Scopus represents exactly.

The indexing of journals in Scopus may not be complete in that a few issues may be missed for some journals (Goodman, 2007; Zhao, 2010). The format of indexing has been changing as well, which makes it necessary to constantly change the computer programs written for processing data downloaded from it.

Before Scopus stabilizes its coverage and indexing, studies that require stable coverage and indexing can use both the ISI databases and Scopus. Specifically, the same search strategy required for the field delineation of a citation analysis study can be performed in both the ISI databases and Scopus and search results downloaded. The dataset from the ISI databases can then be used for citation and co-citation counting, and the dataset from Scopus for information about cited references to inform the interpretation of results.

3.5.2   HOW TO DELINEATE A FIELD USING SCOPUS

Like the ISI databases, Scopus is commercial and for profit, and citation analysis using Scopus requires subscription to or purchase of datasets from this database, which is also quite expensive. For the study of a single small research field or a small number of fields, the Web interface of Scopus that is available to users with a subscription may be sufficient and can be used for all of the commonly used approaches to field delineation discussed earlier. For the study of an entire research enterprise or a large number of large research fields, purchase of datasets from Scopus is often necessary as this type of citation analysis requires large datasets, but only 2,000 records of the results retrieved from a search can be downloaded from the Web interface of Scopus.

For journal-based field delineation, names of the journals that are used to define the research field being studied are searched in Scopus in the Source Title field, one at a time or all at once connected by the Boolean OR operator. Figure 3.3 shows a search for four journals. The Add search field button can be used to add more journals or other fields.

To download search results that are smaller than 2,000 records, select all search results by checking the "All" box in the upper left corner of the main section of the search results page, then click on the Export (not the Download) link next to the check box (Figure 3.4). On the next page, select "Comma separated file, .csv" as the Export Format, and "Complete format" for the Output option; then click on the Export button (Figure 3.5).

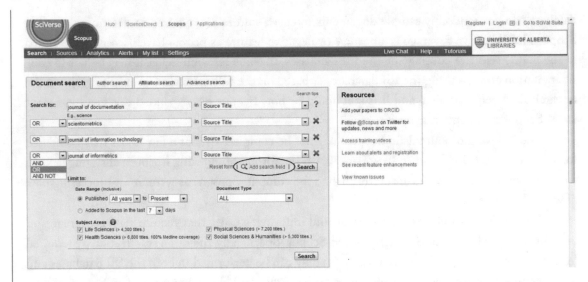

Figure 3.3: Journal-bases field delineation: searching the ISI databases for four journals at a time.

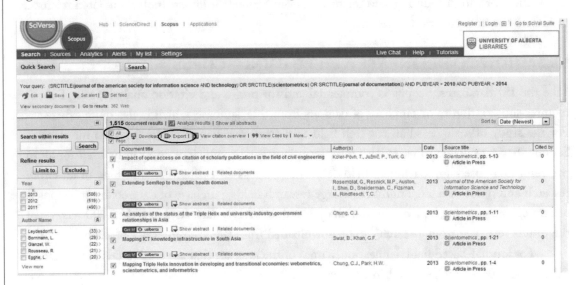

Figure 3.4: Downloading up to 2,000 search results from the ISi datases—Step 1: Mark all for export.

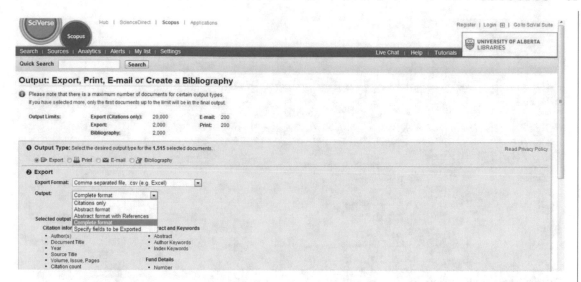

Figure 3.5: Downloading up to 2,000 search results from the ISI datases—Step 2: Choice of export format for download.

If a search results in more than 2,000 records, a series of the same searches for a single year or for a smaller set of journals at a time can be carried out instead. The "Limit to" and "Exclude" options in the Refine results section located on the left side of the search results page can also be used for this purpose (Figure 3.6). For example, if the search in the example shown in Figure 3.3 were expanded to include two more years and four more journals and as a result retrieved 5,000 records, seven searches could be carried out instead, each searching for a single journal and all five years, or five searches, each for all seven journals and a single year. If the search for all journals and all years results in fewer (e.g., 3,500) records than could be achieved by two downloads of 2,000 records, the search could first be refined in the Refine results section by checking three of the five years and then selecting the "Exclude" option. After downloading the search results, return to the search results page with the three years checked, select the "Limit to" option this time, and download the results (Figure 3.6).

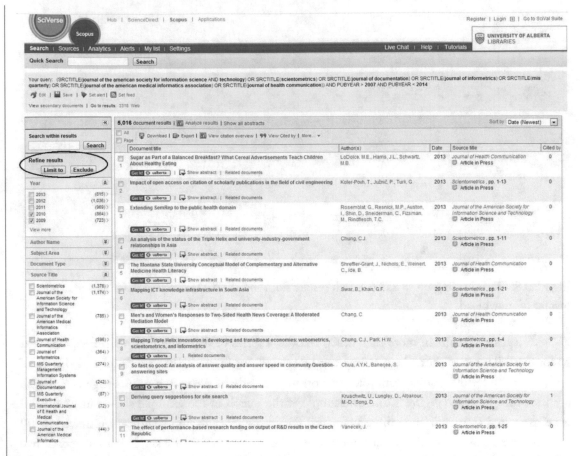

Figure 3.6: Using search refinement to split search results into manageably sized chunks for download.

Field delineation based on subject (e.g., keyword) or author and affiliation searches in Scopus proceeds similarly to the journal-based process above, except that search terms will need to be searched in the corresponding fields (i.e., Article Title, Abstract, Keywords, Authors, and Affiliation).

3.6   FIELD DELINEATION BY COMBINING CITATION DATABASES WITH SUBJECT BIBLIOGRAPHIC DATABASES

Subject (bibliographic) databases refer to bibliographic databases that cover specific subjects or research fields, such as ERIC for education related research and PubMed for biomedical research fields. These databases tend to be more effective for the subject fields covered as they normally use subject headings specific to these subject fields and thus support searches that are specific to these fields. Citation databases, on the other hand, normally cover all research fields and only provide generic search facilities that apply to all research fields. Even when citation databases do provide some kind of indexes specific to some subject fields, such as the two chemistry specific indexes in Scopus (i.e., chemical names and the American Chemical Society CAS registry number), these indexes are often not as comprehensive as those in subject specific databases, and are therefore by no means comparable with these databases (SciVerse, 2012).

For example, MEDLINE is the premier bibliographic database provided by the U.S. National Library of Medicine (NLM) that contains millions of records on journal articles in the life sciences with a concentration on biomedicine; a distinctive feature of it is that the records are extensively and manually indexed with NLM's Medical Subject Headings (MeSH). MeSH specific search options provided in MEDLINE (e.g., searching the term "stem cell" as MeSH term or as MeSH major topic) are therefore very effective. Although both Scopus and the ISI databases cover 100% of MEDLINE, Scopus does not support MeSH specific searches while MEDLINE in Web of Science is a separate database from the ISI citation databases and a search in MEDLINE there does not retrieve records with cited references included.

Datasets retrieved from subject databases therefore can be cleaner and more complete with respect to field delineation than those from generic citation databases within the limit of the coverage of these citation databases. Combining citation databases with subject databases can therefore provide better field delineation for citation analysis, which can be very important for studies that aim to shed light on particularly subtle research policy issues, but at the cost of having to map the search results from subject databases to a citation database. This extra cost, however, has extra benefits in addition to a more complete and cleaner dataset. It:

- allows a way to retrieve a dataset from Scopus that is larger than 2,000 records and where the search cannot be broken down completely into smaller searches,

- serves as a way of normalization and disambiguation of names and cited references that are currently not performed well in the ISI databases or in Scopus, and

- obtains even more information with higher accuracy on cited references than that provided by Scopus' cited references.

These extra benefits and the process of field delineation using this method will be discussed below using the example of combining Scopus and PubMed to retrieve the data required for an all-author co-citation analysis in the stem cell research field. PubMed is a publicly available service by the NLM with MEDLINE at its core. It includes over 18 million rich bibliographic records for biomedical journal articles since 1948 created by information professionals (or provided by journal publishers) and maintained by the NLM.

While the particular method described below will work only for studies on biomedical research areas, as it uses the PubMed database, it can easily be applied to other fields, such as engineering, for which large-scale high-quality bibliographic databases exist. The content below is largely adapted from Zhao and Strotmann (2011a; 2011b) and Strotmann et al. (2010).

3.6.1   JUSTIFICATION OF COMBINING SCOPUS AND PUBMED FOR DELINEATING THE STEM CELL RESEARCH FIELD

Stem cell research is a highly interdisciplinary biomedical research area, and is published in a wide variety of biomedical journals due to the fact that stem cells are fundamental to the workings of each and every organ of the human body. Consequently, stem cells are implicated in a wide range of diseases and also show promise as a research tool and therapeutic vehicle in just as wide a range of areas. In addition, stem cell research logistics require significant support from bioinformatics and biomedical engineering. For a number of quite diverse reasons, there is even quite extensive social science research conducted in this area.

Journal-based field delineation clearly does not work for this type of research field, nor do the keyword searching facilities in generic citation databases which do not generally work well to delimit emerging and interdisciplinary fields, as Zitt and Bassecoulard (2006) show for the nano-sciences, and Suomela and Andrade (2005) for stem cell research. Even if keyword searching in Scopus or the ISI databases were good enough for this purpose, these databases would still not work for the delineation of the large, active, diverse, and highly collaborative stem cell research field. In this field, approximately 10,000 refereed papers are published annually, spread across hundreds of journals, which makes the above-mentioned workarounds for overcoming Scopus's download limit (e.g., searching one year and a few journals at a time) unhelpful. Last authors typically have played a major role in stem cell research like in many other biomedical research fields, which makes it problematic to use the ISI databases that only supports first-author-based citation analysis.

A three-step matching process between PubMed and Scopus was therefore carried out in order to delineate the stem cell field for citation analysis, i.e., to collect a set of records of articles in the stem cell research field that was complete, clean, and included their complete cited references: (1) using PubMed's MeSH term search facility to obtain citing papers, (2) matching these papers to Scopus in order to obtain their cited references, and (3) matching the Scopus cited references to PubMed both to obtain complete data on cited references and to disambiguate (i.e., clean) these cited references.

Scopus was chosen over the ISI databases for this purpose for two main reasons: (1) as discussed in the previous section, searching for the same number of documents using the advanced search facility in Scopus would require only a fraction of the number of queries needed in the ISI databases because of the limit that the ISI databases put on the number of search terms per query, and (2) each cited reference includes terse information in the ISI databases, which makes it extremely tedious to match cited references in the ISI databases back to PubMed records. By contrast, a cited reference in Scopus includes quite extensive information that can be used for the matching: up to eight author names (surname and initials), title, and full journal name, publishing year, volume, and page number.

3.6.2 PROCESS OF MATCHING BETWEEN SCOPUS AND PUBMED FOR FIELD DELINEATION

As mentioned above, a three-step matching process between PubMed and Scopus was carried out.

Step 1. Obtaining a complete and clean set of citing articles on stem cell research in PubMed

Suomela and Andrade (2005), the latter a primary investigator of the Canadian Stem Cell Network at the time, studied the recall and specificity of hundreds of potential search terms for the field of stem cell research. Their results suggest that the PubMed MeSH term search provided an excellent delimitation of the field, while the interdisciplinary nature of the field appeared to make it impossible to construct a keyword search strategy in Scopus or the ISI databases that would match its quality.

Relying on their results, a search for "stem cell" in MeSH terms was therefore conducted in PubMed, with the confidence that the search results would be considerably cleaner and more complete compared with results from keyword or subject searching supported by the ISI databases or Scopus. More than 10,000 records were retrieved for the year 2007 alone (i.e., 10,915), but PubMed supports the download of the full search result set for the years 2004–2009 in XML format, all at once—a feature that is not supported by either the ISI databases or Scopus.

Step 2. Matching PubMed search results to Scopus

Computer programs were then developed to create search strings with information extracted from these downloaded PubMed records which identify records for the same articles in Scopus. To avoid timeout errors in the Scopus database, each search string aims to retrieve 500 articles from Scopus, although the maximum number of downloadable results in Scopus is 2,000 in principle.

For the vast majority of cases, matching records between Scopus and PubMed can be simply done through the PubMed ID (PMID), which is used to identify each paper in PubMed and is indexed in Scopus as a searchable field in its bibliographic records. A search string for 500 articles in Scopus thus consists of 500 PMIDs extracted from the downloaded PubMed records in the format of PMID(3219062), separated by the Boolean OR operator.

Unfortunately, not all records in Scopus have a value in the PMID field, and the PMID values in some records are not valid PubMed IDs. For those records with missing or erroneous values in the PMID field, a different search strategy is used in Scopus queries.

Simply put, the Scopus query constructed for a single article looks for its title or starting and ending page numbers, for last names of its authors, for its source journal's ISSN or title, and for volume and issue numbers. The article title (TITLE) and journal title (SRCTITLE) fields are normalized. Here is a random example:

```
(ISSN(0007-1048) OR SRCTITLE("British Journal of Haematology")) AND VOL-
UME(111) AND ISSUE(2) AND AUTHLAST-NAME(moscardó) AND (TITLE("graft-ver-
sus-tumour effect in non-small-cell lung cancer after allogeneic peripheral
blood stem cell transplantation.") OR (PAGEFIRST(708) AND PAGELAST(710)).
```

As just mentioned, each of the search queries that was created from information extracted from the downloaded PubMed XML records aimed to identify 500 articles in Scopus. That means that an actual search query submitted to Scopus consisted of 500 single article search strings as above, connected with the Boolean OR operator.

To comply with Scopus licensing limitations (Scopus, 2004), which forbid automated downloads, search queries constructed automatically as described above were manually entered in Scopus using its advanced search facility, one at a time, and the complete records of the search results were then downloaded.

A computer program was also developed to remove false positives from the Scopus search results, i.e., records retrieved from Scopus that were not included in the original PubMed download.

The strategies and algorithms described above for matching PubMed records to Scopus worked really well: only about 2% of the PubMed records were not found in Scopus, and less than 1% of the false positives were missed.

Step 3. Matching Scopus cited references to PubMed records

The complete records downloaded from Scopus could now serve as the dataset for citation analysis studies that do not require more than what Scopus can offer. However, the quality of this dataset can be improved by matching Scopus cited references to PubMed records, which may be necessary and important for citation analysis studies that require more accurate and complete data, such as for subtle policy issues. For example, Scopus data on cited references include up to eight of the authors of each cited reference, which can be a problem for citation-based research evaluation in highly collaborative research fields such as the stem cell field, in which large-group collaboration is common. Mapping cited references to their full PubMed records will complete the author lists, mostly with their full names. In addition, Scopus references to the same article may come in many forms, so that identifying the corresponding PubMed records for all of them will solve the problem of disambiguating cited references to a considerably degree.

Note that Scopus' cited references can also be matched back to Scopus source papers in this case as Scopus covers MEDLINE completely. This may be done quite easily with the purchase of the entire Scopus database using the identification numbers of cited references provided, but would require a process similar to Step 2 described above with the downloaded records from Scopus which do not include reference IDs (in fact it is worse, as PMIDs are not included in cited references). This process is much more difficult and time-consuming than the process using PubMed with the support of its Batch Citation Matcher (http://www.ncbi.nlm.nih.gov/pubmed/batchcitmatch), as can be seen below.

There were two reasons for choosing the PubMed Batch Citation Matcher to retrieve the full PubMed records of Scopus cited references rather than directly searching PubMed: (1) the Batch Citation Matcher handles really large queries (e.g., thousands of citations at a time) quite nicely, speeding up the process considerably, and (2) with the exception of the journal name and publication year fields, this tool ignores a field's value if all other fields match—a feature that is useful for correcting erroneous spellings or page numbers found in the Scopus data. The citation matcher thus effectively acts as a disambiguation mechanism for Scopus' cited references, and makes it easy to detect duplicates in the original Scopus data as well.

Computer programs were developed to create search strings from Scopus's data on cited references that look for records of the same articles in PubMed to be issued to the PubMed Batch Citation Matcher. Scopus cited references are quite inconsistent in terms of author names, article titles, journal names, etc.—five to ten different versions of the same reference are not unusual. Mapping these cited references to PubMed records using Batch Citation Matcher can therefore not only complete data on cited references but also help with cleaning (i.e., disambiguating) Scopus' cited reference data because different formats of the same cited reference will be matched to the same PubMed record.

The structure of a query for the Batch Citation Matcher is simple:

```
Journal name | publication year | volume | starting page |first author
name|
```

As an example, "Arterioscler Thromb|1994|14|25|Ahlswede KM|" is the query for this cited reference found in Scopus:

```
Ahlswede, K.M., Williams, S.K., Microvascular endothelial cell sodding of
1-mm expanded polytetrafluoroethylene vascular grafts (1994) Arterioscler
Thromb, 14, p. 25.
```

The PubMed citation matcher returns the PubMed identifier (PMID) corresponding to this article if it is found, or the string "NOT FOUND" otherwise. These PMIDs were then used to retrieve the corresponding full records from PubMed.

The above search queries were manually issued to the PubMed Batch Citation Matcher by email in blocks of several thousand each, and the PMIDs of these articles were obtained in return, also by email. At first, about 90% of the cited references were successfully matched this way.

Attempts were then made to improve the hit rate by modifying and reissuing the queries for those 10% articles that had not been found. Firstly, the queries that returned NOT FOUND were resubmitted, but with the journal name left blank, which identified 55% of the previously unmatched articles. Secondly, the remaining unmatched queries were resubmitted with journal name in place but (a) leaving out the publication year or (b) increasing or (c) decreasing the year of publication by one. These three queries together identified a further 8% of those cited references that had not been found in the previous two steps. In all, the 433,133 cited references contained in the Scopus records for the 2007 stem cell research field literature yielded 414,976 matches in PubMed using this method, with a total hit rate after these three steps of 96%.

In a final step of this mapping, a small computer program was written to automatically download the full PubMed records of these cited references, as long as they were not to documents in the citing set. Using the NCBI EFetch facility, one of its Entrez Programming Utilities available for use with PubMed, this program automatically retrieved the XML-formatted full records for all matched cited references, in blocks of 500 records. Once retrieved, each record was then matched against the original queries that resulted in its PubMed ID to perform some final dataset cleaning.

3.6.3   DATASET OBTAINED AND ITS ADVANTAGES FOR CITATION ANALYSIS

The three-stage matching process thus produced three sets of data: (a) the original download of citing papers from PubMed, (b) the Scopus download that corresponds to (a) but with cited references, and (c) the full PubMed records that corresponded to cited references contained in (b).

A computer program was then developed to assemble these datasets into a form that supports citation analysis. The dataset (c) above was merged with (a) as the two overlap substantially, especially when the citation window is large. The citing-cited-paper relationships were recorded in a separate file during this merging process. For those references that were not found in PubMed, such as books, data extracted from Scopus' cited reference strings were kept but converted into an XML format similar to that of the PubMed records.

The final dataset for citation analysis therefore consists of three sets of XML documents: one that consists of the original download of citing papers from PubMed and of the PubMed records for cited references, one for those references from Scopus whose full records were not found in PubMed, and one for the citing-cited relationship between these papers. These documents can serve as data for all kinds of citation mining studies, and have the following advantages compared with data obtained from any of the citation databases alone:

- They are more accurate as papers are normalized and uniquely identified to a more extensive degree.

- They are in XML format for easier parsing and processing.

- They are cleaner (e.g., the citing-cited relationship is clarified) and more complete (e.g., including full author information for nearly all citing papers and cited references).

3.7   FIELD DELINEATION AND IN-TEXT CITATION ANALYSIS

As discussed earlier, problems with citation databases such as the ISI databases and Scopus have been among the major sources of criticism of citation analysis due to its heavy reliance on these flawed databases (Garfield, 1979; MacRoberts and MacRoberts, 1989; Smith, 1981). Among these problems is their insufficient coverage of some research fields in the social sciences and humanities which has made citation analysis unreliable in these research fields (Moed, 2010).

Although some limitations (e.g., in indexing or downloading) may be worked around by researchers (e.g., Strotmann et al., 2010; Zhao and Strotmann, 2011a), fixing problems in coverage of these databases is completely up to the companies that run these commercial databases. It is therefore very important to find alternative methods and data sources that may alleviate the near-complete reliance on these databases in citation analysis.

In-text citation data from full-text documents may be one such alternative data source. Zhao and Strotmann (2014b) explored the feasibility, benefits, and limitations of in-text author-based citation analysis, and tested how well it worked compared to traditional citation analysis using citation databases. It was found there that in-text citation analysis can work quite as well as traditional citation analysis using citation databases for both author ranking and mapping provided that author name disambiguation is performed properly. If using in-text citation data without any author name disambiguation, ranking authors by citations is not much useful, but author co-citation analysis works well for identifying major research areas and their interrelationships, although caution is required for the interpretation of small research areas and some authors' memberships in specialties.

As with citation analysis using citation databases, in-text citation analysis brings important benefits to citation analysis of research fields but also has its own limitations. Considering how much work it has required to create citation databases and to address the problems they pose for the citation analysis studies relying on them, it is probably worth further study to explore how to fully realize the benefits and address the limitations of in-text citation analysis.

Below is a detailed discussion on the feasibility, benefits, and limitations of in-text citation data for citation analysis, adapted largely from Zhao and Strotmann (2014b).

3.7.1   FEASIBILITY AND BENEFITS OF IN-TEXT CITATION ANALYSIS

Scholarly writing requires that the author of an article (or a book) cite relevant works in the text where they are referenced and list the details of the cited works in the reference list at the end of the article (or in some publication traditions, in footnotes or endnotes). There are a number of standard citation styles that specify the exact details of how in-text citations and reference lists should be written, and each citation style has been adopted by one or more scholarly communities. The APA style specified in the Publication Manual of the American Psychological Association (APA, 2013), for example, requires that all citations in the text be placed in parentheses inside which cited references are separated with semicolons and each cited reference consists of the last names of up to three authors and its publication year. If multiple publications by the same authors are cited in the same parentheses, author names are only listed once followed by the years of the publications separated by semicolons. If more than one publication by the same author(s) in the same year is cited, then these publications are differentiated by adding lower-case letters to the publication year. Alternatively, the authors' last names are listed in the text, followed by a year in parentheses. All this is to be done consistently throughout an article.

As scientific communication has moved toward electronic publishing, journal articles and books are now increasingly available electronically in full text. Technologies for processing text have also advanced dramatically. In fact, for in-text citations clearly delimited by parentheses and following a set of prescribed rules, automatic identification and extraction of in-text citations from full text and the parsing of author names and years from these citations do not have the complex problems that other types of text processing and mining have to deal with (Alako et al., 2005; Frijters et al., 2010; Strotmann and Bleier, 2013), and therefore have the potential to be quite easy and accurate.

The APA citation style is used not only by the Psychology community but also by a number of other scholarly communities especially in the social sciences, such as Linguistics, Sociology, Economics, Criminology, Business, Education, Nursing, and Library and Information Studies. Other widely used citation styles such as Chicago are very similar to APA in terms of their format for in-text citations. In-text citation analysis may therefore extend citation analysis to these research fields, most of which have long been covered insufficiently by citation databases.

In-text citations in the author-year format, delimited by parentheses, can support not only author citation and co-citation counting methods that have been used in citation analysis, but also some weighted counting methods that have the potential to be improvements over traditional methods, as well as citation context analysis (Narin, 1976; Small, 1982).

Currently, the number of citations an author receives from a set of articles is usually calculated as the total number of the author's works that appear in the reference lists of this set of articles, including multiple appearances of the same work. For example, if two works published by author A are cited by article X and three by article Y, the number of citations A receives from X and Y is five no matter how much the two and three cited works overlap, and has nothing to do with how heavily and where these works are used in X and Y. The co-citation count between two authors is traditionally defined as the number of papers that list at least one article from each author's oeuvre in the same reference list. For example, if articles X and Y above also cite one and two articles written by author B respectively, the co-citation count between A and B is two, i.e., two articles (X and Y) that cite them together, and has nothing to do with how many works by A and B are actually cited or how heavily they are cited in X and Y.

It is in principle quite easy to calculate these traditional citation and co-citation counts using in-text citation data. In-text citation strings in the author-year format are first identified and extracted from each citing paper (or book). All in-text citation strings of a citing paper can be combined into a single long string. Whenever this long string contains the last names of both authors A and B, this citing paper contributes one to the co-citation count of authors A and B. The citation count of an author for this citing paper is the number of unique author-year combinations in this long string that contain the name of this author.

However, these traditional citation and co-citation counting methods do not yet take into account how many times or how heavily an article is used in the citing article or where in the citing article it is used. In other words, all citations are treated equally in these methods, which has been another source of criticism of citation analysis. Some articles are real inspirations for the work being developed and are therefore referred to specifically many times in several of the major sections including methodology and discussion. Other articles are simply mentioned once along with many others in the literature review section of the citing article. Researchers often need to weigh if they should cite an article at all in the latter case. It is clearly problematic not to treat the real inspirations for research "better" when using citation counts to measure research impact. Similarly, it is common sense that articles cited in the same parentheses tend to be more closely related than those cited in the same paragraph, those in the same paragraph more closely related than those in the same section, and so on. It is an over-simplification to consider all pairs of cited articles (or cited authors) the same in counting their co-citations as a relatedness measure.

Weighting citations as a potential improvement to straight citation counting has long been proposed (Herlach, 1978; Narin, 1976), and has recently begun to be studied thoroughly and tested in large scales. It has been found that in-text frequency-weighted citation counting is the best of many other full-text features to help spot citations that were considered crucial to the citing papers by their authors (Zhu et al., 2014), and that weighing co-citations by their relative locations can improve the quality of co-citation analysis results (Boyack et al., 2013).

Citation and co-citation counting weighted by in-text citation frequency or location is clearly supported by in-text citation data. Using in-text citation data, the frequency of each cited paper in an article can be counted and the location of each citation can be recorded when the corresponding in-text citation string is extracted. The resulting information can be used to weigh citations or co-citations, leading to potentially better measures for author impact or relatedness. For example, it is relatively easy to calculate a rough citation count weighted by citation frequency using in-text citation data as the number of an author name's total appearances in a citing paper's long in-text citation string, summed over all citing papers. This count is "rough" because an author's name is not always listed whenever the author's work is cited in the text as discussed above about the APA style; however, by normalizing all in-text references to the author-year format before counting, it actually becomes quite reliable (Zhao and Strotmann, 2014b). Counting co-citations weighted by frequency is also feasible along the lines proposed for counting author bibliographic coupling frequencies (Zhao and Strotmann, 2008b). Specifically, the frequency-weighted in-text co-citation count between two authors can be defined mathematically as the size of the intersection of the two multisets of occurrences of the two author names in a citing paper's normalized in-text citation string. For example, if the names of authors A and B appear three and five times respectively in citing article X's long in-text citation string, article X contributes 3, i.e., $\min(3,5)$, to the weighted co-citation count of these two authors. Again, this corresponds mathematically to an intersection of multisets rather than sets of references. Using location to weigh co-citations can be done, for example, by assigning a weight of 4, 3, 2, 1, and 0 to articles (or their authors) cited in the same pair of parentheses, in the same sentence, in the same paragraph, in the same section, and in the same paper, respectively.

3.7.2   LIMITATIONS OF IN-TEXT CITATION ANALYSIS

There have been many criticisms of citation analysis since its introduction, most of which are regarding evaluative citation analysis, i.e., using the citation count (or scores derived from it such as the h-index) to rank journals, researchers, their institutions, or countries for the purpose of research evaluation. Despite these criticisms, citation analysis has played an increasingly important role in research evaluation as shown by the heated discussion generated recently by various university rankings and by the wide and quick spread of use of the h-index in the scholarly world.

By contrast, citation network analysis, i.e., the mapping of research fields using citation links as measures of relatedness between objects (e.g., articles, authors, journals), has not been criticized as much. But it has not drawn quite as much attention either, partly because it is more complex to conduct and has higher requirements for the researchers to have subject domain knowledge when interpreting results. Recent years, however, have seen a dramatic increase in research in the mapping of science of all kinds, mostly citation analysis-based (Zhao and Strotmann, 2014a).

Despite the fact that much of the criticism of citation analysis is focused on the problems of the citation databases on which citation analysis relies, these databases continue to be used as the dominant data sources for citation analysis studies. While in-text citation analysis has its own limitations and problems, the benefits it brings may justify the effort required to address these problems and to work around these limitations, which is comparable to the efforts currently required to address limitations and problems of citation databases.

As seen below, most of the limitations of in-text citation analysis come from its reliance on the availability of the full text of research articles and books and on the use of APA-like standard citation styles. Evaluative citation analysis using in-text citation data has some additional limitations.

Availability of full-text scholarly contents

For all intents and purposes, scholarly publishing has moved to completely digital production by now, which means that practically all recent and current scholarly publications exist in digital format. Many digitization projects have converted past publications from paper to digital and we can expect with confidence to have practically all scholarly publications available in digital format eventually. As a result, in-text citation data can in principle be collected systematically for the purpose of citation analysis studies. In practice, however, many of these full-text materials are still locked away in the hands of commercial companies (e.g., publishers of journals or books), and e-journals subscribed to by researchers' libraries do not usually support the kind of batch download and text-mining of full-text articles that would be required for large-scale in-text citation analysis. For the present study, for example, we had to manually download full-text articles from *JASIST*, one at a time, which was very time-consuming. It is therefore currently difficult to conduct large-scale in-text citation analysis studies using e-journals. The situation with e-books subscribed to by libraries is even worse as there are often no options at all to download, much less process, entire books. Freely available repositories of scholarly publications tend to have a coverage that is not systematic or complete as they are mostly run on the basis of voluntary self-deposit by researchers rather than the systematic collection of materials as is done in citation databases or e-journals. Even PubMed Central, a clearing house for open access full-text publications in the life sciences, downloadable in a large scale, covers only about 5% of the content of its bibliographic database. It is therefore currently problematic to use these repositories as data sources for citation analysis.

Types of citation analysis supported

In-text citation analysis as described here is limited to author citation and co-citation analysis of research fields where standard APA-like citation styles are used. It would require substantially more sophisticated techniques, namely mapping to the text's reference section and expanding the information found there via a bibliographic database, to use it for other types of citation analysis: for journal-based citation analysis as journal names do not appear in-text, for document citation analysis or for any type of bibliographic coupling analysis because author-year combinations do not uniquely identify publications across citing articles, or for the study of research fields that use numbers in superscripts or brackets as in-text citations to link to numbered references at the end of the articles. In these cases, identification of full reference information in the full text would be required for each in-text reference, not to mention the complex disambiguation tasks involved in identifying references to the same item across publications. Some repositories (e.g., PubMed Central), however, can be used directly in this case as they contain markup in the full texts with explicit links to the References section where identifiers for the cited works are included.

Higher requirements for author name disambiguation

In-text author citation analysis is more sensitive to author name ambiguity problems than citation counting using citation databases because only last names are generally available in in-text citation data, as compared to last names and first initials in the ISI databases and full names in Scopus. In-text citation analysis therefore has higher requirements for author name disambiguation. However, especially for evaluation purposes, author name disambiguation has been shown to be necessary as well for studies using citation databases (Strotmann and Zhao, 2012). Author name disambiguation with in-text citation data is possible and also has the potential to be easier and more effective than the same task with citation data from the ISI databases. This is because citation context, citation frequency, and co-occurrence patterns of author names are all excellent sources of information for author name disambiguation (Strotmann and Zhao, 2012), and are available in in-text citation data. However, this remains to be tested in future studies.

Potential impact of weighted citation counting on citing behavior

It has been found that citation indicators can be, and indeed have been, manipulated by parties subjected to research evaluations using these indicators, such as authors in the case of the h-index and journal editors in the case of the journal citation impact factor (Archambault and Lariviere, 2009; Bartneck and Kokkelmans, 2011). The use of citation counts weighted by frequency or location that are supported by in-text citation analysis as discussed above could introduce new opportunities for manipulation. In addition, if weighting by frequency is used, negative citations and citations given for purposes other than use, which have been used to criticize citation analysis, might skew citation analysis results even more heavily than they do now. However, this limitation is not specific to in-text citation analysis as it is caused by weighting and not by citation source, and the potential additional effect of weighting on citing behavior using in-text citation data could in principle be countered by performing citation context sentiment analysis, for example, to identify and properly weigh at least the negative citations, as the citation context is available. In addition, co-citation analysis, whether weighted or not, is not expected to have much impact on citing behavior as there is not much motivation to manipulate the relatedness between authors.

Errors in identifying and parsing in-text citations

Just like indexing cited references in citation databases may introduce errors, it is impossible to completely avoid errors in identifying and parsing in-text citations. While standard in-text citations enclosed in parentheses are quite easy to identify and parse, slightly more sophisticated processing is required when comments are added to in-text citations inside the parentheses, such as "e.g." or "see also," or when author names are dropped in the case of multiple works by the same authors. It is also difficult to correctly identify all in-text citations that list author names (separated by commas) as part of the text followed by the year in the parentheses (e.g., "As Smith, Chen, and Kim (1981) point out...") as there is no consistent delimiter to mark the start of the list of author names. These problems may be alleviated by using advanced text mining techniques at the price of having to deal with more complex issues of full text analysis.

Limited support for all-author citation and co-citation counting

In in-text APA-style citation data, all authors are supposed to be listed for works that have up to five authors when they are cited for the first time in the text, but only the first author is to be provided (followed by "et al.") for the subsequent citations of the same works with three to five authors or if a work has more than five authors (APA, 2013). That means that in-text citation analysis supports traditional first-author based citation and co-citation counting just like citation analysis using the ISI databases, which only indexes the first author of each cited work. In addition, in-text citation analysis supports the preferred all-author-based counting in research fields where the level of collaboration is low, but may not work well for highly collaborative research fields. However, in the social sciences and humanities, with which in-text citation analysis aims to help, this is barely a limitation as collaborations there are rare and normally limited to two or three authors.

3.8   FIELD DELINEATION WITH GOOGLE SCHOLAR AND OTHER CITATION DATA SOURCES ON THE WEB

In addition to the two main commercial citation databases (i.e., the ISI databases and Scopus) that systematically select and index scholarly journal publications (and to a much lesser degree conference and book publications), citation databases (and associated tools) openly available on the public Web have also appeared and been found useful in their own ways. These databases automatically index scholarly publications automatically found on the Web, including their cited references. The most famous of these are Google Scholar for all research fields (http://scholar.google.com) and CiteSeer for computer science research in a broad sense (http://citeseerx.ist.psu.edu/).

Just like the ISI databases and Scopus, Google Scholar and CiteSeer were originally developed as information searching tools rather than tools for citation analysis, and have some amazing features in this regard when compared with traditional information retrieval systems. CiteSeer, for example, facilitates keyword searching (subject words, author names, numbers, etc.) in both citing papers and cited papers. Once a paper has been located, CiteSeer provides virtually all the information related to it: like the ISI databases and Scopus, it provides information that helps evaluate the paper's impact, such as the number of citations it has received and its citation history, and the option of getting related papers by various criteria (including papers that the located paper cites, have cited it, or have been co-cited with it); unlike the ISI databases and Scopus, CiteSeer also provides the context in which the located paper is cited in each paper that cites it in order to help the user evaluate the relevance of the papers that cited the located paper, and it provides links to the full text content in various formats as well as links to the authors' homepages.

As a data source for citation analysis, CiteSeer has been used in citation analysis to study the differences in scholarly communication between the Web and the print world and the effect of Open Access on the citation impact of scholarly publications (Craig et al., 2007; Goodrum, et al., 2001; Lawrence, 2001; Tarrant et al., 2008; Zhao, 2003; 2005a; 2006a). Google Scholar has been compared with the ISI databases and Scopus as a data source for evaluative citation analysis (e.g., Bar-Ilan, 2008; Falagas et al., 2008; Harzing, 2008; 2013; Meho and Yang, 2007). It is found to produce author rankings that are highly correlated with those from the ISI databases and Scopus, although individual researchers' ranks can differ substantially. Google Scholar tends to find many more citations to research papers in certain research fields (such as computer science and economics) than the commercial citation databases, and is therefore important to fair research evaluation in these fields. However, it is much more time-consuming to collect and clean data with Google Scholar, and tools such as Publish or Perish (http://www.harzing.com/pop.htm) have therefore emerged to help with the use of Google Scholar data. Citation network analysis, however, has yet to find a way to use Google Scholar.

There are a few other systems for the collection, storage, and retrieval of research publications available on the public Web, such as arxiv.org for physics and RePEC.org for economics, some of which (e.g., RePEC) also provide citation data. They, however, have been primarily used as data sources for counting downloads in studies on the relationship between downloading and citing research publications, and the citation data they provide have not yet been explored much as data sources for citation analysis (Chu and Krichel, 2007; Brody et al., 2006).

Like any type of citation data sources and tools, including the ISI databases and Scopus, citation data sources and tools on the Web have both benefits and problems.

3.8.1   BENEFITS

Citation data sources and tools on the Web cover a wider variety of document types such as conference papers, technical reports, degree theses, and preprints in addition to journal articles, and provide more complete information about cited references such as titles, all authors, full source names, and citation contexts. These may facilitate a larger variety of inquiries and more sophisticated methods that may be very difficult, if not impossible, with the ISI databases or Scopus, such as comparative analysis between document types, citation context analysis, and weighted citation counting (Narin, 1976; Small, 1982).

Although the journal has served as the primary scholarly communication channel in many research fields, its primary position has always been questioned in some fields in the social sciences and humanities where documents other than journals (e.g., books) are considered at least as important. Furthermore, journals in all fields are facing more challenges with recent developments in the scholarly communication system. The rapid development of information technology has been revolutionizing the way that information is produced and exchanged. As a result, the scholarly communication system is changing to a new model, which emphasizes preprints, conference papers, and the online availability of research papers—more in some fields than others (Goodrum et al., 2001). In physics or computer science, for example, the Web is often researchers' first choice for literature searching (Brown, 2010; Conkling et al., 2010; Youngen, 1997). This means that the study of scholarly communication patterns demonstrated in this part of the literature is increasingly important and that it becomes a more serious problem to use "journal only" data sources for citation analysis, especially for research evaluation.

Citation databases and tools on the Web as data sources for citation analysis support studies that explore new developments in the scholarly communication system in the Web environment as compared to the print world (Brown, 2010; Evans, 2008; Goodrum et al., 2001; Zhao, 2003; 2005a; 2006a). Moreover, they provide additional data on research fields and document types that are not covered adequately by commercial citation databases which have traditionally focused on journals. Combining these Web data and tools with traditional commercial citation databases may result in more in-depth and less biased citation analysis studies.

Last but not least, citation databases and tools on the Web are freely available to anyone who has a connection to the Internet (whereas both the ISI databases and Scopus require an expensive subscription to use their services), which enables citation analysis studies by people who do not have the privilege of accessing these expensive commercial databases. The free and ready access to these Web data and tools can also help with the interpretation of results from citation network analysis studies that use the ISI databases as the data source because information about cited documents, authors, or other objects being studied required for the interpretation is not available in the cited references in the ISI databases but can be obtained easily on the Web in many cases.

3.8.2   PROBLEMS

Citation data sources and tools on the Web are fully automatic in collecting research papers and in indexing these papers, which has caused many of the problems with these tools as data sources for citation analysis (Zhao, 2003; Zhao and Strotmann, 2004).

Nonsystematic coverage of research fields and publications

Citation data sources and tools on the Web index whatever scholarly publications found on the Web (including their cited references) in the target research fields (e.g., Google Scholar for all fields and CiteSeer for broad computer science). The coverage of these tools therefore depends on both the availability of research publications on the Web and the technology used for collecting and indexing these publications.

While the technology is quite effective already and continues to improve, the degree to which scholars publish on the Web varies dramatically between research fields, or even between research areas within the same field, because of publishing traditions, research evaluation practice, or other reasons. For example, scholars in physics, computing science, and economics have been publishing quite extensively on the Web while scholars in other fields have not (Harzing, 2008); unlike scholars in the XML research field who publish heavily on the Web, scholars in the application areas of XML technology such as medical informatics largely publish in journals (Zhao, 2003). In addition, scholarly publications on the Web are mostly based on voluntary self-deposit by researchers rather than systematic collections of materials as done by citation databases. As a result, citation data sources and tools on the Web tend to have a coverage that is not systematic or complete.

Not all papers that meet search criteria are provided

Scholars who are looking for references for their research are often only interested in highly relevant documents. Citation analysts, on the other hand, prefer a complete set of papers that meet certain search criteria. Citation databases on the Web such as GS and CiteSeer normally indicate the total number of documents that meet the criteria but only provide the first few hundreds to the user, ranked by citations or other means. This may be quite sufficient for an IR tool but tends to result in incomplete data for citation analysis. This limit placed on the number of retrieved papers certainly limits the scale of citation analysis studies using these Web data and tools, and therefore their usefulness for citation analysis studies. Documents beyond this limit may be retrieved by computer programs developed to search these databases directly rather than using the interface provided, but still not all documents that met the search criteria could be retrieved. For example, CiteSeer provides only 500 documents to users using its interface, and 1,000 to computer programs searching it directly even if there were more in the database.

No option for downloading search results in a standardized format

The interface and the presentation format for papers and their references tend to change in an IR system, and there is nothing wrong with changing data presentation format as such. The problem with citation data sources and tools on the Web is that there is no option for downloading the search results in a standardized format that is independent of the presentation, so that citation analysis researchers could rely on this stable format to get the data they need.

As a result, data downloaded from these tools are in HTML format. The accuracy of parsing such data depends heavily on features provided in the HTML documents for distinguishing different data segments such as authors, title, and journal name. In the case of CiteSeer, the only such feature for cited papers is that titles are displayed in italics. This feature together with the fixed sequence of presenting data (i.e., authors first, then title, followed by source information) makes it possible to distinguish the basic data segments needed for citation analysis (i.e., the authors, title, and journal), but it is very difficult to go any further.

Not all references are given

Citation data sources and tools on the Web such as CiteSeer do not always provide all references a paper has in its reference list. This may not be important for information searching since no IR systems can exhaust all relevant papers, but may cause validity problems for citation analysis, just as the incompleteness and bias of the ISI databases which have been discussed in the literature as potentially causing validity problems.

Lack of accurate information about date of publishing

A large percentage of papers published on the Web do not have explicit information about the publication date. Papers that do have this information may place it anywhere in the document (in a header, footer, or footnote, for example), which makes it very difficult for a fully automatic citation indexing tool like Google Scholar or CiteSeer to capture this information correctly. As a result, while citation data and tools on the Web may well facilitate citation analysis studies in a general sense and for the purpose of determining overall structures of research fields, it is difficult to carry out time-related studies (such as the evolution of research fields or diffusion of ideas over time) using solely these data and tools.

Errors in parsing various referencing formats and author names

The Web is an extremely diverse environment where papers can be in all kinds of formats and use various referencing conventions. It may be easy for human beings to recognize these different formats but it is not an easy task for a fully automatic citation indexing tool like CiteSeer to make these distinctions. As a result, fully automatic tools tend to produce errors by mixing up information about authors, titles, sources, etc., when uncommon or non-standard writing and referencing formats are encountered. For example, it is found that CiteSeer is more likely to produce errors when indexing papers formatted in two columns than those in single column (Zhao, 2003). Regular individual words are frequently found in an automatically generated "author name" data field, which often happens when a reference starts with the title rather than author names. This type of error is largely if not completely avoided in citation indexes constructed manually, such as the ISI databases.

3.9   OTHER APPROACHES TO FIELD DELINEATION

Some early citation analysis studies built their own citation databases from scratch (Eom, 2003; Zhao, 1990; 1992; 1993). This approach to field delineation ensures a clean dataset for the citation analysis study at hand, but is clearly not practical for large-scale citation analysis studies.

Neither is this approach necessary when the research fields being studied are covered by existing citation databases such as the ISI databases and Scopus. A better approach in these cases would be to supplement downloads from existing citation databases with additional documents that are not covered in these databases but have been determined by the researcher to be necessary for the study at hand. The additional documents can be indexed in the same format as the downloaded records, either manually or by computer programs that citation-index full-text documents just as GS and CiteSeer do to scholarly publications that they identify and collect on the Web.

3.10   ADDITIONAL REMARKS

As citation analysis relies on the collective views of the authors of the datasets used, it is important to perform field delineation carefully.

In general, field delineation can normally be improved by combining multiple data sources. The completeness of the dataset can be improved by supplementing downloads from citation databases with additional documents from other sources as discussed above, or by combining multiple citation databases such as the ISI databases, Scopus, GS, and CiteSeer because these databases do not overlap completely in coverage. The cleanness (as well as the completeness) of the dataset collected can be improved by combining subject bibliographic databases with citation databases as discussed earlier in Section 3.6.

CHAPTER 4

Disambiguation in Citation Network Analysis

4.1   INTRODUCTION

Data cleaning is a fundamental step in all data-intensive research, and network studies require particular care in this respect. Here, data cleaning means one thing foremost: making sure that the nodes and links of the network, including all their respective weights, properly reflect the real-world individuals and their interrelationships that the network models.

In a network model, nodes represent individuals. In a citation network, these may be persons or institutions, documents or journals, or cities or countries, to name a few. For a node to correctly represent an individual, every single occurrence of that individual "in the real world" must be mapped to one and the same node in the network model, and no two distinct individuals may map to the same node in the network; for a link to correctly mirror "the real world," the nodes that it connects must be the "correct" ones in this sense for the individuals whose relationships the link represents in the model. Mathematically speaking, the ideal network maps one-to-one (isomorphically) to the individuals and relations it models.

It is for this reason that data cleaning in network analysis consists primarily of disambiguation: the identification of individuals from the names that refer to them. In the literature, this type of disambiguation is also referred to as named entity identification or, when automated, named entity recognition.

There is an old and venerable tradition in library cataloging and bibliographic database management that maintains authority control files for precisely this purpose. In this tradition, individuals are assigned unique names: Mark Twain is always named Samuel Clemens, and different individuals with that name would be distinguished, for example, by including their respective birth years or dates in their authoritative name forms.

Under the heading of RDA (Resource Description and Access), this tradition is currently undergoing a major reform in the library and information community, in that disambiguating (i.e., "authoritative") name forms are being replaced by universal registered identifiers for individuals in these records, and international registration agencies for such identifiers are being formed. And since many different organizations have long been maintaining their own respective identifier schemes for all types of entities, these same international registries simultaneously tend to maintain mappings between their own registered identifiers and those maintained by other agencies for the same individual.

Internationally unique identifiers have long been maintained for books (ISBN), journals (ISSN), or countries (e.g., 2- or 3-letter ISO country codes). More recently, international registries for individual documents have become popular (e.g., DOI). For individual authors, however, such identifiers have traditionally been maintained on a national basis, and only for major book authors at that. Only now a major promising effort to build and maintain a truly international and universal registry for authors and researchers, the Open Researcher and Contributor ID (ORCID), is starting.

In the long run, bibliographic and citation network studies will therefore be able to rely on bibliographic databases that provide verified identifiers for the individual people, organizations, geographic units, documents, and serials that appear in their records. In the meantime, however, these databases merely contain names or similar designators for most such individuals, not always in authoritative form, and identifying them from their names and from the contexts in which their names appear remains an important data cleaning task in citation analysis.

4.2 NAMES AND DESIGNATIONS IN BIBLIOGRAPHIC RECORDS

A typical bibliographic record will contain quite a number of names: the title that names the work, the name(s) of its author(s), the name of the book series or journal in which it appeared, the name(s) of institution(s) that the authors are affiliated to, names of streets, cities, and countries in author address fields, the name of the publisher, the name of a conference: named works, people, organizations, events, and places.

It sometimes helps to also think of other less obvious parts of a bibliographic record as "naming" things. Classifications and subject headings, for example, designate subfields of research, and the specific form that is found in a bibliographic record serves as the subfield's authoritative "name" in the database.

Most importantly in our context of citation analysis, the designations of documents that have been cited in a work constitute "names" for the cited works. Naming conventions for cited references (e.g., citation styles like APA or reference formats as in the ISI databases), however, vary wildly, both across databases and across the publishing world.

All these "names" have one thing in common: they designate a specific one amongst a large number of individual entities—individual works, places, people, events, organizations, concepts. The individuals thus designated therefore qualify for representation as nodes in a network model.

This means that the fundamental requirement for a "proper" representation of an individual as a node in a network applies, namely, that every occurrence of the same individual be represented in the network by one and the same node. In a nutshell, the construction of a "proper" network model from a set of bibliographic records requires proper identification of the specific individuals that are "meant" by the names as they appear in the record.

4.3 THE NAME AMBIGUITY PROBLEM

Traditional cataloging practices asked the catalogers to ensure that each such individual was provided with a unique name or designation; indeed, traditional bibliographic databases would often require the cataloger to look up any such name in a specially maintained authority control file in order to pick the one specific individual person, organization, or other entity that properly corresponded to the name they enter into the database—and to enter it in precisely the form that the authority control file prescribes for that individual.

In an ideal world, from a citation analyst's perspective, every mention of any such individual should thus be a unique designator reserved for that particular individual—one name, one individual.

The real world, however, is far from perfect in this respect.

Organizations such as university departments change their names frequently; even countries merge (Germany) and split (Czechoslovakia) over time. Not all of an organization's members will always be up-to-date with respect to the most recent such changes, and publishing delays will only add to the chaos that ensues. Name changes are not uncommon among people (e.g., by marriage) or places (e.g., St. Petersburg/Leningrad), either. Amongst artists, pen names are the rule, for example. In a word, individuals may be known under a number of different names over their lifetimes.

Different standards in spelling out an individual's name compound this problem. Special characters in names or titles may be transliterated according to a variety of standards (or kept in their original form). Names, especially of institutions like universities, may be translated to the publication's language (frequently, English), or may be given in their original forms—and if translated, using standardized translations, or again, not. Names of authors whose works have been translated into a large number of languages exist in a number of transliterated or even translated forms, and their works, too, may have appeared in translation under a wide variety of different titles. For cited works, a wide variety of citation styles compounds all of these problems even further.

To summarize, we cannot expect all individuals that we are interested in as citation analysts to appear under one definitive designation, not even in the most well-maintained bibliographic databases; we must expect a serious problem of allonyms.

Neither can we expect every occurrence of the same name in two bibliographic records to refer to the same individual person, or even organization or country; we must also expect a significant homonym problem.

In European countries, the most common surname tends to cover 0.5–2% of the country's population. In East Asia, however, the most common surname may apply to 10% (China) or 40% (Vietnam) of a country's population: the world's most common surname is shared by more than 1 in 100 people on the globe! As given names traditionally come from a small set of Christian names in Europe, it is therefore quite common for people to share exactly the same name there. John Smith, Thomas Müller, Paul Martin, and András Nagy, are typical examples of common full names from English, German, French, and Hungarian language cultures. In East Asia, too, there are commonly used given names, although the pool of given names to choose from tends to be significantly more diverse there. Again, it is quite common for people to be called by exactly the same name in those cultures, too. The name of the recently retired tennis star LI Na (李娜) is a Chinese example.

In citation analysis, one of the most interesting questions to ask about a person, institution, or other unit is how many times their oeuvres have been cited in the international scientific literature. For people, it is often possible to search for their names directly in the cited references that are indexed in a citation database. However, the way that cited references are stored in databases such as the ISI databases exacerbates the duplicate-name problem significantly, because only (transliterated) surnames and initials of (transliterated) given names are entered in these fields. For European names, this means that the same name as it is available in these databases, i.e., the same surname-plus-initial combination, may well be shared by one in one thousand people in a given culture. For East Asian names, transliteration tends to conflate names that are distinct in their original forms, but most seriously, the reduction of given names to single initials means that a full 1%–5% of a large country's population may share a single name as entered as cited author in a citation database. Thus, for many authors it becomes practically impossible to answer this most basic question in citation analysis using the standard search facilities provided by citation databases. Since the Asian Tiger nations have become extremely successful science nations, most databases have begun to at least index the full (transliterated) names of citing authors. By linking cited references to their full records within the database, cited reference searching by full cited author name is increasingly possible in these databases.

For institutions, homonymy is a much less frequent problem, but due to the political history of China, identically named universities, each claiming to continue the tradition of the same pre-revolution institution, may be found in mainland China and in Taiwan, for example.

While science journal article titles tend to be fairly unique, there are certain types of homonymy that occur relatively frequently. Editorials, for example, are frequently titled just that. In addition, book reviews frequently bear the same titles as the books that they review. Furthermore, some long-running longitudinal studies (especially in medical or social science fields) can be expected to report updated results annually as journal papers with nearly identical titles (and indeed nearly identical contents, making these paper series a significant source of false positives in plagiarism detection).

4.4   AMBIGUITY AND POWER LAWS

It is a basic fact of life in bibliometrics that approximate power laws govern many of the most interesting phenomena in the field. Zipf's Law and Bradford's Law are two of these. Power laws and their kin have two characteristics that are important here: there are always a few highest-ranked individuals who, together, accrue as much attention, wealth, citations, collaborators, or whatever it is we are measuring as the lowest 10–50% of the entire population; conversely, if you take enough people from the middle or lower ranks, their combined values will reach those of even the most highly ranked in the population. In practice, what this means to citation analysis is that any single mistake regarding any individual among the top ranks can lead to significant errors in evaluation—but the same is true for ignoring the low-ranked half of the population.

In citation analysis, in particular, just a couple of any given author's or institution's most highly cited publications are, together, cited about as frequently as all the rest combined; in any given mature research field, a few authors' citations together can equal those of all others of the field combined.

In practice, this means that the citation analyst needs to be very sure that all the highly cited works, people, and/or institutions of interest are correctly attributed to each other. Just a single mis-attribution may otherwise invalidate a citation analysis study, especially in an evaluation context. What is worse, even though these extraordinarily highly cited individuals might be discarded as outliers in other types of statistical analysis, it is these very outstanding individuals that are of particular interest in citation analysis, whose extraordinary performance is usually quite a typical phenomenon given the power laws that govern citation distributions.

Conversely, especially with the exploding research contributions from East Asia in many fields of science, it is very important not to bunch all "J. Lee"s or "Y. Wang"s together as one person, as the joint contribution of hundreds of researchers with the same name may rival that of even the most highly cited individual in the same field: this, too, is a characteristic of power laws. It is therefore not enough to properly disambiguate the top tier of the individuals we study. The highly ambiguous names need to be handled reasonably well, too, if we are to be able to rely on the results of a citation analysis study.

This, then, is the real reason why disambiguation is so extremely important in bibliometrics in general, and in citation analysis in particular: power law-like distributions of fundamental phenomena mean that even a single error in attribution can lead to significant errors in evaluation. This is why it is so important to invest heavily in this frequently most expensive aspect of a citation analysis project (estimated at usually 80–90% of the work involved in a citation analysis—e.g., K. Börner, pers. comm., 2012).

4.5   EFFECTS OF AMBIGUITY ON NETWORK ANALYSIS RESULTS

Only very recently have researchers begun looking at what concrete effect the errors in a network model caused by name ambiguities in the data sources may have on the results of popular types of network analysis. The results that they report are quite alarming in the aggregate: not only do typical evaluative analyses of individuals (e.g., citation rankings) suffer significantly from these errors, but there is mounting evidence that even the most basic statistical features of realistic large-scale networks are hugely distorted by ambiguities.

Diesner and Carley (2013), for example, report that "[m]inor changes in accuracy rates of [name disambiguation] lead to comparatively huge changes in network metrics, while the set [of] top-scoring key entities is highly robust. Co-occurrence based link formation entails a small chance of false negatives, but the rate of false positives is alarmingly high."

In fact, Fegley and Torvik (2013) go so far as to dismiss one of the most famous (and most highly cited) recent results in large-scale social network analysis, the exact power-law distribution from preferential attachment (Barabási and Albert, 1999), especially in the case of scientific collaboration networks (Barabási, et al., 2002), as a mere artifact produced by a lack of name disambiguation in the underlying dataset! The ultimate irony here is that Fegley and Torvik's (2013) data are consistent with the interpretation that the cooperation network power law that Barabási observed may in fact have been induced by a power law distribution in the underlying name ambiguities. As Barabási himself has pointed out, power laws in even a relatively small subset of a population will lead to the observation of a power law for the full population.

Similarly, Strotmann and Zhao (2012) find that even highly stable statistical analysis methods of author co-citation analysis fail in the face of large-scale ambiguity errors in the underlying dataset.

While for evaluative bibliometrics the most serious problem is generally the "splitting" of individuals, i.e., the failure to recognize each and every one of an individual's contributions correctly (especially of high-performing individuals), Fegley and Torvik (2013) find that splitting is not the main concern in relational network analysis. Instead, they and Strotmann and Zhao (2012) both find that it is the erroneous "merging" of individuals, i.e., the failure to separate the contributions of multiple individuals correctly because their names are too similar, that causes major distortions of large-scale network analysis results in relational network analysis. Especially East Asian names are prone to extreme amounts of merging, as we can see in the example above. While in European cultures, there are relatively few common given names but a large variety of family names, in Chinese, Korean, and other East Asian cultures the opposite is the case—a small number of surnames is shared by half their populations, but given names are much more varied. The old tradition in scientific publishing to list authors by their surnames and initials works, sort of, when science is done in European-origin cultures, but all bibliographic databases have in recent years had to move to a full-name model as research boomed in the Asian Tiger nations (e.g., PubMed/MEDLINE in 2002).

Given these results, we need to consider briefly what it means to disambiguate a data set for citation analysis before we discuss practical approaches.

As Torvik and Smalheiser (2009) make abundantly clear, it is for all intents and purposes impossible to disambiguate the names of all the individuals in a large dataset completely and fully correctly. With absolute perfection thus out of the question, what remains is to ask when a disambiguation is "good enough," and if (and how) it is possible for a typical researcher to go about disambiguating the dataset well enough.

Unfortunately, there is very little research, if indeed any, into what constitutes "good enough" for a citation analysis study. The few studies that have looked into what goes wrong when individuals are not recognized correctly do give us a hint, though.

First of all, "good enough" usually means that the top-ranked individuals and their most important contributions must be absolutely correctly attributed. Whatever other methods we may find to approximate sufficiently a good disambiguation of our data, in the end it will therefore be necessary to manually double-check, and where necessary fix, the highest-impact individuals' data.

Secondly, it is important to understand that some statistical procedures or network measures are more vulnerable than others to name ambiguities. Typically, local network measures (e.g., node degree) are less affected than global ones (e.g., size of connected component), and evaluative studies (e.g., ranking) are more affected than relational ones (e.g., correlations) (Diesner and Carley, 2013; Strotmann and Zhao, 2012).

For ranking studies, as pointed out already, absolute correctness is paramount, and huge efforts need to be expended to get all the top-ranked individuals just right. When the "individuals" are research institutions, this can be a daunting task.

For correlative studies, on the other hand, a study by Albert et al. (2000) warns us that, while global measures of power-law distributed networks may be quite resilient to uniformly distributed random errors, they are also quite vulnerable to the kind of highly skewed error distributions that we observe for name ambiguities, for example. In the case of an extremely skewed error distribution, they observed that an error rate as low as 10%-20% completely changed the measured values for a fundamental global network metric, namely, connectivity. We can take this as a warning that, as a rule of thumb, we generally need to aim for a roughly 90% (but definitely better than 80%) complete and correct disambiguation. There are plenty of successful bibliometric studies that imply that this level of correctness is also usually quite sufficient for meaningful studies, as long as only "local" measures and correlational statistics are required.

As an aside, we should point out that the requirement of 80% completeness or better applies, in particular, to the underlying citation index's coverage of the field being studied. On the plus side, this means that studies on the life sciences can be relied upon to yield interesting results as long as they solve "well enough" the ambiguity problems inherent in those databases. Results from any citation analysis study on the social sciences or humanities, however, are necessarily highly suspect as long as they rely on these databases and as long as these databases cover less than 80% of the relevant literature in those fields.

4.6 MANUAL DISAMBIGUATION

4.6.1 SMALL NETWORKS

It has been known for a long time that ambiguities in name attribution are a cause for major concern, especially in evaluative citation analysis. White and McCain (1998), for example, explicitly refuse to give an author ranking based on absolute citation numbers as retrieved from the ISI databases for this reason.

For small networks, the best disambiguation method is still the manual one, i.e., the creation and/or maintenance of classic authority control and linkage files for the individuals one is interested in. When maintained actively and professionally over a long time, such files can be accumulated for quite large networks, e.g., for the complete research output of scientists and institutions in small countries like Norway or the Netherlands or for reasonably small research fields (Ley, 2002). However, maintaining such databases at an excellent accuracy level is quite demanding (Ley, 2012), and perfection cannot be guaranteed.

For large datasets, disambiguating them is generally impossible for an individual researcher to do. However, the effective size of the dataset with respect to disambiguation, i.e., the amount of work required to clean it sufficiently, depends on the number of different individuals and name variants that need to be considered.

There are a number of quite effective ways to reduce those numbers, making approximate manual disambiguation feasible even for datasets for networks that derive from a very large number of publications: opting for low-granularity units of analysis, or opting for studying only available well-standardized bibliographic data.

One reason why journals are a preferred unit of study for the purpose of constructing "complete" maps of science is that it means studying (and cleaning) tens of thousands rather than tens of millions of objects if the document or author unit was chosen. The former is quite a feasible number of individuals to clean manually, whereas the latter requires a concerted international effort by many individuals to maintain: the right choice of granularity levels for the unit of analysis in a network can make the difference between feasibility and infeasibility of the manual disambiguation task.

In addition, journal names are a well-maintained component of the records maintained by standard citation databases, so that the number of different spellings for a journal in these databases tends to be fairly small, making the disambiguation task much easier: choosing a well-cleaned, and especially well-standardized, aspect of the dataset you have available can again make all the difference.

Besides journals, high-granularity research aspects include countries, major cities (especially if you are interested in national studies), or major research institutions, for example.

The well-standardized aspects of bibliographic records depend on the database that provides them. For the ISI databases, these include cited references to journal papers, citing journal titles, and cited journal titles. For individual citing publications, those with available DOIs (e.g., Scopus or ISI databases) or PubMed IDs (PubMed and Scopus) fall in this category. Identifiers such as DOIs are rarely provided for cited references still, however.

For many research questions in citation analysis, the interesting entities of analysis are the most highly cited, most prolific, or otherwise top-ranked ones in the literature being studied, and only a relatively small number of these is generally required in such studies: dozens of countries, research fields, or major research institutions, hundreds of researchers, departments, cities, or sub-fields, or a few thousands of publications would cover major developments in quite large sectors of international science quite well, especially when the research question under consideration involves studying a relation that follows a typical approximate power-law distribution of the type that is so common in bibliometrics, and in citation analysis especially.

Suppose, for example, that we want to study the interrelationships between the 100 most highly cited authors in the literature that we study. The disambiguation task in this case means that we need to avoid missing someone who published highly cited papers, and to avoid missing or mis-assigning highly cited papers of those who we study. Suppose further that we use the ISI databases as a data source, and that we study a field where journal papers clearly dominate among citable research publications and where first authors are generally also main authors.

In such a case, a simple procedure for putting together a fairly reliable list of the most highly cited authors of the field manually is as follows:

1. Rank cited authors by last name and first initial, noting for each the number of citations; then rank these authors by their number of citations.

2. Rank cited publications as keyed by the ISI databases by the number of times they are cited.

3. Obtain a list of authors of top ranked publications and their number of citations.

   a. The authors of the first few dozen of most highly cited publications will very likely be among the 100 most highly cited authors that we look for, so begin a table of authors with these.

b. Obtain the full names of these authors by searching for their highly cited works as source papers in the ISI databases, and compile a complete list of publications by each of these authors (by e.g., searching the Web).

c. Then, manually search your data in step 2 in the cited references field for each of these publications, check for the number of papers in your data that cite it, and sum up all the citations to all the publications by each author.

d. Rank this list of authors by their total number of citations obtained this way.

4. Compare this preliminary ranking of top authors with the one in step 1, and take note of those in the latter that do not appear in the former. Process these "missing authors" in rank order, as follows:

a. Use the data in step 2 to identify the dozen or so most highly cited papers that correspond to the name.

b. For this name to correspond to a "real" highly cited author, their citation numbers should sum up to a number that is within a factor of two or so of the lowest in your current preliminary ranking of authors, and almost all of them should, on manual inspection, belong to a single oeuvre (i.e., the same individual).

c. If both these conditions are met, add this author to the preliminary list of highly cited authors using the same method as in step 3 above.

5. Repeat until:

a. you have a list of about twice the number of authors you are interested in (200 in our case), and

b. none of the "authors" in the ranking produced in step 1 above has a higher number of "citations" than, in our case, the number 100 in your preliminary ranking of disambiguated individual authors.

Since citations typically follow a rough power-law distribution, the chances of missing a legitimate member of the "true" top-100 list with this procedure are very slim in our experience, and you only need to disambiguate about twice the number of individuals that you were actually interested in studying, a number that was also quite feasible for manual disambiguation.

This method also works for names of institutions, countries, journals, or other aspects for which a top-ranking list might be of interest.

Not all types of studies allow one to reduce the number of individuals to consider to such a degree, however, but even then there are situations in which approximate manual disambiguation is possible to some degree. With a bit of luck (to be tested appropriately in the study, of course), the resulting network measures that are targeted in the study show sufficient signs of converging to a definitive value (i.e., signs of not changing values much anymore after a while) as the network model is refined, manually, step by step.

4.6.2   LARGE NETWORKS

As we noted earlier in this chapter, research collaboration network studies with individual scientists have been undertaken at very large scales, but lack of name disambiguation has recently been shown to have introduced unexpectedly serious errors in these studies. More specifically, global network characteristics such as density or size of largest component are particularly vulnerable to mis-judgment due to "lumping" errors (Fegley and Torvik, 2013).

For such large-scale author characteristics studies, a relatively simple procedure can produce relatively reasonable estimates. The condition here is that, for a large part of the literature being studied, full author names are available (e.g., as source papers in the ISI databases), and not just surnames plus initials. In this case, the following procedure can sometimes help:

1. Start with a network that estimates individual authors by their surnames and first initial, and calculate the network parameters of interest for the study for this estimated network.

2. Rank surnames by their number of distinct full-name variants (i.e., by number of distinct given name variants for this surname) in the literature. Starting with the surname(s) with the largest number of distinct variants, proceed as follows:

   a. Modify the current network by re-estimating individual authors with this particular surname by using their full names rather than surname-plus-initial, leaving all other estimates unchanged.

   b. Re-calculate the network parameters of interest for the modified network.

3. Repeat until:

   a. the network measures of interest converge, and

   b. the number of distinct variants for the remaining surnames in the list is sufficiently small.

4. Finally, manually merge top-ranked individuals where necessary.

Typically, the number of very common surnames for which it becomes necessary to use the authors' full names rather than first initial as an estimate of individuality is quite small, in the dozens, making this procedure quite feasible under the conditions mentioned above. Especially for exploratory studies, such a procedure can help improve the quality of the estimated network enough to provide useful approximations of global network measures (Strotmann and Bubela, 2010).

In the case where only initials are available for author names, a similar procedure has recently been proposed and tested empirically by Staša Milojević (2013). Note, however, that the findings of Fegley and Torvik (2013) imply that both these methods will likely fail with very large literatures, although the percentage of those author names that are available in full form rather than initials only can push up the size limit below which it can work quite significantly. Strotmann et al. (2010) suggest a practical method for increasing this percentage dramatically in the case of author citation networks, especially for the cited literature, using publicly available services for mass matching cited references to full bibliographic records. One such service is the PubMed Batch Citation Matcher, whose use for disambiguation purposes has been discussed in detail in Chapter 3.

Mutschke (2013) offers an idea for how to optimize the resulting network even further, by analyzing the estimated co-author network that is formed in such a way. He suggests that names whose betweenness centrality in the co-author network (which can be determined interactively using a network visualization tool, say) is far greater than it is to be expected given other characteristics of the node in the network are highly likely to be "anomalous," i.e., the results of "lumping" together several distinct individuals. Names identified in such a manner may also be separated into full-name variants by hand to further improve the quality of the estimated network model.

4.7   ALGORITHMIC DISAMBIGUATION

Due to the sheer scale of the data available in principle for analysis—millions of scientific papers published every year—it would obviously be nice to be able to rely on the computer to perform the arduous disambiguation tasks involved in cleaning data for citation analysis. And indeed, name disambiguation, (named) entity identification, and duplicate detection, the headings under which these tasks are known in computer science, have attracted significant amounts of research over the years. These algorithms tend to achieve 85–95% completeness and correctness rates, which makes them likely quite good enough for a wide range of non-evaluative studies in the sense that we discussed above. Even the most intense of efforts to create software to tackle these problems have failed to achieve perfect success on large datasets, however. For ranking tasks, for example, the quality of any automatic disambiguation is therefore likely insufficient.

Unlike network visualization, automatic disambiguation or matching has yet to be implemented in off-the-shelf software packages, unfortunately. This is one reason why data cleaning remains the most expensive part of any citation analysis—and why few large-scale citation analysis studies have been published that do rely on automatically disambiguated datasets.

4.7.1 AUTHOR NAME DISAMBIGUATION

Author name disambiguation is perhaps the most intensely studied among the several disambiguation tasks. It is important both in evaluative and in citation network analysis—in the former, because it is crucial to identify the complete oeuvres of the researchers that are being evaluated, and in the latter, because highly ambiguous names of researchers distort network structures that rely on name=individual assumptions to such a degree that network measures can become completely useless.

Author name disambiguation could also be called oeuvre identification, as the task is to identify the individuals that may be credited with the publications that are being analyzed in a study. Consequently, it is the metadata of a publication that need to be used to algorithmically identify publications with similar author names as belonging to the same individual author—or not.

There are a few questions that are of interest in designing and building algorithms for disambiguation: Which parts of a typical bibliographic record are most informative when it comes to distinguishing or identifying the authors of a paper that they describe? Which types of algorithms work best? How thorough does the disambiguation have to be, i.e., what kinds and magnitudes of errors can be tolerated in the overall study that it is a part of?

Torvik and Smalheiser (2009) studied the utility of different parts of a bibliographic record in PubMed to distinguish or identify the authors of the papers that it describes, and found that in the biomedical literature there, coauthorship patterns carry the most information in this regard.

There are therefore two types of algorithms that are being explored in the computer and information science literature for author name disambiguation.

The most common of these is clustering using unsupervised machine learning techniques, using a more or less complex similarity measure between bibliographic records to drive it. These types of algorithms and their use in author name disambiguation are reviewed extensively in Smalheiser and Torvik (2009). Torvik's Author-ity may well be the most thorough and successful of the algorithms available in this class, with success rates in the high 90%s. The price for this quality is a cubic time complexity of the algorithm they developed, but that may well be necessary given that they have the very ambitious aim to identify individual needles in a gigantic haystack, namely, those rare pairs of individual authors whose research programs could complement each other fruitfully were they to be introduced to each other.

A second type of name disambiguation algorithm that has been explored more recently is based on network structures. Strotmann et al. (2009b) and Deville et al. (2014) both describe algorithms in this class, the latter considering sufficiently similar author names as belonging to the same individual if they have at least one neighbor in common in either the coauthor or the citation graph. Both report success rates in the 80% ranges, as do most of the less highly tuned algorithms in the class of machine learning clustering reviewed by Smalheiser and Torvik (2009).

These types of algorithms have been applied in the context of research that aims to identify large-scale statistical patterns in author networks. As a basis for author co-citation analysis using dimensionality reduction methods, Strotmann and Zhao (2012) concluded that these simpler network analytic disambiguation methods appear sufficient to produce reasonably reliable results for the large-scale structure of the network despite the relatively low accuracy rates, possibly because they tend to emphasize correcting "lumping" errors at the expense of "splitting" errors.

4.7.2   CITATION LINK DISAMBIGUATION

For these network-based disambiguation algorithms to be able to work, it is obviously necessary to first produce a good model of the network of citing and cited documents in the literature that is being analyzed. We need to decide which particular publication is meant by the author when he or she writes down a reference.

This includes two types of tasks. First, the information contained in the reference may identify a document for which the database contains a full record of metadata describing it, including, typically, one or more unique identifiers for the document. Secondly, for those references that do not identify "source" documents, there may be any number of other references in the dataset that also reference the same "non-source" item, and we will want all such references to be modeled as a link to the same node in the corresponding citation network model. In computer science, both of these tasks are known under the term "matching" rather than "disambiguation."

Sometimes, a reference may contain an identifier such as a DOI or a PubMed ID, in which case matching usually consists of looking up the corresponding document and performing a sanity check to make sure the rest of the reference matches the retrieved document information reasonably well.

Most often, however, the reference will contain a small subset of the full bibliographic information on the document that it refers to. Different databases will contain different subsets and forms of this information. As discussed in Chapter 3, the ISI databases list the first author's surname and initials, a standardized abbreviated form of the source title (book title or journal name), publication year, and volume and number of an article, for example, whereas Scopus provides the names and initials of several authors and the title of the cited work in addition to this information. The cited references in the ISI databases tend to be relatively unique to a cited work, meaning that equality testing between two references tends to suffice for identifying references to the same work, but Scopus references are much less standardized and require more work to match against each other.

Strotmann et al. (2010) show the usefulness of matching references to full bibliographic records rather than each other: these records allow the researcher to access complete bibliographic information for the referenced work rather than relying on the fragmentary information contained in the reference itself. In laboratory-based natural sciences, for example, this is necessary to identify one of the main authors of a publication, namely, the head of the laboratory who tends to be listed as last author of a publication in these fields.

The easiest way to perform this type of matching procedure is to use the search facilities of the databases that one wishes to match against. Different databases have different pros and cons in this respect, but in all cases it is first necessary to separate each reference into its constituent parts in order to reassemble them into a query of the form that the database supports. Strotmann et al. (2012; 2013), Strotmann et al. (2009b), and Strotmann and Zhao (2012) detail some of our experience with doing so for a number of popular databases, including PubMed, Scopus, and the ISI databases.

4.8 BACK TO THE FUTURE: COMPUTER-AIDED DISAMBIGUATION

Even the most thorough automatic disambiguation methods produce less than perfect results. The sheer size of the scientific literature, on the other hand, makes it hard to think that it could be disambiguated completely by hand in all its aspects.

In the future, we will therefore increasingly see hybrid approaches to the disambiguation of individuals in the scientific literature, in which computers, experts, the publishing industry, and the public work together in an open collaboration around the world to resolve this "identity crisis" (Qiu, 2008) in science and technology information as well as it possibly can.

We can already see, on a relatively small scale, how this will work, when considering web services like Mendeley, Google Scholar, ResearchGate, or Wikipedia/DBpedia. A researcher who wishes to set up his or her own publication profile in Google Scholar, for example, is presented with the results of a search in the database for publications carrying her or his name, and asked to identify those of these publications that indeed belong to her or his oeuvre. The researcher may also manually add metadata records for publications not (yet) indexed in Google Scholar. In ResearchGate, the scholar may additionally upload full texts of published or even unpublished work, as well as data and original figures or tables, to round out their research profiles. Later, whenever Google Scholar indexes a new scientific publication, its software will notify the author whenever similar documents that they have likely co-written are located, asking him or her to verify if this is indeed his or her publication. Both Google Scholar and ResearchGate, as well as other similar services, provide permanent addresses for these profiles, which effectively serve as identifiers for the individuals that created them.

Google Scholar will also scan full texts of new publications for references to publications for which it has indexed the metadata, and makes these available to scholars. To allow individual researchers to manually help improve this particular automatic disambiguation outcome, this service provides two possibilities. First, if a cited reference cannot be mapped to a specific document in the database, the reference itself becomes a placeholder for a full publication, to be claimed (or not) by a researcher in his or her profile. Secondly, to help with complex publication histories or simply with downright cataloging or citation errors, which are surprisingly common, Google Scholar allows a researcher to identify publications that appear to be different as actually referring to the same work of the author.

More and more research institutions are being asked to provide to their funders or to the public regular accounts of their research performance, i.e., that of their affiliated members. The "current research information systems" (CRISs) that are deployed for such a purpose tend to be initialized with content in a similar manner, in that automatic searches in databases are counter-checked by the researchers who are employed in these institutions; however, there is an important difference. To minimize this (ab)use of the highly valuable time of their researchers, institutions will often provide them with professional cataloger and indexer services, ensuring at the same time an independent verification (and quality control) of the information that they use for subsequent reports.

For well-known researchers, Wikipedia adds yet another twist, where the public manually enters and/or verifies details of the most important works of these individuals.

To summarize: we are seeing a development toward a large number of more or less public databases that are initialized via algorithmic extraction and disambiguation of authors, institutions, oeuvres, and references from full texts, and which then undergo manual quality control by authors, information professionals, or the general public. The information professionals among them may be employed by publishers, libraries, or database vendors. Some of these databases will include cross-links to equivalent entries in other databases, just as the Scopus or the ISI record of a publication may contain its PubMed ID and most bibliographic databases will include DOIs of the indexed items wherever available.

The increase in manual quality control feeds back into the development of higher-quality disambiguation algorithms, as the initial unsupervised machine learning algorithms used in the start-up phase of the service evolve into supervised machine learning via professional quality control.

As these developments converge into a collaborative and openly available system of authority files for scientific and technological publications and for the people and institutions involved in them, bibliometric analysis, and particularly citation analysis, can be expected to be able to produce increasingly reliable results from the constantly improving data source that this system will eventually be able to provide for this purpose.

CHAPTER 5

Visualization of Citation Networks

5.1   WHY CITATION NETWORK VISUALIZATION?

A picture is worth a thousand words, they say. In citation analysis, we can paraphrase: a picture may be more informative than a thousand numbers—a visualization of the interrelationships between cited and/or citing objects may reveal more structure than the corresponding table of objects and their citation interrelationships.

Take as an example one of the many citation network visualizations from Katy Börner's book *Atlas of Science* (Börner, 2010), many of which have been traveling the world since 2005 as part of the *Places and Spaces* science exhibit she curates and on display at the accompanying website sci-maps.org. The "World Map of Science" as shown in Figure 5.1 was chosen as a "brilliant display of the year" in a 2006 *Nature* news article (Marris, 2006). This visualization is based on a co-citation analysis of one year's worth of science journal publications, about 800,000 in total, as indexed in the ISI databases. Imagine the information overload entailed by looking at a table of 800,000 x 800,000 co-citation counts of science publications.

Not that this map of science visualizes this gigantic table fully, of course. In citation analysis visualizations, the number of documents, journals, or authors covered in the underlying study is usually much too large for the human mind to be able to grasp such detail, which is why statistical clustering or dimensionality reduction methods are used for whittling down the number of visualized objects down to, typically, a few hundred or a couple of thousand. In this map of science, the documents were clustered into about 800 "paradigms" of science with about a thousand documents each on average. As usual, co-citation counts of papers were used as a similarity measure in the document clustering phase, and a similar metric to measure the correlation between the resulting 800 or so paper clusters. It is this 800 x 800 matrix of "paradigms" and their correlations that the map of science visualizes, combined with information on each of the 800 or so paradigms, such as the number of publications it comprises (size), which field of science it belongs to (color), and salient common terms in titles and abstracts of the papers in this area. The latter three carry the same kind of information as a simple table would, whereas the grey scale value of a link between two nodes representing two "paradigms" indicates the strength of the correlation between them, and thus a data entry in the 800 x 800 matrix mentioned earlier. Not that all entries in the matrix are visualized as links, though: only connections with strengths exceeding a certain threshold are shown. Again, this is a common technique in co-citation visualizations, for the simple reason that co-citation matrices tend to be quite dense, and drawing all non-zero links would simply cover the entire image with links.

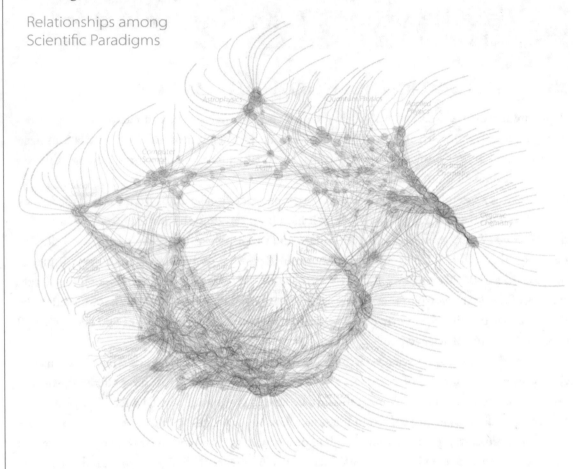

Figure 5.1: Global Map of Science from article co-citation analysis (Boyack et al., 2007, reproduced here in the latest version as posted on http://wbpaley.com/brad/mapOfScience/).

It is the layout of the map of science that truly provides the visual sense of the observer with information that goes well beyond what could be discerned easily from a corresponding table. The creators of this particular map used a spring-embedded layout algorithm to place nodes representing similar "paradigms" close to each other on the map, while those representing dissimilar ones are placed more or less independently from each other, and the whole set of nodes is spread relatively evenly across the canvas.

The resulting network visualization tells an interesting story. "Paradigms" tend to cluster into discernible sub-fields of the sciences (sub-fields of physics in one region of the map, social science areas in another). On the right, the map reflects the traditional hierarchy of the hard sciences—mathematics, physics, chemistry, and biology building on each other—although there is much more detail to be seen, and the hierarchy becomes a succession on a circle rather than on a straight line. The map places the medical sciences next on this circle (and thus, presumably, the hierarchy), followed by neuro-sciences and the social sciences. Computer science, however, clearly does not fit into this traditional hierarchy anymore, instead visually closing the circle with strong correlations to mathematics and physics on the one hand, and to the social sciences and neuro-sciences on the other, i.e., with connections to both the top and the bottom of the traditional hierarchy of the sciences.

Major visual gaps in this map of science, which we could interpret as delimiting potential top-level classifications of the sciences, would suggest quite a non-traditional set of university faculties, however: (a) physics and chemistry; (b) life sciences, cognitive sciences, and medicine; (c) social sciences; (d) mathematics and computer science. Moreover, the visualization raises the question as to what degree it primarily reflects the traditional hierarchy of the sciences or independent clusters of research, a question that Fanelli and Glänzel (2013) weigh in favor of the former.

To summarize what we have discussed so far:

- Citation analysis visualizations usually combine what we termed evaluative and relational citation analysis results. Node sizes tend to reflect evaluative results—the larger a node, the more citations it represents. Links, on the other hand, represent relational citation analysis results—the stronger the link, the more highly co-cited or the more strongly bibliographically coupled the nodes are that it connects.

- The layout of nodes and links in a citation network visualization tends to be created automatically using any of a number of automatic graph layouting algorithms. Done well, it can reflect an interpretable global relational citation structure.

- Network visualizations tend to summarize rather than directly represent the underlying citation network. Basically, there are two summarization methods typically used: (a) selecting a subset of nodes and links to draw, or (b) clustering nodes and visualizing relationships between clusters. Combinations of these two are possible, too, as we will see below.

- A picture is worth a thousand words when it serves to illustrate a story. The intelligibility requirement for network visualizations imposes strict limits for the number and density of nodes and links on them. Getting this aspect right can be more an art than a science.

- Citation network visualizations cannot tell a story without any words at all. As in country maps, it is necessary to attach a name to outstanding features for their viewers to be able to orient themselves in them. Especially in visualizations of such abstract networks, the names for large-scale features are frequently the result of an interpretation by the creators of the visualization rather than automatically generated labels.

Under these conditions, citation network visualizations can be very useful to illustrate the results of a citation analysis. Perhaps even more importantly, they can be quite useful as explorative tools that help with the discovery of patterns.

While we do not know if Fanelli and Glänzel were inspired to investigate this question by this particular visualization, we can nevertheless present this as an interesting example of how visualizations could serve as exploration tools, helping to generate hypotheses that are to be tested.

5.2   CAUTIONARY TALES

While citation network visualizations can help the eye identify true patterns in huge amounts of data, caution is required when interpreting these patterns: as with Fanelli and Glänzel (2013), additional research is usually required to verify that observed patterns are more than just figments of the imagination or mere artifacts of one of the many components of the analysis that led to them.

5.2.1   DATABASE ARTIFACTS

The relative sizes of research areas as visualized in the world map of science in Figure 5.1 are most probably database artifacts, for example. Especially the small size of the social sciences cluster at the top left of Figure 5.1 is unlikely to reflect reality: the coverage of social science publications in the ISI databases is well known to be very incomplete, with estimates in the 10–50% range (compared to 90–98% in the life sciences) (e.g., Chi, 2012, 2013). Numbers of publications and numbers of citations in the social sciences are therefore both heavily underestimated, so that the numbers and sizes of social science nodes as well as the number and strengths of links connecting them to the other sciences will be underestimated in this map.

Figure 5.2 illustrates this point nicely. It, too, is a world map of science, and it, too, is part of the *Places and Spaces* exhibit of science maps (scimaps.org), but this time a click-stream model is used to estimate sizes and correlations between clusters. Here, the social sciences are shown as a huge and complex cluster at the center (Bollen et al., 2009) rather than as a small appendix in the periphery of science as in Figure 5.1. The "truth" about the social sciences probably lies somewhere between the two.

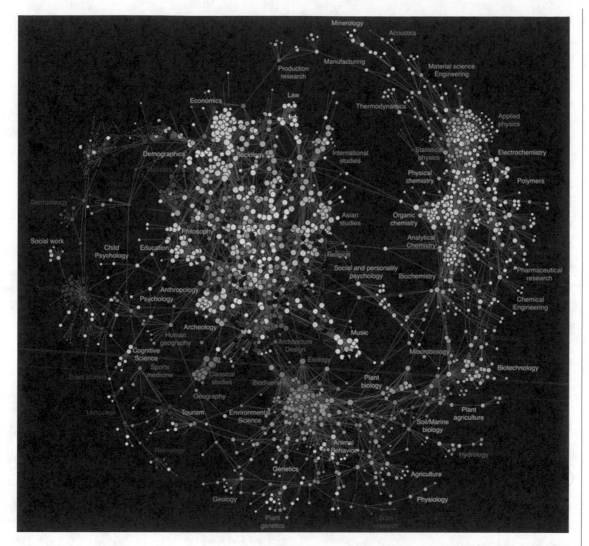

Figure 5.2: Global Map of Science from article click stream data (Bollen et al., 2009).

5.2.2   VISUALIZATION ARTIFACTS

Our second cautionary tale regards the limitations of visualization techniques themselves. Notice that there is no clearly delineated mathematics cluster in Figure 5.1, and no mathematics cluster at all in Figure 5.2. Again, this is clearly a problem given the fundamental importance of mathematics research in the science enterprise. In Figure 5.2, this may be in part due to the relatively small size of the mathematics fields, which may have caused them to fail to go beyond the click-count threshold imposed on the visualization—this is one presumably quite common type of visualization artifact.

In Figure 5.1, however, a number of mathematics "paradigms" are noticeable, centered at the top of the figure: the advantage of clustering rather than filtering is that relatively small areas will still be represented in the resulting visualization. Still, the narrative that Figure 5.1 suggests about the Field of Mathematics is likely largely a visualization artifact. Mathematics publications are famous both for the extreme care taken in citing relevant literature and for the extremely small number of citations that even researchers and publications of the highest quality receive within that field. Whenever a mathematical result becomes useful to another field of research, be it physics, biology, the social sciences, or computer science, the number of citations that it will receive from those application areas will almost certainly dwarf those it receives from within mathematics itself. In a visualization like Figure 5.1, this means that mathematics is shown as a field that has little or no identity of its own—the structure of mathematics as depicted here is that of its application areas instead.

With most automatic visualization techniques, small groups will appear incoherent in this way as a visualization artifact, a fact that needs to be taken into account whenever interpreting one. This also very likely puts a severe limit to the validity of clustering techniques that use majority votes of 2D-visualization runs as a clustering method (Boyack and Klavans, 2010; Klavans and Boyack, 2011, Boyack et al., 2013), as they are likely to miss this important class of clusters.

This type of visualization artifact can also happen with quite large and tightly coupled groupings, because this effect is in part caused by the need to show in two dimensions a phenomenon that frequently requires quite a large number of dimensions to do it justice, i.e., to place nodes and links in relation to each other in such a way that each and every link's length directly corresponds to the strength of the relationship between the two nodes that it connects. It is therefore usually a good idea to at least run a visualization in three dimensions in addition to the two-dimensional depiction used for publication in order to double check if the structures suggested by the latter still appear in the former.

5.2.3 INFORMATIVE VS. HEAVY LINKS

The missing mathematics cluster in Figure 5.2 also illustrates another central problem of network visualizations, namely, how to choose the most important or relevant parts of a network that should be included in the visualization. It is clear that the visualization in Figure 5.1 found better answers to this question than that in Figure 5.2 as indicated by how the field of mathematics was presented there.

The fundamental problem here is that frequencies, sizes, or weights tend to correlate with the importance or relevance of the information that they convey only locally, i.e., within a group of quite similar entities. But who would seriously consider the mathematics research fields unimportant compared to the life sciences simply because the numbers of researchers, publications, and citations they accrue are a minuscule fraction of the corresponding numbers there? In different fields, and even in different subfields of the same field, publication and citation cultures differ significantly, as does coverage in the citation databases.

This phenomenon is surprisingly common: in information science, for example, a "global" view would indicate that it is completely dominated by computer science if size was all that mattered (Boyack and Klavans, 2011a); in stem cell research, the research sub-community that investigates stem cell research ethics is of utmost importance to the field and highly regarded as such by the research community there, but it is tiny by biomedical research group size standards even if good-sized by ethics research area standards.

Information theory tells us that something is informative if it adds something new to the overall picture. The most relevant and most interesting things are those that surprise us while being linked with things we (thought we) knew.

There are two main techniques in visualization that allow one to address this issue. One of these we met above: by clustering the entire dataset in such a way that all clusters are visualizable and none need to be left out, even small sub-fields can separate out as their own clusters and contribute to the overall view. The second technique can improve on this one: instead of clustering the data for visualization, which assign each entity to exactly one cluster, use a statistical technique like factor analysis or latent Dirichlet allocation, which consider each entity as potentially contributing to more than one topic. In this case, we can also obtain link weights by informativeness rather than counts.

5.3 THREE DECADES OF CO-CITATION NETWORK VISUALIZATIONS OF THE LIBRARY AND INFORMATION SCIENCE FIELD

Visualization has been a part of published citation network analysis studies for decades, albeit at a much smaller scale than that of Figure 5.1 and 5.2.

Especially in author co-citation analysis (ACA) studies, LIS field maps were included from the very beginning as shown by Figure 5.3 taken from White and Griffith (1981), which introduced ACA. These tended to be multi-dimensional scaling (MDS) maps, with the exception of Rosengren's (1968) node-and-link author co-mention network visualizations.

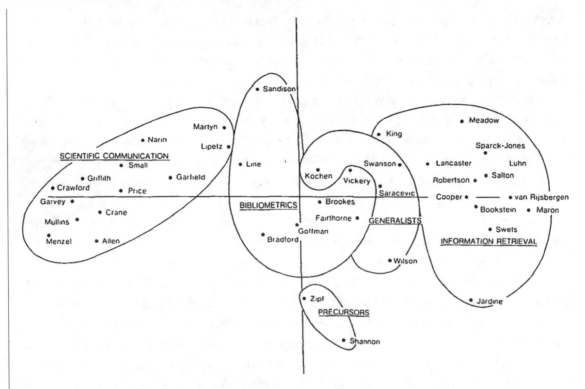

Figure 5.3: ACA MDS map of LIS 1972–79 (White and Griffith, 1981, p. 165).

Since White and McCain's (1998) seminal paper sub-titled "visualizing a discipline," it has become something of a tradition to use the field of library and information science as a test case not just for citation analysis techniques but in particular for the informativeness of different visualization techniques or visualization systems.

Like White and Griffith (1981), White and McCain (1998) mainly use the SPSS implementation of multidimensional scaling (MDS) as a visualization technique, which places the individuals (in their case, individual authors) on a two-dimensional map based on statistical analysis, but leaving out all links (Figure 5.4 taken from their paper). They described the visual appearance of their map as "looking rather like Australia" with well-populated coasts and empty wastes in the center—an effect that later researchers identified as an artifact of MDS (e.g., van Eck and al. 2010).

Noting that "specialties are better conveyed by factor analysis," White and McCain (1998) based their interpretation of the intellectual structure of information science not so much on the MDS visualization as on the factor analysis results that they obtained for their author co-citation matrix from SPSS. Among other interesting features, they noticed that the factor matrix indicated that information science is split into two sub-fields—"literatures" and "retrieval" they called them—that are separated by a deep chasm.

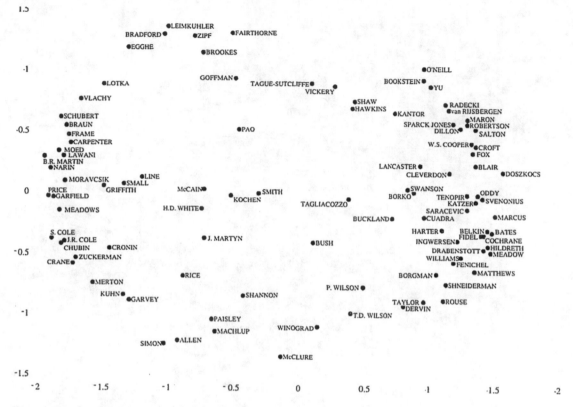

Figure 5.4: **ACA MDS map of LIS 1988–1995** (White and McCain, 1998, p. 347).

Zhao and Strotmann (2008a) went on to analyze and visualize the intellectual structure of the information science field a decade on—during the first decade of the rise to prominence of the World Wide Web. Although they purposely used many of the same methods as White and McCain (1998), they did not use MDS to visualize their results, but rather introduced a simple technique for directly visualizing the factor matrix that White and McCain (1998) had found so informative before. And indeed, their visualization clearly showed that fundamental structural dichotomy within information science that several authors had observed (but never "seen") before (Figure 5.5): their technique led to an image that succeeded—for the first time—in "telling" this particular story.

Their success led later researchers to test their own visualization methods and systems on the same dataset with the express goal of using theirs as a benchmark.

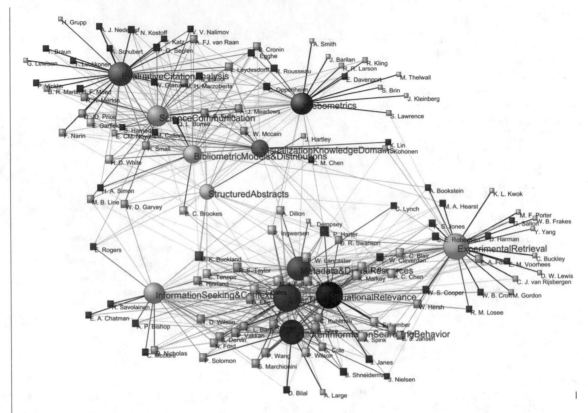

Figure 5.5: Factor analysis visualization of LIS 1996–2005 (Zhao and Strotmann, 2008a).

Van Eck and al. (2010) tested their optimization of the MDS algorithm called VOS and their VOSviewer implementation of that algorithm (Figure 5.6) on the dataset. Their paper points out that, like the Zhao and Strotmann method, the VOS algorithm visually separates the two main camps of the information science field more clearly compared to MDS: the ability to tell this particular story from that particular dataset has become a benchmark for the quality of citation network visualization techniques.

Chen et al. (2010) applied the then-current version of Chaomei Chen's citation network visualization system CiteSpace to this dataset (Figure 5.7 taken from their paper). Their focus was on whether CiteSpace identifies closely similar clusters to those found by the factor analysis in Zhao and Strotmann's (2008a), and then tested three automatic labeling techniques for those clusters against the manually assigned labels there. This visualization, too, can be interpreted to show the two-camp structure of LIS (retrieval on the left, literatures on the right), although it appears to show stronger links across the divide between the two camps (e.g., between clusters #3 and #10) than within the camps (e.g., between clusters #2 and #3 in the literatures camp and between clusters #7 and #10 in the retrieval camp).

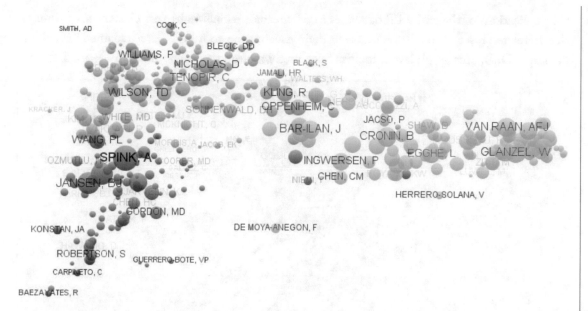

Figure 5.6: **VOS** visualization of **LIS** (van Eck and al., 2010).

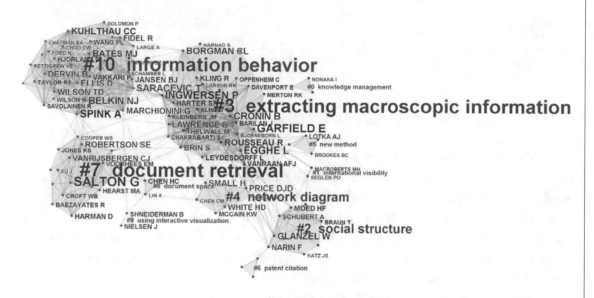

Figure 5.7: CiteSpace ACA visualization of LIS with automatically extracted cluster labels (Chen et al., 2010).

Boyack and Klavans (2011a) also highlight this feature in their visualization of this field from a "global" perspective (Figure 5.8). Their analysis was based on clustering several years' worth of the publications of the entire ISI databases into "threads"—small multi-year clusters of continuous closely related research publications, using their visualization tool DrL (later renamed vxOrd and then openOrd). This graph layout tool was also used to create the science map in Figure 5.1.

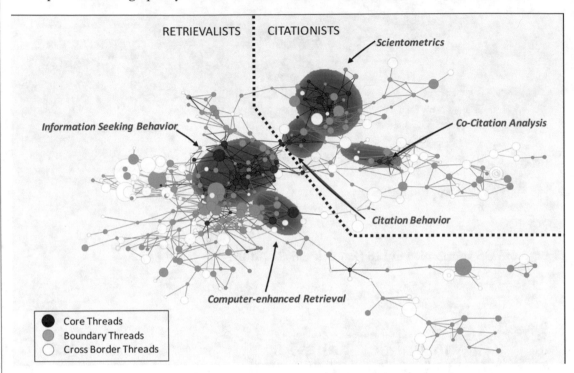

Figure 5.8: Research "thread" visualization of LIS (Boyack and Klavans, 2011a).

Meanwhile, Zhao and Strotmann (2014a) have refined their visualization technique to improve its informativeness even further, by relying on the fact that factor analyses of co-citation matrices with the theoretically preferred oblique rotation produce two factor matrices, namely, the structure matrix, which is usually very dense, and the pattern matrix, which is usually very sparse. They now use the structure matrix to calculate a stable and informative automatic layout, but highlight the more informative link structure of the pattern matrix to avoid information overload (Figure 5.9). Their visualization of a more recent time slice of LIS publications indicates that some bridging between the two main camps of the field is beginning to succeed.

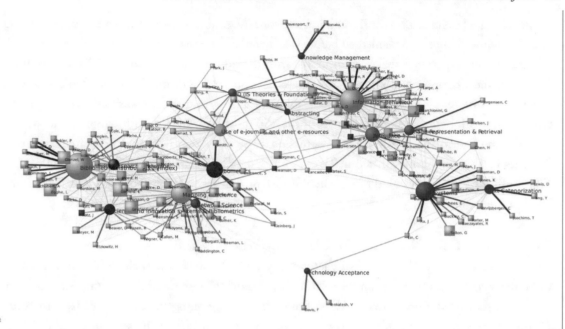

Figure 5.9: **Factor Analysis visualization of LIS 2006–2010** (Zhao and Strotmann, 2014a).

5.4   VISUALIZATION OF CITATION NETWORKS USING PAJEK

This section describes in detail how the Zhao and Strotmann visualizations presented in their published articles (2008a; 2008b; 2008c; 2011a; 2011b; 2012; 2014a) are produced using the popular general-purpose social network visualization system Pajek (Batagelj and Mrvar, 2007). Even though they use Pajek to visualize the factor structures resulting from factor analysis of matrices of author co-citation counts or bibliographic coupling frequencies, the visualization techniques they use apply to other types of bibliometric networks, which will be illustrated below by an example as well.

Please note that in addition to effective use of general-purpose statistical analysis and network visualization tools, software packages specifically developed for citation network visualizations have also emerged over the years. Well-known examples include CiteSpace and VOSviewer. These packages can produce visualizations directly from data downloaded from major citation databases (e.g., Web of Science, Scopus). This means on the one hand that researchers using these packages are not required to go through the many steps often needed when using generic tools as presented below, but on the other hand they also tend to lose the precise control over their studies such as performing name disambiguation when necessary and cleaning citation networks to be visualized. For example, VOSviewer treats allonyms as different individuals in its visualizations, and does not support manual examinations of the citation networks (e.g., author co-citation matrices) to be visualized to allow allonyms to be merged before visualization. As a result, researchers using these packages can in our experience feel uncomfortable with the interpretation of the visualization results.

All the examples and visual maps in this section are based on the same citation network so that the differences between the visualizations produced in different ways are easily seen. The citation network is the co-citation matrix of the 150 most highly cited information scientists used in Zhao and Strotmann (2014a). The information science research field was delineated as all publications in 11 core journals (listed in Table 2.4 in Chapter 2) during the time period 2006–2010. First-author counting was used to identify the 150 most highly cited authors and to calculate their co-citation counts.

5.4.1   FACTOR ANALYSIS OF BIBLIOMETRIC DATA

As discussed in Chapter 2, the goal of Factor Analysis (FA) is to seek a small number of meaningful underlying factors that explain the relationships among a large number of items, and has been used in author cocitation analysis (ACA) from the very beginning to reveal specialty structures of research fields and authors' memberships in one or more such specialties (White and Griffith, 1981). FA applied in ACA has been shown to provide clear and revealing results as to the nature of a discipline (White and McCain, 1998).

In addition to the specialty groupings of a research field that other multivariate analysis techniques such as Cluster Analysis can also identify, FA can assign individual authors to more than one specialty, can indicate the level of association between authors and the specialties to which they belong, and can provide measures of "the degree of relationship between specialties" (White and Griffith, 1982, p. 260), i.e., more information on the structural interactions between specialties.

In this sense, factors in FA are dimensions that span (much of) the observed variance, and the analyzed objects (e.g., authors) are placed in the multidimensional space spanned by them. FA has been limited to being used on relatively small datasets, but recent developments in dimensionality reduction algorithms, namely, Latent Dirichlet Allocation (LDA) type methods, show great promise as a future replacement for FA. With this type of methods, it is possible to process nearly arbitrarily large datasets with comparable results. Bleier and Strotmann (2013) have begun experimenting with using LDA instead of FA with visualizations of the type we present here.

Rotation is normally necessary in FA to obtain meaningful factor structures. There are two types of rotation methods in FA: orthogonal and oblique. Theoretically, an orthogonal rotation assumes that resulting factors are not correlated, and works best for revealing independent dimensions of the underlying structure being studied. An oblique rotation, by contrast, is not restricted to keeping the extracted factors independent of each other, and therefore works better at separating out factors when it can be expected theoretically that the resulting factors would in reality be correlated (Hair, et al., 1998).

In the case of ACA, large factors are interpreted as specialties within a research field, and the correlation between different factors can therefore be expected to be fairly high, as it would represent interdisciplinary research or cross-disciplinary dissemination between specialties. Indeed, high correlations between factors were found in different fields, with the highest correlation between two factors reported in a given study ranging from 0.39–0.65 (McCain, 1990b; White and Griffith, 1982; Zhao, 2006a). An oblique rotation, therefore, appears theoretically more appropriate for ACA although orthogonal rotation methods have also been used with meaningful results in ACA studies in practice (White and McCain, 1998; Zhao and Strotmann, 2008a). As an additional advantage, an oblique rotation produces more information that can be used to interpret the results: a component correlation matrix to indicate the degree of correlation between resulting factors, and two matrices (instead of one with orthogonal rotation) to show the factor structures: pattern matrix and structure matrix (McCain, 1990b; White and Griffith, 1982; Zhao and Strotmann, 2008a). Loadings in the pattern matrix represent the unique contribution of individual authors (variables) to specialties (factors), whereas loadings in the structure matrix, which are "simple correlations between variables and factors," are determined both by an author's unique contribution to each factor and by the correlation among factors (Hair, et al., 1998, p. 113). In order to focus on important relationships between authors and factors, only loadings greater than a threshold (e.g., 0.3 in the examples below) are normally retained in these result matrices.

Any of these factor matrices can be visualized using the method described below. With an oblique rotation, the combination of pattern matrix and structure matrix makes the visual map even more informative, as discussed below. We will use the structure matrix as an example in the description of visualization of individual factor matrices. We will then discuss how to combine pattern and structure matrix into a single map.

5.4.2   CONVERSION OF FACTOR ANALYSIS RESULTS FROM SPSS TO PAJEK NETWORK FORMAT

Factor matrices need to be converted to the network file format required by Pajek (i.e, .net file format) in order to be read into the Pajek program for visualization. Here we describe the steps and algorithms for a simple computer program to do the conversion. But it will become clear that the conversion can also be done manually (e.g., for small matrices) directly from the SPSS output to the final Pajek .net file.

Export a factor matrix from the SPSS output file to a spreadsheet file.

This is simply done by right-clicking on the matrix in the SPSS output file and choosing Export. Figure 5.10 shows what a structure matrix exported from the SPSS output looks like. This is from the factor analysis of the co-citation matrix of 150 authors explained at the beginning of Section

5.4. Note in particular that the factors are only numbered (i.e., without meaningful labels) in the SPSS output, and that author names do not contain spaces any more.

	1	2	3	4	5	6	7	8	9	10	11	12	13	14	15	16
ColeJ	.870			-.513	-.338			.467	-.380			.339				-.371
ColeS	.859			-.665				.417	-.440			.318				-.406
AksnesD	.855			-.739	-.305				-.471							-.467
SeglenP	.849			-.743	-.365			.360	-.459							-.386
VanraanA	.823			-.762	-.328			.320	-.490			.308				-.539
MacrobertsM	.807			-.555	-.472			.521	-.662			.321				-.319
NederhofA	.781			-.648	-.455			.322	-.451							-.603
MertonR	.767			-.535	-.416	.300		.497	-.593			.433				-.438
BordonsM	.749			-.724	-.363				-.442			.498				-.595
FisherK		.953					-.388						.349	.305	-.386	
PettigrewK		.937					-.322						.316		-.380	
SavolainenR		.934					-.427						.346	.334	-.392	
ChatmanE		.931					-.305								-.369	
SonnenwaldD		.930					-.371	.319					.338	.302	-.357	
CaseD		.930					-.472	.327					.463	.353	-.425	
NahlD		.927					-.454						.364	.405	-.364	
ShneidermanB							-.538				-.344			.786		
ChenH			.606				-.446				-.623			.749		
JorgensenC														.725		
JansenB		.552	.377				-.660				-.375		.307	.703		
NielsenJ							-.598				-.313			.702		
BrownJ		.383													-.848	
Nonakal															-.780	
DavenportT															-.753	
TijssenR		.501		-.392					-.645			.518				-.832
MeyerM		.375		-.372					-.459			.419				-.806
HicksD		.687		-.564	-.342				-.483			.380				-.798
EtzkowitzH		.311							-.374			.456				-.798
NarinF		.606		-.496					-.653			.462				-.781
ZittM		.585		-.610					-.590			.486				-.778
KatzJ		.627		-.502					-.432			.586				-.737

Extraction Method: Principal Component Analysis.
Rotation Method: Oblimin with Kaiser Normalization.

Figure 5.10: Structure matrix in a spreadsheet exported from SPSS (above the blank line: top of file; below the blank line: bottom of file).

Convert spreadsheet files to CSV files.

Double click the spreadsheet file to open it in a spreadsheet program. Remove all spurious information (i.e., the first three rows and the last row in Figure 5.10) from the spreadsheet and then save it as a CSV file (preferably tab-separated values format). Figure 5.11 shows excerpts of the CSV file in tab-separated value format corresponding to those shown in Figure 5.10.

	A	B	C	D	E	F	G	H	I	J	K	L	M	N	O	P	Q
1	ColeJ	0.87			-0.513	-0.338			0.467	-0.38			0.339				-0.371
2	ColeS	0.859			-0.665				0.417	-0.44			0.318				-0.406
3	AksnesD	0.855			-0.739	-0.305				-0.471							-0.467
4	SeglenP	0.849			-0.743	-0.365			0.36	-0.459							-0.386
5	VanraanA	0.823			-0.762	-0.328			0.32	-0.49			0.308				-0.539
6	MacrobertsN	0.807			-0.555	-0.472			0.521	-0.662			0.321				-0.319
7	NederhofA	0.781			-0.648	-0.455			0.322	-0.451							-0.603
8	MertonR	0.767			-0.535	-0.416	0.3		0.497	-0.593			0.433				-0.438
9	BordonsM	0.749			-0.724	-0.363				-0.442			0.498				-0.595
10	FisherK		0.953					-0.388						0.349	0.305	-0.386	
11	PettigrewK		0.937					-0.322						0.316		-0.38	
12	SavolainenR		0.934					-0.427						0.346	0.334	-0.392	
13	ChatmanE		0.931					-0.305								-0.369	
14	SonnenwaldD		0.93					-0.371	0.319					0.338	0.302	-0.357	
15	CaseD		0.93					-0.472	0.327					0.463	0.353	-0.425	
16	NahlD		0.927					-0.454						0.364	0.405	-0.364	
17																	
18	ShneidermanB							-0.538				-0.344			0.786		
19	ChenH			0.606				-0.446				-0.623			0.749		
20	JorgensenC														0.725		
21	JansenB		0.552	0.377				-0.66				-0.375		0.307	0.703		
22	NielsenJ							-0.598				-0.313			0.702		
23	BrownJ		0.383													-0.846	
24	Nonakal															-0.78	
25	DavenportT															-0.753	
26	TijssenR	0.501			-0.392					-0.645			0.518				-0.832
27	MeyerM	0.375			-0.372					-0.459			0.419				-0.806
28	HicksD	0.687			-0.564	-0.342				-0.483			0.38				-0.798
29	EtzkowitzH	0.311								-0.374			0.456				-0.798
30	NarinF	0.606			-0.496					-0.653			0.462				-0.781
31	ZittM	0.585			-0.61					-0.59			0.486				-0.778
32	KatzJ	0.627			-0.502					-0.432			0.586				-0.737
33																	
34																	

Figure 5.11: Structure matrix in a CSV file of tab-separated value format (above the blank line: top of file; below the blank line: bottom of file).

Convert CSV files to Pajek network files (.net format).

Figure 5.12 shows what the .net file as converted from the CSV file in Figure 5.11 looks like. As we can see, a .net file is a text file and is quite easy to create by writing a little computer program and would not be difficult to create manually using any text editor and the data in the SPSS output file. The Python script we have been using for this purpose is included as Appendix 5.4.2.

A .net file consists of two parts: vertices and edges. The first part is for factors and authors visualized as nodes (called vertices in Pajek) in a map. This part starts with the keyword *Vertices followed by ($n+m$) and (optionally) by m where n is the number of factors and m the number of authors. This is followed by factors and authors, one on each line. The order of these vertices is arbitrary, but they are numbered in the .net file and their index numbers must be used correctly to represent them in the edges that follow. Edges in the second part correspond to cell values in a factor matrix. Each cell value (i.e., a factor loading greater than a threshold, e.g., 0.3) represents the strength of the relationship between an author and a factor, and is visualized as a line connecting the corresponding author and factor. Each cell value is represented in the .net file on a separate line containing the index of the factor, the index of the author, and the value itself separated by a blank. The edge declaration "18 1 0.855" in Figure 5.12, for example, means that a line of strength (i.e., loading) 0.855 connects node 18 (author "Aksnes, D") and node 1 (factor "Research evaluation").

```
*Vertices 166                                              146 "Tenopir, C"
1 "research evaluation" circle fos 18 lc Blue x_fact 1.2 y_fact 1.2   147 "Thelwall, M"
2 "Info seeking and use"                                   148 "Tijssen, R"
3 "IR systems"                                             149 "Vakkari, P"
4 "h-index and other mathematical bibliometric distributions"   150 "Vanraan, A"
5 "webometrics"                                            151 "Vanrijsbergen, C"
6 "LIS foundations"                                        152 "Vaughan, L"
7 "relevance"                                              153 "Venkatesh, V"
8 "Use of e-journals and other e-resources"               154 "Vinkler, P"
9 "Mapping of science"                                     155 "Voorhees, E"
10 "technology acceptance"                                 156 "Waddington, C"
11 "text categorization (esp with machine learning)"       157 "Wagner, C"
12 "network science"                                       158 "Wang, P"
13 "Abstract and Abstracting"                              159 "White, H"
14 "image retrieval"                                       160 "White, R"
15 "KM"                                                    161 "Wildemuth, B"
16 "science and innovation systems and bibliometrics"      162 "Wilson, P"
17 "Ahlgren, P" box fos 12 lc Black x_fact 1.2 y_fact 1.2  163 "Wilson, T"
18 "Aksnes, D"                                             164 "Xu, J"
19 "Allan, J"                                              165 "Yang, Y"
20 "Baezayates, R"                                         166 "Zitt, M"
21 "Barabasi, A"                                           *Edges
22 "Bar-ilan, J"                                           52 1 0.87
23 "Barry, C"                                              52 4 -0.513
24 "Bates, M"                                              52 5 -0.338
25 "Bawden, D"                                             52 8 0.467
26 "Beaver, D"                                             52 9 -0.38
27 "Belkin, N"                                             52 12 0.339
28 "Bensman, S"                                            52 16 -0.371
29 "Bilal, D"                                              53 1 0.859
30 "Bollen, J"                                             53 4 -0.665
31 "Bordons, M"                                            53 8 0.417
32 "Borgatti, S"                                           53 9 -0.44
33 "Borgman, C"                                            53 12 0.318
34 "Borlund, P"                                            53 16 -0.406
35 "Borner, K"                                             18 1 0.855
36 "Bornmann, L"                                           18 4 -0.739
37 "Boyack, K"                                             18 5 -0.305
38 "Braun, T"                                              18 9 -0.471
39 "Brin, S"                                               18 16 -0.467
40 "Brown, J"                                              135 1 0.849
41 "Buckland, M"                                           135 4 -0.743
42 "Buckley, C"                                            135 5 -0.365
43 "Budd, J"
44 "Burrell, Q"
45 "Bystrom, K"
```

......

Figure 5.12: Structure matrix in .net file format (left: top of file; right: bottom of file).

Note that the factors in the example file shown in Figure 5.12 were given meaningful labels. In fact, the conversion from CSV to Pajek format is a good time to add those labels if they have already been determined at that time. If not, assigning labels of the form "Factor 1," "Factor 2," etc., works just fine, too.

How the factor and author nodes and their labels should appear in the visual map can be specified by adding corresponding information on each line of the vertices. For example, adding the string (without the quotation marks) "circle fos 18 lc Blue x_fact 1.2 y_fact 1.2" to the end of the first factor line makes all of the factor nodes to appear as circles with labels in font size ("fos") 18 and label color ("lc") blue, and adding the string "box fos 12 lc Black x_fact 1.2 y_fact 1.2" to the end of the first author line makes all author nodes square boxes with labels in size 12 and black color. Both types of nodes are scaled up in visualized size by a factor of 1.2 in all directions, retaining proportions but improving visibility. The shapes, sizes, and colors can be set and fine-tuned according to specific needs and preferences.

5.4.3 VISUALIZATION WITH LOADING SUMMARIES AS NODE SIZES AND DEGREE COLORING

Figure 5.13 is an example of such visualizations. On this map, authors are represented by square nodes and factors by circular nodes, each appropriately labeled. The sizes of nodes in these maps carry auxiliary information. An author node is proportional in size to the author's total loading on all factors combined, and the size of a factor node corresponds to the sum of the loadings on this factor by all authors who load sufficiently (i.e., 0.3 or higher in this case) on it. In this way, the size of a node is an approximate indicator of its overall significance in the map.

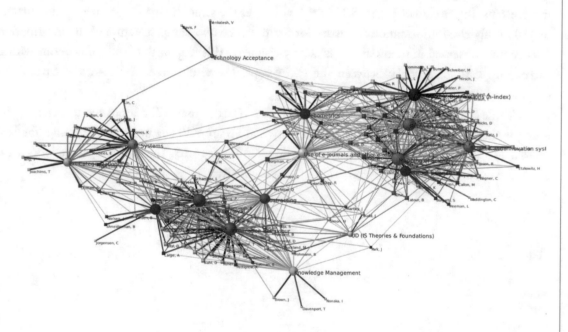

Figure 5.13: Visualization of structure matrix with loading summaries as node sizes and degree coloring.

In addition, node colors represent the number of links to or from a node to other nodes in the map (i.e., its degree). This feature is not that useful in the visualizations of structure matrices due to the large number of co-loadings as shown in Figure 5.13, but can be quite useful when the links in the visualizations are from the pattern matrices as shown in Figure 5.9. The degree information for author nodes can be used to study authors' research breadth as it shows visually that some authors belong to only one specialty or two (e.g., yellow and green square nodes in Figure 5.9 respectively) while some others have memberships in multiple specialties.

The thickness of a line that connects an author with a factor is proportional to the value of the loading of this author on this factor, as is its grey-scale value, with darker lines corresponding to higher loadings. Dashed lines indicate loadings of opposite signs. Throughout, only sufficiently high loadings of absolute value 0.3 or higher are considered. In this way, a map preserves all the relevant information that is contained in a large table of author loadings on factors as in the SPSS output file.

The layout of the map is produced using Pajek's implementation of the Kamada-Kawai graph layout algorithm (Batagelj and Mrvar, 2007) and using loadings as similarity measure between author and factor nodes. The result is a map that is visually informative and true to the factorization it represents. In the case of Figure 5.13 which visualizes the structure matrix of a co-citation matrix of 150 highly cited information scientists, for example, the two-camp structure of the information science field observed in many studies is clearly visible on this map with dense connections within each camp and sparse links between the two camps. The visual maps in Zhao and Strotmann (2008a; 2008b; 2008c) are of this type.

Table 5.1 provides the steps for creating these types of maps. The input file to Pajek in the example there is the structure matrix .net file shown in Figure 5.12 (named as structure.net for easy reference) and the output is the visualization shown in Figure 5.13. The same steps also work with a .net file created from the pattern matrix of a factor analysis, of course.

Table 5.1: Steps for creating maps with loading summaries as node sizes

1. Start up Pajek.

2. In the Pajek menu, choose *File -> Network -> Read*, and select the structure.net file created above. Make sure to choose the option *Files with type: HTML with SVG* in the file chooser menu that pops up.

3. As the loadings can be negative, adjust them by choosing *Network -> Create new network -> Transform -> Line Values -> Absolute* from the Pajek menu.

4. To determine the node colors, choose *Network -> Create partition -> Degree -> All* from the Pajek menu. This creates a grouping where all authors that have the same number of factors that they load on will be members of the same group, and all members in the same group will be given the same color.

5. To determine node sizes, choose *Network -> Create vector -> Centrality -> Weighted degree -> All* from the Pajek menu.

6. To fine-tune the visualization, it sometimes helps to scale the link strengths in this network. To do this, choose *Network -> Create new network -> Transform -> Line Values -> Multiply by*, and enter a multiplier (3.0 is a good value in our experience) in the input box that pops up.

7. Visualize the network by choosing *Draw -> Network + first partition + first vector*. A visualization window pops up, and it is usually a good idea to maximize it before proceeding.

1. Choose *Options -> Values of Lines -> Similarities* from the Pajek visualization window menu. This option uses a factor loading as measuring the similarity of an author to a factor and displays an author node in the map the more closely to a factor node the higher this similarity is.

2. Choose both *Options -> Lines -> GreyScale* and *Options -> Lines -> Different Widths* from the Pajek visualization window menu. Pajek remembers these settings between sessions, so that you do not usually need to perform these settings more than once.

3. Hit *Ctrl-K* to re-draw the map. We normally do this a few times until we are satisfied with the map. This is equivalent to choosing *Layout -> Energy -> Kamada-Kawai -> Free* or, in recent Pajek versions, *Layout -> Energy -> Kamada-Kawai -> Separate Components*.

4. Finally, save the visualization result as an SVG file (or rather, an HTML file with an associated SVG file) by choosing *Export -> 2D -> SVG -> General*, and entering the file name for the HTML file to be saved, say, structureMap.htm. Make sure to choose the option *Files with type: HTML with SVG* in the file chooser menu that pops up. A corresponding SVG file called structureMap.svg will also be save automatically. If the 3D look of nodes is preferred, before saving the visualization result, choose *Export -> Options* from the visualization window menu, enable the option *SVG: 3D Effect on Vertices* in the configuration window that pops up, and then close the options window.

Note that when a map is re-drawn, the layout changes with the pattern matrix, but remains largely stable with the structure matrix. The map from the pattern matrix, therefore, is only used to show the sizes of specialties and authors' memberships in specialties whereas the map from the structure matrix shows the interrelationships between the specialties (e.g., the two-camp structure of the information science field observed in several previous studies).

5.4.4 VISUALIZATION WITH NODE SIZES REFLECTING CITEDNESS

The above visualization is very informative, but does have one drawback—highly cited authors in the field are not easily identified visually.

To remedy this as did Strotmann and Zhao (2012) and Zhao and Strotmann (2014a), we can create an additional file to make available the citation counts of authors for Pajek to use in its visualization so that the node sizes correspond to their citation counts. In this case, we also need to calculate appropriate summary citation counts for the members of a factor to assign to the factor nodes.

To calculate a factor's member citation count, we first determine the members of the factor (defined as those authors who load more highly in the absolute on this factor than on any other factor) and their loadings on this factor. We then sum up the citation counts of all member authors, weighted by their absolute loadings (i.e., their citation counts multiplied by their loadings on this factor).

These citation counts, both for authors and for factors, are then put into a text file saved with the extension .vec, say, citations.vec. The first line of this file contains the keyword *Vertices, and each line of the rest of the file, ordered in the same order as the vertices (i.e., factors and authors) in the .net file above of the factor matrix being visualized (e.g., structure.net), contains a single number, the citation count for the corresponding author or the member citation count for the corresponding factor on each line.

The visualization proceeds as in Table 5.1, except that Step 5 is replaced by loading citations. vec and scaling it for improved visualization as described in Table 5.2 below.

Table 5.2: Steps for using citation counts as node sizes
5.1. Load citation counts vector file by choosing *File -> Vector -> Read* and opening this file, e.g., citations.vec.
5.2. To scale the citation count to get a good visualization, subsequently choose *Vector -> Transform -> Multiply by* and enter the scale factor in the window that pops up. For the well-sized research field in this example, we used a scale factor of 0.05.

Figure 5.14 is the visual map created this way from the same structure matrix as for Figure 5.13. It shows everything that Figure 5.13 shows, plus the citation impact of authors and specialties. For example, a quick glance of the map can spot the most influential authors such as Leydesdorff, Garfield, and Salton.

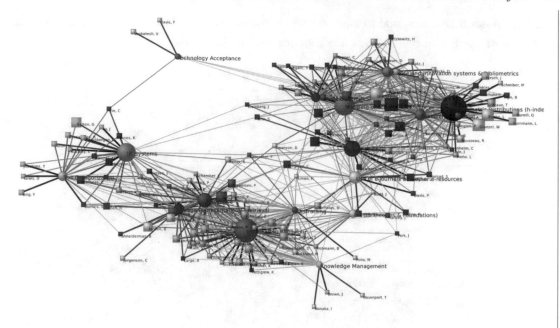

Figure 5.14: Visualization of structure matrix with citation counts as node sizes.

5.4.5 VISUALIZATION WITH NODE COLOR REFLECTING FACTOR MEMBERSHIP

So far, the node colors in our visualization have reflected the degree to which an author bridges specialties (or more precisely, how many factors this author co-loads on), which can be quite useful for analyzing authors' characteristics as shown in Zhao and Strotmann (2008a; 2008b), for example. Factor node colors have however tended to be unintelligible to the human observer as they were chosen based on the number of authors who co-load on them.

An obvious alternative node coloring in this visualization is by factorization—a factor node and all authors who are primarily members of that factor are assigned the same color in this case. Figure 5.15 shows an example, which is the same map as Figure 5.14 but with this new node coloring. Examples can also be found in Strotmann and Zhao (2012).

To create visualizations with this alternative coloring, we need to create a Pajek clusters file with the extension .clu, say, membership.clu. This has the same format as the citations.vec file described in the previous section. The first line of this file contains the keyword *Vertices, and the rest of the lines, ordered in the same order as the vertices (i.e., factors and authors) in the .net file above of the factor matrix being visualized (e.g., structure.net), contain a single integer on each line. This integer is used by Pajek to assign a color in the visualization. Assign a different number to each of the factors and put the number in the .clu file on the line corresponding to the factor itself, and to all those lines that correspond to authors that are members of the factor. In case an author is not a member of any factor, this author's line contains the number zero.

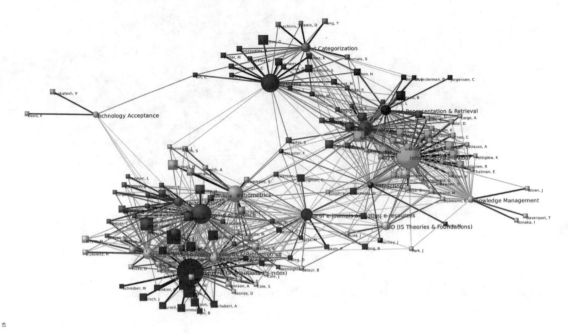

Figure 5.15: Structure with citation count node sizes and factor membership coloring.

Given this file membership.clu, the visualization proceeds as in Table 5.1 above, except for loading this file in Step 4 as described in Table 5.3 below:

Table 5.3: Step for coloring by factor membership
1. Load (*File -> Partition -> Read*) the file membership.clu.

Clearly, both node coloring methods are useful. Which one is better to use depends on the researcher and on the purpose of the visualization.

5.4.6 COMBINING PATTERN AND STRUCTURE MATRIX VISUALIZATIONS

As discussed above, the main SPSS output of a factor analysis with an oblique rotation is a pattern matrix and a structure matrix. These two matrices each have their pros and cons for visualization.

As shown in Figures 5.13, 5.14, and 5.15, the dense connections between authors and factors in the structure matrix, on the one hand, help produce quite stable layouts that in the aggregate tend to visualize fairly meaningful interrelationships between specialties of a research field, but on the other hand often clutter the map and make node labels (especially author nodes) difficult to read and the number of an author's memberships in specialties less meaningful. Although authors' primary memberships can be shown clearly on the map by the coloring method described above, it is difficult to see the names of authors on the map and which authors bridge which specialties. In addition, loadings in this matrix are theoretically not purely authors' memberships in specialties (factors) but a combination of authors' memberships and the correlations between factors.

In the pattern matrix, however, most authors load substantially (e.g., 0.3 or higher) on only one factor, with only a few authors (interpreted as bridging authors) linked to more than one factor (i.e., specialty). Its sparse link structure results in a visual map that is uncluttered and shows the sizes of specialties and authors' memberships in specialties clearly as shown in Figure 5.16, which is a visualization of the pattern matrix from the same factor analysis as the structure matrix used for Figures 5.13, 5.14, and 5.15. But a pattern matrix does not contain enough information to produce a stable layout, sometimes even, as in this example, producing a network with several unconnected components. The layout of the map, therefore, does not readily show the interrelationships between specialties such as the two-camp structure of this field.

For these reasons, we either need to create a map for each of the pattern and structure matrices as in Zhao and Strotmann (2008a; 2008b), with one showing the sizes of specialties and authors' memberships in specialties and the other the interrelationships between the specialties, or we can visualize the two matrices as a combined map in order to utilize the advantages of both parts of the factor analysis result as in Strotmann and Zhao (2012) and Zhao and Strotmann (2014a).

In order to combine the two matrices, we need to create both the structure.net and the pattern.net files, corresponding to the structure and pattern matrices respectively, as described above. Given these and the citation count and factor membership Pajek input files discussed previously, we first produce coordinated visualizations for the two files in Pajek, and then merge the two into a single joint visualization using, e.g., Inkscape, an open-source vector graphics editor. Table 5.4 provides the steps.

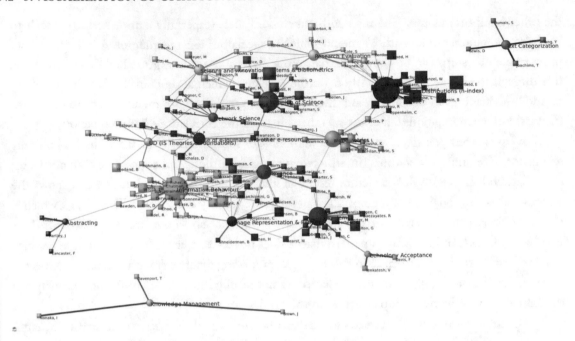

Figure 5.16: Visualization of pattern matrix with citation count node sizes and factor membership coloring.

Figure 5.17 (merged.svg) is the result of these steps. It is an uncluttered map with a stable layout showing clearly the level of impact of each author (author node size), the significance of each specialty (factor node size), the interrelationships between specialties and authors (map layout and background links), and the memberships of each author in specialties (links and node colors). The links from the structure matrix are retained as a muted background as a visual cue to the motivation for the node layout.

Table 5.4: Steps for combining structure and pattern matrices into a single map

1. Visualize the structure.net file as described in Table 5.1, following the steps up to and including Step 7(3), possibly modified according to Table 5.2 and/or Table 5.3. Take note of the network number assigned by Pajek for Network 1 in the main Pajek window and as the title of the Pajek visualization window as you do so. Also take note of the contents of the Partition 1 and Vector 1 fields in the main Pajek window that you use for the visualization in Step 7(3).

2. Before continuing with Step 7(4) in Table 5.1, choose *Graph-Only* from the Pajek visualization window menu and then save the visualization of the structure matrix to an SVG file as described in Step 7(4).

3. Do not close Pajek (this is important!), but continue to the coordinated visualization of the pattern matrix.

4. Now follow the instructions to load and prepare the pattern.net file as in Table 5.1, up to and including Step 6. Take note of the network number assigned by Pajek for Network 1 as you complete Step 6 there.

5. We re-use the structure matrix layout of Step 2 above for the pattern matrix layout as follows, for a coordinated visualization of structure and pattern matrices.

   i.   In the main Pajek window, select the network number you noted for the network derived from the structure.net file in Step 2 as Network 1, and the network number for the one derived from the pattern.net file in Step 4 as Network 2.

   ii.   Transfer the links of the pattern network to the structure network by choosing *Nets -> Cross-Intersection -> Second*. This enables us to visualize the pattern network in the same stable layout as the structure network that we already visualized.

   iii. At this point, the Partition and the Vector chosen in the main Pajek window should still be those derived from the pattern.net file. If not, choose those that you noted in Step 1 above from the drop-down lists of partitions and vectors, respectively.

   iv.   Now switch over to the Pajek visualization window by choosing *Draw-> Draw-Partition-Vector* from the menu. The map should show the author and factor nodes still arranged as they were for the structure matrix visualization, but with fewer lines connecting them.

   v.   If there are no labels attached to the nodes in this window because of Step 2, choose *Options -> Mark Vertices Using -> Labels* from the visualization window menu to activate their display.

   vi.   Finally, save this as an SVG file (and HTML) as in Step 7(4) in Table 5.1, say, as pattern.htm and pattern.svg.\

6. Merge and clean the two SVG files, pattern.svg and structure.svg, manually.

   i.   Start Inkscape, and open both pattern.svg and structure.svg in two separate windows.

   ii.   Create a new empty Inkscape image.

   iii. In the structure.svg window, select everything (Ctrl-A) and copy it (Ctrl-C).

   iv.   In the New image window, paste (Ctrl-V) the structure map into the new drawing.

   v.   In the New image window, add a new layer on top of the structure map (top layer). Select the top layer.

   vi.   Switch over to the pattern.svg window, select all, group, and copy as before.

   vii. After switching back to the New drawing window, paste the content of pattern.svg into the top layer of the New drawing.

   viii. The pattern and structure graphs now need to be aligned manually so that corresponding nodes overlap exactly. This is easiest to do by first moving the newly pasted pattern network roughly into place when the image is completely visible on the screen, and then zooming in to nudge it into place exactly.

   ix.   Finally, adjust the opacity levels for the top and the middle layers for the best visual effect. We used an opacity level of 20% for the structure layer and 100% for the pattern layer.

   x.   The result can now be saved, say as merged.svg.

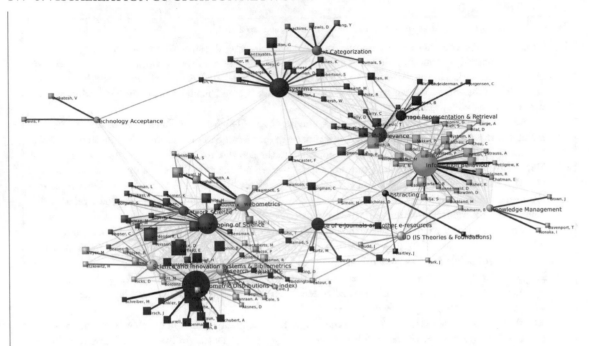

Figure 5.17: Combined visualization.

Figure 5.17 is essentially the same map as Figure 5.9, with the only difference being the coloring method. Figure 5.17 uses factor membership coloring which gives the same color to a factor and all its members, i.e., all authors who load primarily on it, as described in detail in Section 5.4.5. Figure 5.9 uses degree coloring which represents the number of factors on which an author loads (i.e., its degree) in the case of author nodes (i.e., squares in the figures) as described in Section 5.4.3.

These two images also serve as illustration of the point made earlier in Section 5.4.6 about the stability of the layouts produced from the structure matrix. Although these two visualizations have different orientations and appear different at first sight, closer examination will show that the relative positions of both factor and author nodes remain more or less the same. As a result, a researcher will arrive at the same interpretations regarding the interrelationships between specialties and authors using these two maps.

5.4.7 FINE-TUNING THE MAPS

While the SVG file output from Pajek is already a very useful visualization as is, incorporating it into a publication usually requires cleaning it up a bit and then converting it to an image format that is recognized by your favorite word processing application or journal publisher. Table 5.5 provides the steps for doing this.

Table 5.5: Steps for fine-tuning SVG files from Pajek

1. We load the SVG file into Inkscape. Within this editor, we can perform manual cleanup operations such as
   i. Resizing and/or re-coloring node labels. If you did not have any meaningful labels in the original CSV file, you can also edit the factor labels at this point.
   ii. Repositioning node labels to minimize overlap between labels, nodes, and lines to improve legibility of the map. Pajek does not have any algorithms for optimized label positioning, unfortunately. Note: be careful *not* to accidentally reposition any nodes or links while you do so, as this would invalidate the resulting map!
2. The final result can then be saved as PDF, for example, to get an infinite resolution image. Usually, you will need to save it as an image file, however.
   i. To do so, we choose *Export Bitmap...* from the Inkscape menu.
   ii. In the Export Bitmap options window that pops up, we choose *Drawing* as *Export area* and choose a *Bitmap size* by specifying a number for the dpi (dots per inch) field as prescribed by the publisher. We also enter a file name. The output format is PNG.
3. The PNG format will need to be converted to JPEG, usually. We use the open-source program Gimp for this purpose, simply loading it into the program as PNG file and then saving it as a file in JPEG format. When a large number of images need to be converted, we sometimes use ImageMagick for batch conversion instead.

5.4.8 VISUALIZATION OF BIBLIOMETRIC NETWORKS WITHOUT FACTOR ANALYSIS

Essentially, the visualization method described above works with a table where a large number of rows group into a small number of columns by the relationships between these rows and columns. In the case of a factor matrix, the columns are factors, the rows are authors, and their relationships are authors' loadings in factors.

Clearly, any table with this structure, i.e., the interrelationships between groups of objects measured by objects' relatedness with the groups, can be visualized with this method.

For example, diseases are related to molecular substances, and how closely a disease is related to a molecular substance can be measured bibliometrically by their co-occurrences in research articles, i.e., the number of research articles that are indexed under both this disease and this molecular substance. A matrix of 20 diseases by 100 substances can be created this way with the values being co-occurrences if we are interested in investigating how these 20 diseases are related to these 100 substances and to each other through these substances. Both diseases and substances can be identified by the frequency of their occurrence in research articles. This 20 (column) x 100 (row) matrix can then be visualized using the method described in this chapter, with the 20 diseases corresponding to factors and 100 substances to authors.

Figure 5.18 shows the result of visualizing a matrix of co-occurrences of 20 major diseases in the nervous system with 100 major substances identified by the frequency of their occurrence in research articles on nerve systems during the 1965–2012 time period. This visualization, which has aided the investigation of molecular association networks of nervous system diseases in Hu et al. (2013), used the simplest method described in this chapter, i.e., visualization with node size being (the sum of) cell value and node color the number of factors (i.e., diseases here) that an author loads on (i.e., a substance is related to here). The methods described above that improve on coloring and node size can be similarly adapted to this set of data as well.

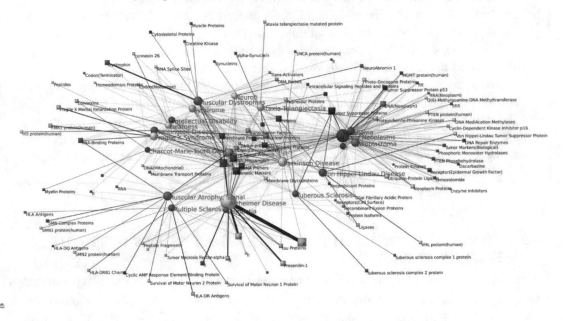

Figure 5.18: Visualization of diseases and molecular substances co-occuring in research papers (Hu et al., 2013).

5.5   CONCLUDING REMARKS

In citation analysis, it is true, as we have seen in this chapter, that a picture can be worth a thousand words. On the other hand, it also became clear that different methods can produce different pictures for the same underlying facts, and that some of these methods are better than others at telling that story of a thousand words. Somewhat paradoxically, it is also true that the abstract pictures that are produced via citation network analysis and visualization are unable to tell that story without a large number of words—labels—to help the mind orient itself as the eye explores the picture.

Citation network visualization has had a long tradition in citation analysis because it can help the researcher bring interpretable order into huge datasets. Various generic statistical analysis and network visualization tools have been used for citation network visualization over the years and software packages specifically developed for this purpose have also emerged, such as CiteSpace and VOSviewer. The latter can produce visualizations directly from data downloaded from major citation databases (e.g., Web of Science, Scopus). This means that researchers using these packages on the one hand are not required to go through the many steps often needed when using generic tools as presented in this chapter, but on the other hand tend to lose the precise control over the quality of the network data for their studies and as a result tend to feel uncomfortable with the interpretation of the visualization results.

Informative visualizations of bibliometric networks can be created with general purpose network analysis and visualization tools such as Pajek as shown in this chapter. We hope that the details provided here on how to create these visualizations will enable researchers to use these types of visual maps in their own research, and help promote more creative use of these tools in Bibliometrics.

Appendix 3.3

```
<PubmedArticle>
    <MedlineCitation Owner="NLM" Status="MEDLINE">
        <PMID Version="1">23825632</PMID>
        <DateCreated>
            <Year>2013</Year>
            <Month>07</Month>
            <Day>04</Day>
        </DateCreated>
        <DateCompleted>
            <Year>2014</Year>
            <Month>02</Month>
            <Day>07</Day>
        </DateCompleted>
        <DateRevised>
            <Year>2014</Year>
            <Month>11</Month>
            <Day>13</Day>
        </DateRevised>
        <Article PubModel="Electronic-Print">
            <Journal>
                <ISSN IssnType="Electronic">1932-6203</ISSN>
                <JournalIssue CitedMedium="Internet">
                    <Volume>8</Volume>
                    <Issue>6</Issue>
                    <PubDate>
                        <Year>2013</Year>
                    </PubDate>
                </JournalIssue>
                <Title>PloS one</Title>
                <ISOAbbreviation>PLoS ONE</ISOAbbreviation>
            </Journal>
            <ArticleTitle>Mapping molecular association networks of ner-
vous system diseases via large-scale analysis of published research.</
ArticleTitle>
            <Pagination>
                <MedlinePgn>e67121</MedlinePgn>
            </Pagination>
            <ELocationID EIdType="doi" ValidYN="Y">10.1371/journal.
pone.0067121</ELocationID>
            <Abstract>
```

```
                <AbstractText>Network medicine has been suc-
cessfully to elicit the structure of large-scale molecular interaction
networks. Its main proponents have claimed that this approach to integra-
tive medical investigation should make it possible to identify functional
modules of interacting molecular biological units as well as interac-
tions themselves. This paper takes a significant step in this direction.
Based on a large-scale analysis of the nervous system molecular medicine
literature, this study analyzes and visualizes the complex structure of
associations between diseases on the one hand and all types of molecular
substances on the other. From this analysis it then identifies functional
co-association groups consisting of several types of molecular sub-
stances, each consisting of substances that exhibit a pattern of frequent
co-association with similar diseases. These groups in turn exhibit inter-
linking in a complex pattern, suggesting that such complex interactions
between functional molecular modules may play a role in disease etiology.
We find that the patterns exhibited by the networks of disease - molec-
ular substance associations studied here correspond well to a number of
recently published research results, and that the groups of molecular
substances identified by statistical analysis of these networks do appear
to be interesting groups of molecular substances that are interconnected
in identifiable and interpretable ways. Our results not only demonstrate
that networks are a convenient framework to analyze and visualize large-
scale, complex relationships among molecular networks and diseases, but
may also provide a conceptual basis for bridging gaps in experimental and
theoretical knowledge.</AbstractText>
```

```
            </Abstract>
            <AuthorList CompleteYN="Y">
                <Author ValidYN="Y">
                    <LastName>Hu</LastName>
                    <ForeName>Xiaojun</ForeName>
                    <Initials>X</Initials>
                    <AffiliationInfo>
                        <Affiliation>Medical Information Centre, Zhe-
jiang University School of Medicine, Hangzhou, China. xihu@zju.edi.cn</
Affiliation>
                    </AffiliationInfo>
                </Author>
                <Author ValidYN="Y">
                    <LastName>Zhao</LastName>
                    <ForeName>Dangzhi</ForeName>
                    <Initials>D</Initials>
                </Author>
                <Author ValidYN="Y">
                    <LastName>Strotmann</LastName>
                    <ForeName>Andreas</ForeName>
                    <Initials>A</Initials>
```

```xml
            </Author>
        </AuthorList>
        <Language>eng</Language>
        <PublicationTypeList>
            <PublicationType UI="D016428">Journal Article</Publica-
tionType>
            <PublicationType UI="D013485">Research Support, Non-U.S.
Gov't</PublicationType>
        </PublicationTypeList>
        <ArticleDate DateType="Electronic">
            <Year>2013</Year>
            <Month>06</Month>
            <Day>25</Day>
        </ArticleDate>
    </Article>
    <MedlineJournalInfo>
        <Country>United States</Country>
        <MedlineTA>PLoS One</MedlineTA>
        <NlmUniqueID>101285081</NlmUniqueID>
        <ISSNLinking>1932-6203</ISSNLinking>
    </MedlineJournalInfo>
    <ChemicalList>
        <Chemical>
            <RegistryNumber>0</RegistryNumber>
          <NameOfSubstance UI="D015415">Biological Markers</NameOf-
Substance>
        </Chemical>
        <Chemical>
            <RegistryNumber>0</RegistryNumber>
            <NameOfSubstance UI="D026901">Membrane Transport Pro-
teins</NameOfSubstance>
        </Chemical>
    </ChemicalList>
    <CitationSubset>IM</CitationSubset>
    <CommentsCorrectionsList>
        <CommentsCorrections RefType="Cites">
          <RefSource>Mov Disord. 2011 May;26(6):1056-71</RefSource>
            <PMID Version="1">21626551</PMID>
        </CommentsCorrections>
        <CommentsCorrections RefType="Cites">
          <RefSource>Nat Rev Genet. 2011 Jan;12(1):56-68</RefSource>
            <PMID Version="1">21164525</PMID>
        </CommentsCorrections>
        <CommentsCorrections RefType="Cites">
            <RefSource>BMC Bioinformatics. 2011;12:435</RefSource>
            <PMID Version="1">22070195</PMID>
```

```
            </CommentsCorrections>
            <CommentsCorrections RefType="Cites">
                <RefSource>Blood. 2012 Jan 5;119(1):308-19</RefSource>
                <PMID Version="1">22049513</PMID>
            </CommentsCorrections>
            <CommentsCorrections RefType="Cites">
                <RefSource>Mol Syst Biol. 2012;8:565</RefSource>
                <PMID Version="1">22252388</PMID>
            </CommentsCorrections>
            <CommentsCorrections RefType="Cites">
                 <RefSource>Epilepsy Res. 2012 Feb;98(2-3):104-15</Ref-
Source>
                <PMID Version="1">22055355</PMID>
            </CommentsCorrections>
            <CommentsCorrections RefType="Cites">
                      <RefSource>J Neurol Neurosurg Psychiatry. 2012
Apr;83(4):430-6</RefSource>
                <PMID Version="1">22138181</PMID>
            </CommentsCorrections>
            <CommentsCorrections RefType="Cites">
                 <RefSource>Neurology. 2012 Apr 17;78(16):1237-44</Ref-
Source>
                <PMID Version="1">22491861</PMID>
            </CommentsCorrections>
            <CommentsCorrections RefType="Cites">
               <RefSource>Chem Biodivers. 2012 May;9(5):841-7</RefSource>
                <PMID Version="1">22589086</PMID>
            </CommentsCorrections>
            <CommentsCorrections RefType="Cites">
                  <RefSource>Hiroshima J Med Sci. 2012 Mar;61(1):1-6</
RefSource>
                <PMID Version="1">22702213</PMID>
            </CommentsCorrections>
            <CommentsCorrections RefType="Cites">
                <RefSource>PLoS One. 2012;7(7):e41750</RefSource>
                <PMID Version="1">22911851</PMID>
            </CommentsCorrections>
            <CommentsCorrections RefType="Cites">
               <RefSource>Biochem J. 2000 Dec 1;352 Pt 2:511-8</RefSource>
                <PMID Version="1">11085945</PMID>
            </CommentsCorrections>
            <CommentsCorrections RefType="Cites">
                  <RefSource>J Cell Biol. 2002 Jun 24;157(7):1187-96</
RefSource>
                <PMID Version="1">12082079</PMID>
            </CommentsCorrections>
```

```
<CommentsCorrections RefType="Cites">
    <RefSource>Nat Genet. 2002 Jul;31(3):316-9</RefSource>
    <PMID Version="1">12006977</PMID>
</CommentsCorrections>
<CommentsCorrections RefType="Cites">
    <RefSource>Mol Cancer Ther. 2002 Mar;1(5):347-55</Ref-
Source>
    <PMID Version="1">12489851</PMID>
</CommentsCorrections>
<CommentsCorrections RefType="Cites">
        <RefSource>Bioinformatics. 2002 Dec;18(12):1553-61</
RefSource>
        <PMID Version="1">12490438</PMID>
</CommentsCorrections>
<CommentsCorrections RefType="Cites">
    <RefSource>Science. 1991 Oct 4;254(5028):97-9</RefSource>
    <PMID Version="1">1925564</PMID>
</CommentsCorrections>
<CommentsCorrections RefType="Cites">
    <RefSource>Brain Pathol. 1991 Jul;1(4):279-86</RefSource>
    <PMID Version="1">1669718</PMID>
</CommentsCorrections>
<CommentsCorrections RefType="Cites">
     <RefSource>BMJ. 1995 Apr 29;310(6987):1085-6</RefSource>
     <PMID Version="1">7742666</PMID>
</CommentsCorrections>
<CommentsCorrections RefType="Cites">
        <RefSource>Science. 1955 Jul 15;122(3159):108-11</Ref-
Source>
        <PMID Version="1">14385826</PMID>
</CommentsCorrections>
<CommentsCorrections RefType="Cites">
 <RefSource>BMC Bioinformatics. 2004 Oct 8;5:147</RefSource>
        <PMID Version="1">15473905</PMID>
</CommentsCorrections>
<CommentsCorrections RefType="Cites">
 <RefSource>Mol Microbiol. 2005 Oct;58(2):349-57</RefSource>
        <PMID Version="1">16194224</PMID>
</CommentsCorrections>
<CommentsCorrections RefType="Cites">
        <RefSource>Bioinformatics. 2005 Sep 1;21 Suppl 2:ii252-
8</RefSource>
        <PMID Version="1">16204114</PMID>
</CommentsCorrections>
<CommentsCorrections RefType="Cites">
    <RefSource>JAMA. 2007 Apr 11;297(14):1551-61</RefSource>
```

```
                    <PMID Version="1">17426274</PMID>
            </CommentsCorrections>
            <CommentsCorrections RefType="Cites">
                    <RefSource>Proc Natl Acad Sci U S A. 2007 May
22;104(21):8685-90</RefSource>
                    <PMID Version="1">17502601</PMID>
            </CommentsCorrections>
            <CommentsCorrections RefType="Cites">
                <RefSource>N Engl J Med. 2007 Jul 26;357(4):404-7</Ref-
Source>
                    <PMID Version="1">17652657</PMID>
            </CommentsCorrections>
            <CommentsCorrections RefType="Cites">
                ·<RefSource>Proc Natl Acad Sci U S A. 2008 Jan 8;105(1):145-
50</RefSource>
                    <PMID Version="1">18162536</PMID>
            </CommentsCorrections>
            <CommentsCorrections RefType="Cites">
                    <RefSource>Nucleic Acids Res. 2008 Jan;36(Database is-
sue):D901-6</RefSource>
                    <PMID Version="1">18048412</PMID>
            </CommentsCorrections>
            <CommentsCorrections RefType="Cites">
                    <RefSource>Science. 2008 May 30;320(5880):1172-3</Ref-
Source>
                    <PMID Version="1">18511680</PMID>
            </CommentsCorrections>
            <CommentsCorrections RefType="Cites">
                    <RefSource>Recent Results Cancer Res. 2009;171:217-39</
RefSource>
                    <PMID Version="1">19322547</PMID>
            </CommentsCorrections>
            <CommentsCorrections RefType="Cites">
                <RefSource>PLoS Med. 2009 Jul 21;6(7):e1000097</RefSource>
                    <PMID Version="1">19621072</PMID>
            </CommentsCorrections>
            <CommentsCorrections RefType="Cites">
                    <RefSource>PLoS Comput Biol. 2009 Jul;5(7):e1000450</
RefSource>
                    <PMID Version="1">19649302</PMID>
            </CommentsCorrections>
            <CommentsCorrections RefType="Cites">
                <RefSource>Nature. 2009 Sep 10;461(7261):218-23</RefSource>
                    <PMID Version="1">19741703</PMID>
            </CommentsCorrections>
            <CommentsCorrections RefType="Cites">
```

```
            <RefSource>J Alzheimers Dis. 2009;17(2):259-65</RefSource>
                <PMID Version="1">19221408</PMID>
            </CommentsCorrections>
            <CommentsCorrections RefType="Cites">
                <RefSource>Hum Mol Genet. 2010 Apr 15;19(R1):R12-20</
RefSource>
                <PMID Version="1">20413653</PMID>
            </CommentsCorrections>
            <CommentsCorrections RefType="Cites">
                    <RefSource>Proc Natl Acad Sci U S A. 2010 Jun
1;107(22):10256-61</RefSource>
                <PMID Version="1">20479234</PMID>
            </CommentsCorrections>
            <CommentsCorrections RefType="Cites">
                <RefSource>Target Oncol. 2010 Sep;5(3):161-5</RefSource>
                <PMID Version="1">20725792</PMID>
            </CommentsCorrections>
            <CommentsCorrections RefType="Cites">
                <RefSource>Neurosurgery. 2011 Jun;68(6):N14-5</RefSource>
                <PMID Version="1">21778941</PMID>
            </CommentsCorrections>
        </CommentsCorrectionsList>
        <MeshHeadingList>
            <MeshHeading>
                <DescriptorName MajorTopicYN="N" UI="D015415">Biological
Markers</DescriptorName>
                <QualifierName MajorTopicYN="N" UI="Q000378">metabolism</
QualifierName>
            </MeshHeading>
            <MeshHeading>
                <DescriptorName MajorTopicYN="Y" UI="D035843">Biomedical
Research</DescriptorName>
            </MeshHeading>
            <MeshHeading>
                <DescriptorName MajorTopicYN="N" UI="D016000">Cluster
Analysis</DescriptorName>
            </MeshHeading>
            <MeshHeading>
                <DescriptorName MajorTopicYN="Y" UI="D019295">Computa-
tional Biology</DescriptorName>
            </MeshHeading>
            <MeshHeading>
                <DescriptorName MajorTopicYN="N" UI="D006801">Humans</
DescriptorName>
            </MeshHeading>
            <MeshHeading>
```

```
                        <DescriptorName MajorTopicYN="N" UI="D026901">Membrane
Transport Proteins</DescriptorName>
                    <QualifierName MajorTopicYN="N" UI="Q000378">metabolism</
QualifierName>
                </MeshHeading>
                <MeshHeading>
                     <DescriptorName MajorTopicYN="N" UI="D008870">Microtu-
bules</DescriptorName>
                    <QualifierName MajorTopicYN="N" UI="Q000378">metabolism</
QualifierName>
                </MeshHeading>
                <MeshHeading>
                   <DescriptorName MajorTopicYN="N" UI="D009046">Motor Neu-
rons</DescriptorName>
                     <QualifierName MajorTopicYN="N" UI="Q000473">pathology</
QualifierName>
                </MeshHeading>
                <MeshHeading>
                     <DescriptorName MajorTopicYN="N" UI="D009132">Muscles</
DescriptorName>
                      <QualifierName MajorTopicYN="N" UI="Q000503">physiopa-
thology</QualifierName>
                </MeshHeading>
                <MeshHeading>
                   <DescriptorName MajorTopicYN="N" UI="D009422">Nervous
System Diseases</DescriptorName>
                  <QualifierName MajorTopicYN="N" UI="Q000276">immunology</
QualifierName>
                   <QualifierName MajorTopicYN="Y" UI="Q000378">metabolism</
QualifierName>
                    <QualifierName MajorTopicYN="N" UI="Q000473">pathology</
QualifierName>
                      <QualifierName MajorTopicYN="N" UI="Q000503">physiopa-
thology</QualifierName>
                </MeshHeading>
                <MeshHeading>
                  <DescriptorName MajorTopicYN="N" UI="D009857">Oncogenes</
DescriptorName>
                     <QualifierName MajorTopicYN="N" UI="Q000235">genetics</
QualifierName>
                </MeshHeading>
                <MeshHeading>
                      <DescriptorName MajorTopicYN="N" UI="D015398">Signal
Transduction</DescriptorName>
                </MeshHeading>
                <MeshHeading>
```

```
                    <DescriptorName MajorTopicYN="N" UI="D014158">Transcrip-
tion, Genetic</DescriptorName>
                </MeshHeading>
                <MeshHeading>
                    <DescriptorName MajorTopicYN="N" UI="D015533">Transcrip-
tional Activation</DescriptorName>
                </MeshHeading>
            </MeshHeadingList>
            <OtherID Source="NLM">PMC3692415</OtherID>
        </MedlineCitation>
        <PubmedData>
            <History>
                <PubMedPubDate PubStatus="ppublish">
                    <Year>2013</Year>
                    <Month/>
                    <Day/>
                </PubMedPubDate>
                <PubMedPubDate PubStatus="received">
                    <Year>2013</Year>
                    <Month>3</Month>
                    <Day>5</Day>
                </PubMedPubDate>
                <PubMedPubDate PubStatus="accepted">
                    <Year>2013</Year>
                    <Month>5</Month>
                    <Day>13</Day>
                </PubMedPubDate>
                <PubMedPubDate PubStatus="epublish">
                    <Year>2013</Year>
                    <Month>6</Month>
                    <Day>25</Day>
                </PubMedPubDate>
                <PubMedPubDate PubStatus="entrez">
                    <Year>2013</Year>
                    <Month>7</Month>
                    <Day>5</Day>
                    <Hour>6</Hour>
                    <Minute>0</Minute>
                </PubMedPubDate>
                <PubMedPubDate PubStatus="pubmed">
                    <Year>2013</Year>
                    <Month>7</Month>
                    <Day>5</Day>
                    <Hour>6</Hour>
                    <Minute>0</Minute>
                </PubMedPubDate>
```

```
            <PubMedPubDate PubStatus="medline">
                <Year>2014</Year>
                <Month>2</Month>
                <Day>8</Day>
                <Hour>6</Hour>
                <Minute>0</Minute>
            </PubMedPubDate>
        </History>
        <PublicationStatus>epublish</PublicationStatus>
        <ArticleIdList>
            <ArticleId IdType="doi">10.1371/journal.pone.0067121</Arti-
cleId>
            <ArticleId IdType="pii">PONE-D-13-09728</ArticleId>
            <ArticleId IdType="pubmed">23825632</ArticleId>
            <ArticleId IdType="pmc">PMC3692415</ArticleId>
        </ArticleIdList>
    </PubmedData>
</PubmedArticle>
```

Appendix 5.4.2

A PYTHON SCRIPT FOR CONVERSION OF A FACTOR ANALYSIS RESULT MATRIX TO A NETWORK REPRESENTATION

The following simple Python script converts a factor analysis result matrix (factors x members) from comma-separated values (CSV) format to a graph in Pajek's .net format.

```python
def factorsCsv2Net(csvFn,netFn,codec='utf-8'):
    import codecs

    f=codecs.open(csvFn,'r',codec)
    l=f.read().splitlines()
    factors = [[field.strip().replace('"','')
            for field in line.split(',')]
            for line in l]
    factornames = factors[0][1:]
    factors = factors[1:]
    vertices = sorted([f[0] for f in factors])
    vertexdeclarations = dict(zip(factornames+vertices,
                    range(1,len(factornames)+len(vertices)+1)))
    edges = [ [(f[0],i,x)
        for x,i in zip(f[1:],range(1,len(factors[0])))
        if x]
        for f in factors]
    e=[]
    for ed in edges:
        e=e+ed
    edgedeclarations = [(vertexdeclarations[name],
                vertexdeclarations[factornames[factor-1]],
                loading)
                for name,factor,loading in e]
    of=codecs.open(netFn,'w','latin1','replace')
    print>>of, ('*Vertices '+str(len(vertexdeclarations))+'\n'
            +'\n'.join([' '.join([str(vertexdeclarations[vertex]),
                        quotestring(vertex)])
                    for vertex
                    in sorted(vertexdeclarations,
                        lambda x,y:cmp(vertexdeclarations[x],
```

```
                                    vertexdeclarations[y])))])
                  +'\n'
                  +'*Edges\n'
                  +'\n'.join([' '.join([str(name),
                                  str(factor),
                                  loading])
                              for name,factor,loading
                              in edgedeclarations]))
    of.close()

def quotestring(s):
    return '"'+s+'"'
```

Bibliography

Adam, D. (2002). Citation analysis: The counting house. *Nature*, 415, 726–729. DOI: 10.1038/415726a. DOI: 10.1038/415726a.

Ahlgren, P., Jarneving, B., and Rousseau, R. (2003). Requirements for a cocitation similarity measure, with special reference to Pearson's correlation coefficient. *Journal of the American Society for Information Science*, 54, 550–560. DOI: 10.1002/asi.10242. 46

Ahlgren, P., Jarneving, B., and Rousseau, R. (2004a). Author cocitation and Pearson's r. *Journal of the American Society for Information Science and Technology*, 55(9), 843. DOI: 10.1002/asi.20030. 46

Ahlgren, P., Jarneving, B., and Rousseau, R. (2004b). Rejoinder: In defense of formal methods. *Journal of the American Society for Information Science and Technology*, 55(10), 936. DOI: 10.1002/asi.20029. 46

Alako, B. T. F., Veldhoven, A., van Baal, S., Jelier, R., Verhoeven, S., Rullman, T., Polman, J., and Jenster, G. (2005). CoPub Mapper: Mining MEDLINE based on search term co-publication. *BMC Bioinformatics* 6, article 51. DOI: 10.1186/1471-2105-6-51. DOI: 10.1186/1471-2105-6-51. 90

Albert, R., Jeong, H.W., and Barabási, A.L. (2000). Error and attack tolerance of complex networks. *Nature* 406, 378-382. DOI: 10.1038/35019019. 107

Andres, A. (2009). *Measuring academic research: How to undertake a bibliometric study*. Atlanta, Georgia: Neal-Schuman Publishers, Inc. DOI: 10.1533/9781780630182. 19

Anselin, L. (1988). *Spatial econometrics: Methods and models*. Springer. DOI: 10.1007/978-94-015-7799-1. 7

APA style [Website]. (2013). American Psychological Association. Retrieved from http://www.apastyle.org/. 90, 95

Archambault, E., and Lariviere, V. (2009). History of the journal impact factor: Contingencies and consequences. *Scientometrics*, 79(3), 635-649. DOI: 10.1007/s11192-007-2036-x. 94

Ardanuy, J. (2012). Scientific collaboration in Library and Information Science viewed through the Web of Knowledge: The Spanish case. *Scientometrics*, 90(3), 877–890. DOI: 10.1007/s11192-011-0552-1. 62

Arunachalam, S. (1998). Citation analysis: Do we need a theory? *Scientometrics*, 43, 141–142. DOI: 10.1007/BF02458402. 15

Author identifier (2013). SciVerse. Retrieved from http://www.info.sciverse.com/scopus/scopus-in-detail/tools/authoridentifier.

Bagatelj, V. (2003). Efficient algorithms for citation network analysis. Retrieved from ArXiv Computing Research Repository at http://arxiv.org/abs/cs/0309023. 48

Barabási, A.L., and Albert, R. (1999). Emergence of scaling in random networks. *Science*, 286, 509–512. DOI: 10.1126/science.286.5439.509. 106

Barabási, A.L. Gulbahce, N., and Loscalzo, J. (2011). Network medicine: A network-based approach to human disease. *Nature Reviews Genetics*. nature.com. DOI: 10.1038/nrg2918. 47

Barabási, A.L., Jeong, H., Neda, Z, Ravasz, E, Schubert, A., and Vicsek, T. (2002). Evolution of the social network of scientific collaborations. *Physica A*, 311, 590–614. DOI: 10.1016/S0378-4371(02)00736-7. 106

Bar-Ilan, J. (2008). Which h-index? A comparison of WoS, Scopus and Google Scholar. *Scientometrics*, 74(2), 257–271. DOI: 10.1007/s11192-008-0216-y. 96

Bartneck, C., and Kokkelmans, S. (2011). Detecting h-index manipulation through self-citation analysis. *Scientometrics*, 87(1), 85–98. DOI: 10.1007/s11192-010-0306-5. 94

Bassecoulard, E., Lelu, A., and Zitt, M. (2007). A modular sequence of retrieval procedures to delineate a scientific field: From vocabulary to citations and back. In *Proceedings of the 11th International Conference on Scientometrics and Informetrics* (pp. 74–84), June 25-27, 2007, Madrid, Spain. 8, 61

Batagelj, V., and Mrvar, A. (2007). Pajek: Program for analysis and visualization of large networks. Retrieved from http://vlado.fmf.uni-lj.si/pub/networks/pajek/. 129, 136

Bayer, A. E., and Folger, J. (1966). Some correlates of a citation measure of productivity in science. *Sociology of Education*, 39, 381–390. DOI: 10.2307/2111920. 13

Bensman, S. J. (2001). Urquhart's and Garfield's Laws: The British controversy over their validity. *Journal of the American Society for Information Science and Technology*, 59(9), 714–724. DOI: 10.1002/asi.1122. 73

Bensman, S. J. (2004). Pearson's r and author cocitation analysis: A commentary on the controversy. *Journal of the American Society for Information Science and Technology*, 55(10), 935–936. DOI: 10.1002/asi.20028. 46

Bergmark, D. (2000). Automatic extraction of reference linking information from online documents (Tech. Rep. TR 2000-1821). Ithaca, NY: Cornell University.

Bleier, A., and Strotmann, A. (2013). Author name co-mention analysis: Testing a poor man's author co-citation analysis method. *Proceedings of the 14th International Society for Scientometrics and Informetrics Conference*. July 15–19, 2013. Vienna, Austria. 130

Book Citation Index (2013). Web of Knowledge. Retrieved from http://wokinfo.com/products_tools/multidisciplinary/bookcitationindex.

Bollen, J., van de Sompel, H., Hagberg, A., Bettencourt, L., Chute, R., et al. (2009). Clickstream data yields high-resolution maps of science. *PloS ONE* 4(3), e4803. DOI: 10.1371/journal.pone.0004803. 120, 121

Borgman, C. L., and Furner, J. (2002). Scholarly communication and bibliometrics. *Annual Review of Information Science and Technology*, 36, 3–72. DOI: 10.1002/aris.1440360102. 3, 5, 12, 21

Borgman, C.L. (Ed.). (1990). *Scholarly communication and bibliometrics*. Newbury Park, CA: Sage Publications, Inc. 6, 11, 13, 14, 15, 68

Börner, K. (2010). *Atlas of Science: Visualizing What We Know*. The MIT Press. DOI: 10.1007/s11192-011-0409-7.

Börner, K., Maru, J. T., and Goldstone, R. L. (2004). The simultaneous evolution of author and paper networks. *Proceedings of the National Academy of Sciences of the United States of America*, 101(Suppl. 1), 5266–5273. DOI: 10.1073/pnas.0307625100. 47

Börner, Katy, Soma Sanyai and Alessandro Vespignani. (2008). Network science. *Annual Review of Information Science and Technology*, 41: 537–607. DOI: 10.1002/aris.2007.1440410119. 18

Bornmann, L. (2010). Towards an ideal method of measuring research performance: Some comments to the Opthof and Leydesdorff (2010) paper. *Journal of Informetrics* 4(3) 441. DOI: 10.1016/j.joi.2010.04.004. 25

Bornmann, L., and Daniel, H.-D. (2008). What do citation counts measure? A review of studies on citing behavior. *Journal of Documentation*, 64: 45–80. DOI: 10.1108/00220410810844150. 12

Boyack, K. W, Börner, K., and Klavans, R. (2007). Mapping the structure and evolution of chemistry research. *Proceedings of the 11th International Conference of the International Society for Scientometrics and Informetrics*, June 25–27, 2007, Madrid, Spain. 47

Boyack, K. W., Börner, K., and Klavans, R. (2009). Mapping the structure and evolution of chemistry research. *Scientometrics*, 79(1), 45-60. DOI: 10.1007/s11192-009-0403-5. DOI: 10.1007/s11192-009-0403-5. 24, 40

Boyack, K.W., and Klavans, R. (2010). Co-citation analysis, bibliographic coupling, and direct citation: Which citation approach represents the research front most accurately? *Journal of the American Society for Information Science and Technology*, 61(12), 2389–2404. DOI: 10.1002/asi.21419. 122

Boyack, K. W., and Klavans, R. (2011a). Using global mapping to create more accurate document-level maps of research fields. *Journal of the American Society for Information Science and Technology* 62, 1–18. DOI: 10.1002/asi.21444. 23, 123, 127, 128

Boyack, K. W., and Klavans, R. (2011b). Multiple dimensions of journal specificity: Why journals can't be assigned to disciplines. *Proceedings of the 13th International Conference on Scientometrics and Informetrics* (pp. 123–133), July 4–7, 2011, Durban, South Africa. 27

Boyack, K. W., Klavans, R., and Börner, K. (2005). Mapping the backbone of science. *Scientometrics*, 64(3), 351–374. DOI: 10.1007/s11192-005-0255-6. 5, 23, 40, 47

Boyack, K. W., Klavans, R., Paley, W. B., and Börner, K. (2007). Mapping, illuminating, and interacting with science. *ACM SIGGRAPH 2007 Sketches*, SIGGRAPH'07, Article number 2. DOI: 10.1145/1278780.1278783. 118

Boyack, K.W., Small, H., and Klavans, R. (2013). Improving the accuracy of co-citation clustering using full text. *Journal of the American Society for Information Science and Technology*, 64(9), 1759–1767. DOI: 10.1002/asi.22896. 15, 35, 91, 122

Brin, S., and Page, L. (1998). The anatomy of a large-scale hypertextual Web search engine. *Computer Networks and ISDN Systems*, 30(1–7), 107–117. DOI: 10.1016/S0169-7552(98)00110-X. 9

Brody, T., Harnad, S., and Carr, L. (2006). Earlier Web usage statistics as predictors of later citation impact. *Journal of the American Society for Information Science and Technology*, 57, 1060–1072. DOI: 10.1002/asi.20373. 96

Brooks, F. P. (1975). The mythical man-month (Vol. 1995). Reading, MA: Addison-Wesley. 7

Brown, C. M. (2007). The role of Web-based information in the scholarly communication of chemists: Citation and content analyses of American Chemical Society Journals. *Journal of the American Society for Information Science and Technology*, 58(13), 2055–2065. DOI: 10.1002/asi.20666. 7

Brown, C. M. (2010). Communication in the sciences. *Annual Review of Information Science and Technology*, 44, 287–316. DOI: 10.1002/aris.2010.1440440114. 7, 97

Brown, C. M., and Ortega, L. (2005). Information-seeking behavior of physical science librarians: Does research inform practice? *College and Research Libraries*, 66(3), 231–247. DOI: 10.5860/crl.66.3.231.

Brunvand, A., and Pashkova-Balkenhol, T. (2008). Undergraduate use of government information: What citation studies tell us about instruction strategies. *Libraries and the Academy* 8(2), 197-209. DOI: 10.1353/pla.2008.0014. 7

Bubela, T., Strotmann, A., Adams, R., and Morrison, S. (2010). Commercialization and collaboration: Competing policies in publicly funded stem cell research? *Cell stem cell*, 7 (1), 25–30. DOI: 10.1016/j.stem.2010.06.010. 25

Carter, G. M. (1974). *Peer review, citations, and biomedical research policy: NIH grants to medical school faculty*. Santa Monica, California: Rand Corporation. Available online at http://www.rand.org/content/dam/rand/pubs/reports/2008/R1583.pdf. 13

Chang, Y. W., and Huang, M. H. (2012). A study of the evolution of interdisciplinarity in library and information science: Using three bibliometric methods. *Journal of the American Society for Information Science and Technology*, 63(1), 22-33. DOI: 10.1002/asi.21649. 8

Chen, C. M. (2006). CiteSpace II: Detecting and visualizing emerging trends and transient patterns in scientific literature. *Journal of the American Society for Information Science and Technology*, 57(3), 359–377. DOI: 10.1002/asi.20317. 47

Chen, C., and Carr, L. (1999). Trailblazing the literature of hypertext: Author co-citation analysis (1989-1998). In *Proceedings of the 10th ACM Conference on Hypertext and Hypermedia: Returning to Our Diverse Roots* (pp. 51-60). Available online: http://www.pages.drexel.edu/~cc345/papers/ht99.pdf. DOI: 10.1145/294469.294486. 65

Chen, C., Ibekwe-SanJuan, F., and Hou, J. (2010). The structure and dynamics of cocitation clusters: A multiple-perspective cocitation analysis. *Journal of the American Society for Information Science and Technology*, 61(7), 1386–1409. DOI: 10.1002/asi.21309. 9, 50, 126, 127

Chen, H. (1999). Visualizing semantic spaces and author cocitation networks in digital libraries. *Information Processing and Management*, 35, 401–420. DOI: 10.1016/S0306-4573(98)00068-5. 9

Chen, H., Houston, A. L., Sewell, R. R., and Schatz, B. R. (1998a). Internet browsing and searching: User evaluations of category map and concept space techniques. *Journal of the American Society for Information Science*, 49, 582–603. DOI: 10.1002/(SICI)1097-4571(19980515)49:7<582::AID-ASI2>3.0.CO;2-X. 9

Chen, H., Martinez, J., Kichhoff, A., Ng. T. D., and Schatz, B. R. (1998b). Alleviating search uncertainty through concept associations: Automatic indexing, co-occurrence analysis, and parallel computing. *Journal of the American Society for Information Science*, 49, 206–216. DOI: 10.1002/(SICI)1097-4571(199803)49:3<206::AID-ASI3>3.0.CO;2-K. 9

Chi, P.S. (2012). Bibliometric characteristics of political science research in Germany. *Proceedings of the ASIS&T 2012 Annual Meeting*. DOI: 10.1002/meet.14504901115. 120

Chi, P.S. (2013). Do non-source items make a difference in the social sciences? *Proceedings of the 14th International Society for Scientometrics and Informetrics Conference*. July 15–19, 2013. Vienna, Austria. 120

Chu, H., and Krichel, T. (2007). Downloads vs. citations: Relationships, contributing factors and beyond. In *Proceedings of the 11th International Conference of the International Society for Scientometrics and Informetrics*, June 25–27, 2007, Madrid, Spain. 96

Conkling, T., Harwell, K., McCallips, C., Nyana, S., and Osif, B. (2010). Research material selection in the pre-web and post-web environments: An interdisciplinary study of bibliographic citations in doctoral dissertations. *Journal of Academic Librarianship*, 36(1), 20–31. DOI: 10.1016/j.acalib.2009.11.003. 97

Cooke, R., and Rosenthal, D. (2011). Students use more books after library instruction: An analysis of undergraduate paper citations. *College and Research Libraries*, 72(4), 332–343. DOI: 10.5860/crl-90. 7

Cornelius, B., Landström, H., and Persson, O. (2006). Entrepreneurial studies: The dynamic research front of a developing social science. *Entrepreneurship Theory and Practice*, 30, 375–398. DOI: 10.1111/j.1540-6520.2006.00125.x. 38, 65

Cota, R. G., Ferreira, A. F., Nascimento, C., Gonçalves, M. A., and Laender, A. H. F. (2010). An unsupervised heuristic-based hierarchical method for name disambiguation in bibliographic citations. *Journal of the American Society for Information Science and Technology*, 61(9), 1853–1870. DOI: 10.1002/asi.21363.

Craig, I., Plume, A., McVeigh, M., Pringle, J., and Amin, M. (2007). Do open access articles have greater citation impact?: A critical review of the literature. *Journal of Informetrics*, 1(3), 239–248. Available online: http://www.publishingresearch.net/Citations-SummaryPaper3_000.pdf.pdf. DOI: 10.1016/j.joi.2007.04.001. 96

Crane, D. (1972). *Invisible colleges: Diffusion of knowledge in scientific communities*. Chicago: University of Chicago Press. 11

Cronin, B. (1984). *The citation process: The role and significance of citations in scientific communication*. London: Taylor Graham. 4, 12

Cronin, B., and Meho, L. I. (2006). Using the h-index to rank influential information scientists. *Journal of the American Society for Information Science and Technology*, 57(9), 1275–1278. DOI: 10.1002/asi.20354. 64

CrossRef [Website]. (2013). Retrieved from http://www.crossref.org.

Cui, L. (1999). Rating health Web sites using the principles of citation analysis: A bibliometric approach. *Journal of Medical Internet Research*, 1(1). Retrieved from http://www.jmir.org/1999/1/e4/index.htm. DOI: 10.2196/jmir.1.1.e4. 18

Culnan, M. J., O'Reilly, C. A., and Chatman, J. A. (1990). Intellectual structure of research in organizational behavior, 1972-1984: A cocitation analysis. *Journal of the American Society for Information Science*, 41, 453–458. DOI: 10.1002/(SICI)1097-4571(199009)41:6<453::AID-ASI13>3.0.CO;2-E. 44

Dahling, R. L. (1962). Shannon's information theory: The spread of an idea. In Katz, E., et al. (eds.), *Studies of innovation and of communication to the public* (pp. 119–139). Stanford, CA: The Institute. 6

Data Collection. (2013). CWTS Leiden Ranking. Retrieved from http://www.leidenranking.com/methodology/datacollection. 65

Davis, J. M. (1970). The transmission of information in psychiatry. In *Proceedings of the American Society for Information Science Annual Meeting*: Vol. 7 (pp. 53 – 56). New York: Greenwood Publishing. 6

De Bellis, N. (2009). *Bibliometrics and citation analysis: From the Science Citation Index to Cybermetrics*. Lanham, Maryland: Scarecrow Press. 19

De May, M. (1982). *The cognitive paradigm*. Boston, MA: D. Reidel. [now University of Chicago Press] DOI: 10.1007/978-94-009-7956-7. 11

Deville, P., Wang, D.S., Sinatra, R., Song, C.M., Blondel, V.D., and Barabási, A.L. (2014). Career on the move: Geography, stratification, and scientific impact. *Scientific Reports*, 4, Article number: 4770. DOI: 10.1038/srep04770. 113

Diesner, J., and Carley, K.M. (2013). Error propagation and robustness of relation extraction methods. *Presentation at XXXIII International Sunbelt Social Network Conference*, Hamburg, Germany, May 2013. 106, 107

Ding, Y. (1998). Scholarly communication and bibliometrics: II. Scholarly communication process (Literature Review). *International Forum on Information and Documentation*, 23(3), 3–19. 63

Ding, Y., Chowdhury, G. G., Foo, S., and Qian, W. (2000). Bibliometric information retrieval system (BIRS): A Web search interface utilizing bibliometric research results. *Journal of the American Society for Information Science*, 51, 1190–1204. DOI: 10.1002/1097-4571(2000)9999:9999<::AID-ASI1031>3.0.CO;2-B. 9

Ding, Y., and Cronin, B. (2011). Popular and/or prestigious? Measures of scholarly esteem. *Information Processing and Management*, 47, 80–96. DOI: /10.1016/j.ipm.2010.01.002.

Ding, Y., Liu, X., Guo, C., and Cronin, B. (2013). The distribution of references across texts: Some implications for citation analysis. *Journal of Informetrics*, 7, 583–592. DOI: 10.1016/j.joi.2013.03.003. 15

Dubin, D. (2004). The most influential paper Gerard Salton never wrote. *Library Trends*, 52(4), 748–764.

Edge, D. O. (1979). Quantitative measures of communication in science: A critical review. *History of Science*, 17, 102–134. 12, 13, 68

Egghe, L. (2000). New informetric aspects of the Internet: Some reflections, many problems. *Journal of Information Science*, 26, 329–335. DOI: 10.1177/016555150002600505. 18

Egghe, L., and Rousseau, R. (1990). *Introduction to informetrics*. New York: Elsevier Science. 68

Endersby, J. W. (1996). Collaborative research in the social sciences: Multiple authorship and publication credit. *Social Science Quarterly*, 77, 375–392. 29, 73

Eom, S. B. (2003). *Author co-citation analysis using custom bibliographic databases: An introduction to the Sas approach*. Lewiston, NY: Edwin Mellen Press. 100

Eom, S. B. (2008). *Author cocitation analysis: Quantitative methods for mapping the intellectual structure of an academic discipline*. Hershey, PA: IGI Global.

Eom, S. B., and Farris, R. S. (1996). The contributions of organizational science to the development of decision support systems research subspecialties. *Journal of the American Society for Information Science*, 47(12), 941–952. DOI: 10.1002/(SICI)1097-4571(199612)47:12<941::AID-ASI7>3.0.CO;2-2. 65

Érdi, P., Makovi, K., Somogyvári, Z., Strandburg, K., Tobochnik, J., Volf, P., and Zalányi L. (2013). Prediction of emerging technologies based on analysis of the US patent citation network. *Scientometrics*, 95(1), 225-242. DOI: 10.1007/s11192-012-0796-4. 10

Etzkowitz, H., and Leydesdorff, L. (2000). The dynamics of innovation: from National Systems and "Mode 2" to a Triple Helix of university-industry-government relations. *Research Policy*, 29(2), 109-123. DOI: 10.1016/S0048-7333(99)00055-4. 10

European Patent Office [Website]. (2013). Retrieved from http://worldwide.espacenet.com.

Evans, J. (2008). Electronic publication and the narrowing of science and scholarship. *Science*, 321, 395–399. DOI: 10.1126/science.1150473. 97

Fairthorne, R. A. (1969). Empirical hyperbolic distributions (Bradford-Zipf-Mandelbrot) for bibliometric description and prediction. *Journal of Documentation*, 25, 319–343. DOI: 10.1108/eb026481. 17

Falagas, M. E., Pitsouni, E. I., Malietzis, G. A., and Pappas, G. (2008). Comparison of PubMed, Scopus, Web of Science, and Google Scholar: Strengths and weaknesses. *FASEB Journal*, 22(2), 338–342. DOI: 10.1096/fj.07-9492LSF. 96

Fanelli, D., and Glänzel, W. (2013). Bibliometric evidence for a hierarchy of the sciences. *PLoS ONE* 8(6): e66938. DOI: 10.1371/journal.pone.0066938. 119, 120

Fegley, B.D., and Torvik, V.I. (2013). Has large-scale named-entity network analysis been resting on a flawed assumption? *PLoS ONE* 8(7): e70299. DOI: 10.1371/journal.pone.0070299. 106, 111, 112

Fiorenzo, F., Domenico, M., and Luca, M. (2013). The effect of database dirty data on h-index calculation. *Scientometrics*, 95(3), 1179–1188. DOI: 10.1007/s11192-012-0871-x. 64

Fiszman, M., Demner-Fushman, D., Kilicoglu, H., and Rindflesch, T.C. (2009). Automatic summarization of MEDLINE citations for evidence-based medical treatment: A topic-oriented evaluation. *Journal of Biomedical Informatics*, 42, 801–813. DOI: 10.1016/j.jbi.2008.10.002. 9

Frijters, R., van Vugt, M., Smeets, R., van Schaik, R., de Vlieg, J., and Alkema, W. (2010). Literature mining for the discovery of hidden connections between drugs, genes and diseases. *PLOS Computational Biology*, 6(9), article e1000943. DOI: 10.1371/journal.pcbi.1000943. 90

Garfield, E. (1979). *Citation indexing—its theory and application in science, technology, and humanities*. New York: John Wiley and Sons. 2, 3, 13, 14, 15, 19, 52, 68, 69, 73, 89

Garfield, E. (1985). In tribute to Derek John de Solla Price: A citation analysis of Little science, big science. *Scientometrics*, 7, 487–503. DOI: 10.1007/BF02017163. 7

Garfield, E., Malin, M. W., and Small, H. (1978). Citation data as science indicators. In Y. Elkana, J. Lederberg, R. K. Merton, A. Thackray, and H. Zuckerman (eds.), *Toward a metric of science: The advent of science indicators* (pp. 179-207). New York: John Wiley.

Garfield, E., Pudovkin, A.I., and Istomin, V.S. (2002). Algorithmic citation-linked historiography: mapping the literature of science. In Elaine G. Toms (Ed.) *Proceedings of the 65th Annual Meeting of the American Society for Information Science and Technology* (ASIS&T), Vol: 39, pp. 14–24. DOI: 10.1002/meet.1450390102. 48

Glänzel, W. and Czerwon, H. J. (1996). A new methodological approach to bibliographic coupling and its application to the national, regional and institutional level. *Scientometrics*, 37, 195–221. DOI: 10.1007/BF02093621. 25

Goodman, D. (2007). Update on Scopus and Web of Science. *The Charleston Advisor*, 8(3), 15. 79

Goodrum, A. A., McCain, K. W., Lawrence, S., and Giles, C. L. (2001). Scholarly publishing in the Internet age: A citation analysis of computer science literature. *Information Processing and Management*, 37, 661–675. DOI: 10.1016/S0306-4573(00)00047-9. 96, 97

Griffith, B. C. (1990). Understanding science: Studies of communication and information. In C. L. Borgman (ed.), *Scholarly communication and bibliometrics* (pp. 31-45). Newbury Park, CA: Sage Publications, Inc. 12

Gross, T., and Taylor, A. G. (2005). What have we got to lose?: The effect of controlled vocabulary on keyword searching results. *College and Research Libraries*, 66(3), 212–230. DOI: 10.5860/crl.66.3.212. 67

Gu, Y. N. (2004). Global knowledge management research: A bibliometric analysis. *Scientometrics*, 61(2), 171–190. DOI: 10.1023/B:SCIE.0000041647.01086.f4. 63

Hair, J. F., Anderson, R. E., Tatham, R. L., and Black, W. C. (1998). *Multivariate data analysis* (5th ed.). Upper Saddle River, NJ: Prentice Hall. 42, 45, 55, 130, 131

Harter, S. P. and Kim, H. K. (1996). Electronic Journals and Scholarly Communication: A Citation and Reference Study. *Proceedings of the Midyear Meeting of the American Society for Information Science*, San Diego, CA, May 20-22, 1996, pp. 299–315. DOI: 10.3998/3336451.0003.212. 15

Harzing, A. (2008). *Google Scholar: A new data source for citation analysis. Publish or Perish*. Available online: http://www.harzing.com/pop_gs.htm. 96, 98

Harzing, A. (2013). A preliminary test of Google Scholar as a source for citation data: a longitudinal study of Nobel Prize winners. *Scientometrics*, 94(3), 1057–1075. DOI: 10.1007/s11192-012-0777-7. 96

Hemminger, B. M., Lu, D., Vaughan, K. T. L., Adams, S. J. (2007). Information seeking behavior of academic scientists. *Journal of the American Society for Information Science and Technology*, 58(14), 2205–2225. DOI: 10.1002/asi.20686. 7

Henzinger, M., and Lawrence, S. (2004). Extracting knowledge from the World Wide Web. *Proceedings of the National Academy of Sciences of the United States of America* 101(Suppl. 1), 5186–5191. DOI: 10.1073/pnas.0307528100. 47

Henzinger, M., Sunol, J., and Weber, I. (2010). The stability of the h-index. *Scientometrics*, 84(2), 465–479. DOI: 10.1007/s11192-009-0098-7. 64

Herlach, G. (1978). Can retrieval of information from citation indexes be simplified? Multiple mention of a reference as a characteristic of the link between cited and citing article. *Journal of the American Society for Information Science*, 29, 308–310. DOI: 10.1002/asi.4630290608. 91

Hicks, D. (1987). Limitations of co-citation analysis as a tool for science policy. *Social Studies of Science*, 17, 295–316. DOI: 10.1177/030631287017002004. 5

Hirsch, J. E. (2005). An index to quantify an individual's scientific research output. *Proceedings of the National Academy of Sciences of the United States of America*, 102(46), 16569-16572. DOI: 10.1073/pnas.0507655102. 59

Hitchcock, S., Carr, L., Harris, S., Hey, J. M. N., and Hall, W. (1997). Citation linking: Improving access to online journals. *Proceedings of the 2nd ACM International Conference on Digital Libraries*, 1997, 115–122. DOI: 10.1145/263690.263804. 8

Hitchcock, S., Carr, L., Jiao, Z., Bergmark, D., Hall, W., Lagoze, C., and Harnad, S. (2000). Developing services for open eprint archives: Globalization, integration and the impact of links. Retrieved from http://opcit.eprints.org/dl00/dl00.html. 8

Hjørland, B. (2013). Citation analysis: A social and dynamic approach to knowledge organization. *Information Processing & Management*, 49(6), 1313-1325. DOI: 10.1016/j.ipm.2013.07.001. 9

Hou, W., Li, M., and Niu, D. (2011). Counting citations in texts rather than reference lists to improve the accuracy of assessing scientific contribution. *BioEssays*, 33, 724–727. DOI: 10.1002/bies.201100067. 15

Hu, X., Zhao, D., and Strotmann, A. (2013). Mapping molecular association networks of nervous system diseases via large-scale analysis of published research. To appear in *PLOS ONE*. DOI: 10.1371/journal.pone.0067121. 47, 48, 146

Huang, M. H., and Chang, Y. W. (2012). A comparative study of interdisciplinary changes between information science and library science. *Scientometrics*, 91(3), 789-803. DOI: 10.1007/s11192-012-0619-7. 8

Ingwersen, P. (1998). The calculation of Web impact factors. *Journal of Documentation*, 54, 236–243. DOI: 10.1108/EUM0000000007167. 18

Jarneving, B. (2005). A comparison of two bibliometric methods for mapping of the research front. *Scientometrics*, 65, 245–263. DOI: 10.1007/s11192-005-0270-7. 38

Jarneving, B. (2007). Bibliographic coupling and its application to research-front and other core documents. *Journal of Informetrics*, 1, 287–307. DOI: 10.1016/j.joi.2007.07.004. 38

Jeong, Y.K., Song, M., and Ding, Y. (2014). Content-based author co-citation analysis. *Journal of Informetrics*, 8, 197–211. DOI: 10.1016/j.joi.2013.12.001.

Kayongo, J. and Helm, C. (2012). Relevance of library collections for graduate student research: A citation analysis study of doctoral dissertations at Notre Dame. *College and Research Libraries*, 73, 47–67. DOI: 10.5860/crl-211. 8

Keen, P. G. W. (1987). MIS research: current status, trends and needs. In R. A. Buckingham, R. A. Hirschheim, F. F. Land, and C. J. Tully (eds.), Information systems education: recommendations and implementation (pp. 1–13). Cambridge: Cambridge University Press. 13

Kessler, M. M. (1963). Bibliographic coupling between scientific papers. *American Documentation*, 14, 10–25. DOI: 10.1002/asi.5090140103. 38

Klavans, R., and Boyack, K.W. (2006). Quantitative evaluation of large maps of science. *Scientometrics*, 68(3), 475–499. DOI: 10.1007/s11192-006-0125-x.

Klavans, R., and Boyack, K.W. (2011). Using global mapping to create more accurate document-level maps of research fields. *Journal of the American Society for Information Science and Technology*, 62(1), 1–18. DOI: 10.1002/asi.21444. 122

Kohl, D. F., and Davis, C. H. (1985). Ratings of journals by ARL library directors and deans of library and information science schools. *College and Research Libraries*, 46, 40–47. DOI: 10.5860/crl_46_01_40.

Kreuzman, H. (2001). A co-citation analysis of representative authors in philosophy: Examining the relationship between epistemologists and philosophers of science. *Scientometrics*, 51, 525–539. DOI: 10.1023/A:1019647103469. 43, 46

Lange, L.L. (2001). Citation counts of multi-authored papers – First-named authors and further authors. *Scientometrics*, 52, 457–470. DOI: 10.1023/A:1014299917063. 29

Larivière, V., Sugimoto, C.R., and Cronin, B. (2012). A bibliometric chronicling of library and information science's first hundred years. *Journal of the American Society for Information Science and Technology*, 63, 997–1016. DOI: 10.1002/asi.22645. 62

Lawrence, S. (2001). Online or invisible? *Nature*, 411(6837), 521. DOI: 10.1038/35079151. 96

Lenk, P. (1983). Mapping of fields based on nominations. *Journal of the American Society for Information Science*, 34, 115–122. DOI: 10.1002/asi.4630340204. 13

Levitt, J., and Thelwall, M. (2009a). The most highly cited Library and Information Science articles: Interdisciplinarity, first authors and citation patterns. *Scientometrics*, 78(1), 45–67. DOI: 10.1007/s11192-007-1927-1. 62

Levitt, J., and Thelwall, M. (2009b). Citation levels and collaboratin within library and information science. *Journal of the American Society for Information Science and Technology*, 60(3), 434-442. DOI: 10.1002/asi.21000. 62

Levitt, J., Thelwall, M., and Oppenheim, C. (2011). Variations between subjects in the extent to which the social sciences have become more interdisciplinary. *Journal of the American Society for Information Science and Technology*, 62(6), 1118-1129. DOI: 10.1002/asi.21539. 62

Ley, M. (2002). The DBLP computer science bibliography. *Lecture Notes in Computer Science*, 2476, 1–10. DOI: 10.1007/3-540-45735-6_1. 108

Ley, M. (2012). Personal communication. 108

Leydesdorff, L. (2006). Can scientific journals be classified in terms of aggregated journal-journal citation relations using the Journal Citation Reports? *Journal of the American Society for Information Science and Technology*, 57(5), 601-613. DOI: 10.1002/asi.20322. 71

Leydesdorff, L. (2007). Betweenness centrality as an indicator of the interdisciplinarity of scientific journals. *Journal of the American Society for Information Science and Technology*, 58 (9), 1303–1319. DOI: 10.1002/asi.20614. 47

Leydesdorff, L. (2008). Caveats for the use of citation indicators in research and journal evaluations. *Journal of the American Society for Information Science and Technology*, 59(2), 278-287. DOI: 10.1002/asi.20743. 17, 27

Leydesdorff, L., and Bornmann, L. (2011). How fractional counting of citations affects the impact factor: Normalization in terms of differences in citation potentials among fields of science. *Journal of the American Society for Information Science and Technology*, 62: 217–229. DOI: 10.1002/asi.21450. 26, 31

Leydesdorff, L., and Rafols, I. (2009). A global map of science based on the ISI subject categories. *Journal of the American Society for Information Science and Technology*, 60(2), 348-362. DOI: 10.1002/asi.20967. 27

Leydesdorff, L., and Vaughan, L. (2006). Co-occurrence matrices and their applications in information science: Extending ACA to the web environment. *Journal of the American Society for Information Science and Technology*, 57(12), 1616–1628. DOI: 10.1002/asi.20335. 41, 45, 46, 66

Lievrouw, L. A. (1990). Reconciling structure and process in the study of scholarly communication. In C. L. Borgman (ed.), *Scholarly communication and bibliometrics* (pp. 59-69). Newbury Park, CA: Sage Publications, Inc. 11

Lievrouw, L. A., Rogers, E. M., Lowe, C. U., and Nadel, E. (1987). Triangulation as a research strategy for identifying invisible colleges among biomedical sciences. *Social Networks*, 9, 217–238. DOI: 10.1016/0378-8733(87)90021-9. 11

Lin, X., White, H.D., and Buzydlowski, J.W. (2003). Real-time author co-citation mapping for online searching. *Information Processing and Management*, 39(5), 689–706. DOI: 10.1016/S0306-4573(02)00037-7.

Lindsey, D. (1980). Production and citation measures in the sociology of science: the problem of multiple authorship. *Social Studies of Science*, 10, 145–162. DOI: 10.1177/030631278001000202. 68, 73

Liu, M.X.. (1993). The complexities of citation practice: A review of citation studies. *Journal of Documentation*, 49: 370–408. DOI: 10.1108/eb026920. 12

Liu, N. C. and Cheng, Y. (2005). The academic ranking of world universities. *Higher Education in Europe*, 30(2), 127–136. DOI: 10.1080/03797720500260116. 71

Long, J. S., McGinnis, R. and Allison, P. D. (1980). The problem of junior-authored papers in constructing citation counts. *Social Studies of Science*, 10, 127–143. DOI: 10.1177/030631278001000201. 68

MacRoberts, M. H., and MacRoberts, B. R. (1989). Problems of citation analysis: A critical review. *Journal of the American Society for Information Science*, 40, 342–349. DOI: 10.1002/(SICI)1097-4571(198909)40:5<342::AID-ASI7>3.0.CO;2-U. 12, 13, 14, 15, 68, 69, 71, 89

Marris, E. (2006). 2006 Gallery: Brilliant display. *Nature*, 444, 985-991. DOI: 10.1038/444985a. 117

Marshakova, I. V. (1973). A system of document connections based on references. *Scientific and Technical Information Serial of VINITI*, 6, 3–8. 5, 33

McCain, K. W. (1984). Longitudinal author cocitation mapping: the changing structure of macroeconomics. *Journal of the American Society for Information Science*, 35, 351–359. DOI: 10.1002/asi.4630350607. 5

McCain, K. W. (1986). Cocited author mapping as a valid representation of intellectual structure. *Journal of the American Society for Information Science*, 37, 111–122. DOI: 10.1002/(SICI)1097-4571(198605)37:3<111::AID-ASI2>3.0.CO;2-D. 13, 14, 52

McCain, K. W. (1988). Evaluating cocited author search performance in a collaborative specialty. *Journal of the American Society for Information Science*, 39, 428–431. DOI: 10.1002/(SICI)1097-4571(198811)39:6<428::AID-ASI7>3.0.CO;2-P. 68

McCain, K. W. (1990a). Mapping authors in intellectual space: Population genetics in the 1980s. In C. L. Borgman (ed.), *Scholarly communication and bibliometrics* (pp. 194–216). Newbury Park, CA: Sage. 26, 42

McCain, K. W. (1990b). Mapping authors in intellectual space: A technical overview. *Journal of the American Society for Information Science*, 41, 433–443. DOI: 10.1002/(SICI)1097-4571(199009)41:6<433::AID-ASI11>3.0.CO;2-Q. 21, 25, 35, 43, 44, 48, 52, 54, 131

McCain, K. W. (1991). Mapping economics through the journal literature: An experiment in journal cocitation analysis. *Journal of the American Society for Information Science*, 42(4), 290–296. DOI: 10.1002/(SICI)1097-4571(199105)42:4<290::AID-ASI5>3.0.CO;2-9. 33

McCain, K. W. (2011). Eponymy and obliteration by incorporation: The case of the "Nash Equilibrium." *Journal of the American Society for Information Science and Technology*, 62(7), 1412–1424. DOI: 10.1002/asi.21536. 6

McCain, K. W., and Salvucci, L. J. (2006). How influential is Brooks' Law: A longitudinal citation context analysis of Frederick Brooks 'The Mythical Man-Month.' *Journal of Information Science*, 32, 277–295. DOI: 10.1177/0165551506064397. 7

Meester, W. (2013). Towards a comprehensive citation index for the arts and humanities. *Research Trends*, 32. Retrieved from http://www.researchtrends.com/issue-32-march-2013/towards-a-comprehensive-citation-index-for-the-arts-humanities/. 78

Meho, L. I., and Sonnenwald, D. H. (2000). Citation ranking versus peer evaluation of senior faculty research performance: A case study of Kurdish scholarship. *Journal of the American Society for Information Science*, 51, 123–138. DOI: 10.1002/(SICI)1097-4571(2000)51:2<123::AID-ASI4>3.0.CO;2-N. 3

Meho, L. I., and Spurgin, K. M. (2005). Ranking the research productivity of library and information science faculty and schools: An evaluation of data sources and research methods. *Journal of the American Society for Information Science and Technology*, 56(12), 1314–1331. DOI: 10.1002/asi.20227. 64

Meho, L. I., and Yang, K. (2007). Impact of data sources on citation counts and rankings of LIS faculty: Web of Science versus Scopus and Google Scholar. *Journal of the American Society for Information Science and Technology*, 58, 2105–2125. DOI: 10.1002/asi.20677. 64, 66, 96

Merton, R. K. (1942). Science and technology in a democratic order. *Journal of Legal and Political Sociology*, 1, 115–126. 12

Milojević, S. (2013). Accuracy of simple, initials-based methods for author name disambiguation. *Journal of Informetrics*, Volume 7, Issue 4, October 2013, Pages 767–773. DOI: 10.1016/j.joi.2013.06.006. 112

Moed, H. F. (2010). *Citation analysis in research evaluation* (2nd ed.). Dordrecht: Springer. 3, 4, 19, 65, 66, 68, 71, 73, 89

Moed, H. F., and Vriens, M. (1989). Possible inaccuracies occurring in citation analysis. *Journal of Information Science*, 15, 95–107. DOI: 10.1177/016555158901500205. 13

Morris, S. A., and Van der Veer Martens, B. (2009). Mapping research specialties. *Annual Review of Information Science and Technology*, 42, 213–295. DOI: 10.1002/aris.2008.1440420113. 49

Morris, S., and Yen, G. (2004). Crossmaps: Visualization of overlapping relationships in collections of journal papers. *Proceedings of the National Academy of Sciences of the United States of America*, 101(Supplement 1), 5291–5296. Available online: http://www.pnas.org/content/101/suppl.1/5291.full. DOI: 10.1073/pnas.0307604100. 47

Mullins, N. C. (1973). *Theory and theory groups in contemporary American sociology*. New York: Harper and Row. DOI: 10.1002/1520-6696(197510)11:4<405::AID-JHBS2300110415>3.0.CO;2-1. 11

Mullins, N. C., Hargens, L. L., Hecht, P. K., and Kick, E. L. (1977). The group structure of cocitation clusters: A comparative study. *American Sociological Review*, 42, 552–562. DOI: 10.2307/2094554. 11, 13, 14

Mutschke, P. (2013). Anomaly detection in centrality computations. *Presentation at XXXIII International Sunbelt Social Network Conference*, Hamburg, Germany, May 2013. 112

Narin, F. (1976). *Evaluative bibliometrics: the use of publication and citation analysis in the evaluation of scientific activity*. Cherry Hill, NJ: Computer Horizons. 90, 91, 97

Nicolaisen, J. Citation analysis. (2007). *Annual Review of Information Science and Technology*, 41: 609–641. DOI: 10.1002/aris.2007.1440410120. 12, 14

Nisonger, T. E., and Davis, C. H. (2005). The perception of library and information science journals by LIS education deans and ARL library directors: A replication of the Kohl-Davis study. *College and Research Libraries*, 66, 341–377. DOI: 10.5860/crl.66.4.341.

O'Rand, A. M. (1992). Mathematizing social science in the 1950s: The early development and diffusion of game theory. In Weintraub, R. E. (ed.), *Toward a history of game theory* (pp.

107–205). Durham, NC: Duke University Press. DOI: 10.1215/00182702-24-Supplement-177. 6

Oehler, K. (1990). Speaking axiomatically: Citation patterns to early articles in general equilibrium theory. *History of Political Economy*, 22(1), 101–112. DOI: 10.1215/00182702-22-1-101. 6

OpenURL. (2009). OCLC Research. Retrieved from http://www.oclc.org/research/activities/openurl.html?urlm=159705.

Osareh, F. (1996). Bibliometrics, citation analysis and co-citation analysis: A review of literature II. *Libri*, 46, 217–225. DOI: 10.1515/libr.1996.46.4.217. 14, 68

Otte, Evelien, and Rousseau, R. (2002). Social network analysis: A powerful strategy, also for the information sciences. *Journal of Information Science*, 28: 441–453. DOI: 10.1177/016555150202800601. 18

Peritz, B. C. (1992). On the objectives of citation analysis: Problems of theory and method. *Journal of the American Society for Information Science*, 43, 448–451. DOI: 10.1002/(SICI)1097-4571(199207)43:6<448::AID-ASI5>3.0.CO;2-9. 3, 12

Persson, O. (1994). The intellectual base and research fronts of JASIS 1986-1990. *Journal of the American Society for Information Science*, 45, 31–38. DOI: 10.1002/(SICI)1097-4571(199401)45:1<31::AID-ASI4>3.0.CO;2-G. 38, 65

Persson, O. (2001). All author citations versus first author citations. *Scientometrics*, 50(2), 339–344. DOI: 10.1023/A:1010534009428.

Ponzi, L. J. (2002). The intellectual structure and interdisciplinary breadth of Knowledge Management: A bibliometric study of its early stage of development. *Scientometrics*, 55(2), 259–272. DOI: 10.1023/A:1019619824850. 63

Porter, A., Zhang, Y., and Newman, N. (2013). Topic extraction methods. *Workshop at The 14th the International Society for Scientometrics and Informetrics Conference*. July 15–19, 2013. Vienna, Austria. 41

Price, D. J. S. (1963). Big science, little science. Columbia University, New York. 7

Qiu, J. (2008). Scientific publishing – identity crisis. *Nature*, 451, 766-767. DOI: 10.1038/451766a. 115

Rauhvargers, A. (2011). Global university rankings and their impact. Retrieved from http://www.eua.be/Libraries/Publications_homepage_list/Global_University_Rankings_and_Their_Impact.sflb.ashx. 17, 71

Reinsfelder, T. L. (2012). Citation analysis as a tool to measure the impact of individual research consultations. *College and Research Libraries*, 73(3), 263–277. DOI: 10.5860/crl-261. 7

Rice, R. E., Borgman, C. L., Bednarski, D., and Hart, P. J. (1989). Journal-to-journal citation data: Issues of validity and reliability. *Scientometrics*, 15, 257–282. DOI: 10.1007/BF02017202. 13

Rogers, E. M. and Cottrill, C. A. (1990). An author co-citation analysis of two research traditions: Technology transfer and the diffusion of innovations. In C. L. Borgman (ed.), *Scholarly communication and bibliometrics* (pp. 157–165). Newbury Park, CA: Sage. 6

Rosengren, K.E. (1968). *Sociological Aspects of the Literary System*. Stockholm: Natur och Kultur.

Rousseau, R. (1997). Sitations: an exploratory study. *Cybermetrics*, 1(1). Retrieved from http://www.cindoc.csic.es/cybermetrics/articles/v1i1p1.html. 18

Rousseau, R., and Zuccala, A. (2004). A classification of author co-citations: Definitions and search strategies. *Journal of the American Society for Information Science and Technology*, 55(6), 513–529. DOI: 10.1002/asi.10401. 36

Rousseau, R., Garcia-Zorita, C., and Sanz-Casado, E. (2013). The h-bubble. *Journal of Informetrics*, 7(2), 294–300. DOI: 10.1016/j.joi.2012.11.012. 19, 59

Rowley, J. (1994). The controlled versus natural indexing languages debate revisited: a perspective on information retrieval practice and research. *Journal of Information Science*, 20(2), 108–118. DOI: 10.1177/016555159402000204. 67

Rudd, E. (1977). The effect of alphabetical order of author listing on the careers of scientists. *Social Studies of Science*, 7, 268–269. DOI: 10.1177/030631277700700208. 73

Saracevic, T. (1975). Relevance: A review of and a framework for the thinking on the notion in information science. *Journal of the American Society for Information Science*, 26(6), 321–343. DOI: 10.1002/asi.4630260604. 67

Sarafoglou, N., and Paelinck, J. (2008). On diffusion of ideas in the academic world: The case of spatial econometrics. *The Annals of Regional Science*, 42(2), 487–500. DOI: 10.1007/s00168-007-0162-2. 7

Schneider, J. W., and Borlund, P. (2004). Introduction to bibliometrics for construction and maintenance of thesauri: Methodical considerations. *Journal of Documentation*, 60(5), 524–549. DOI: 10.1108/00220410410560609. 9

Schneider, J. W., Larsen, B., and Ingwersen, P. (2009). A comparative study of first and all-author co-citation counting, and two different matrix generation approaches applied for author co-citation analyses. *Scientometrics*, 80(1), 103–130. DOI: 10.1007/s11192-007-2019-y. 45

Schneider, J., and Borlund, P. (2004). Introduction to bibliometrics for construction and maintenance of thesauri: Methodological considerations. *Journal of Documentation* 60(5), 524–549. DOI: 10.1108/00220410410560609.

SciVerse. (2012). *Content coverage guide*. Retrieved from http://files.sciverse.com/documents/pdf/ContentCoverageGuide-jan-2013.pdf. 77, 78, 83

Scopus. (2004). *Terms and Conditions*. Available at http://www.scopus.com/scopus/standard/termsandconditions.url. 86

Scopus Help. (2013). *SciVerse*. Retrieved from http://help.scopus.com/. 76

Shaw, W. M. (1985). Critical thresholds in co-citation graphs. *Journal of the American Society for Information Science*, 36, 38–43. DOI: 10.1002/asi.4630360104. 5

Shiffrin, R. M., and Börner, K. (2004). Mapping knowledge domains. *Proceedings of the National Academy of Sciences of the United States of America*, 101(Suppl. 1), 5183–5185. DOI: 10.1073/pnas.0307852100. 47

Smalheiser, N. R. and Torvik, V. I. (2009). Author name disambiguation. *Annual Review of Information Science and Technology* (B. Cronin, Ed.), 43, 287–313. DOI: 10.1002/aris.2009.1440430113. 113

Small, H. (1973). Cocitation in the scientific literature: A new measure of the relationship between two documents. *Journal of the American Society for Information Science*, 24, 265–269. DOI: 10.1002/asi.4630240406. 5, 33

Small, H. (1974). Multiple citation patterns in science literature: The circle and hill models. *Information Storage and Retrieval*, 10, 393–402. DOI: 10.1016/0020-0271(74)90046-1. 5

Small, H. (1976). Structural dynamics of scientific literature. *International Classification*, 3(2), 67–74. 12

Small, H. (1977). A co-citation model of a scientific specialty: A longitudinal study of collagen research. *Social Studies of Science*, 7, 211–238. DOI: 10.1177/030631277700700202. 5, 14, 47

Small, H.G. (1978). Cited Documents as Concept Symbols. *Social Studies of Science* 8 (3) p. 327-340. 6

Small, H. (1981). The relationship of information science to the social sciences: A co-citation analysis. *Information Processing and Management*, 17, 39–50. DOI: 10.1016/0306-4573(81)90040-6. 5

Small, H. (1982). Citation context analysis. In B. J. Dervin and M. J. Voigt (eds.), *Progress in communication sciences* (Vol. 3, pp. 287–310). Norwood, NJ: Ablex. 90, 97

Small, H. (1998). Citations and consilience in science. *Scientometrics*, 43(1), 143–148. DOI: 10.1007/BF02458403. 6

Small, H. (1999a). On the shoulders of giants. *Bulletin of the American Society for Information Science*, 25(2), 23–25. 21

Small, H. (1999b). Visualizing science by citation mapping. *Journal of the American Society for Information Science*, 50, 799–813. DOI: 10.1002/(SICI)1097-4571(1999)50:9<799::AID-ASI9>3.0.CO;2-G. 2, 4, 5, 40

Small, H., and Greenlee, E. (1980). Citation context analysis of a co-citation cluster: Recombinant-DNA. *Scientometrics* 2(4), 277-301. DOI: 10.1007/BF02016349. 6

Small, H., and Sweeney, E. (1985). Clustering the Science Citation Index using co-citations: I. A comparison of methods. *Scientometrics*, 7(3-6), 391–409. DOI: 10.1007/BF02017157. 26

Smart, J. C., and Bayer, A. E. (1986). Author collaboration and impact: A note on citation rates of single and multiple authored articles. *Scientometrics*, 10(5-6), 297–305. DOI: 10.1007/BF02016776. 29

Smith, L. C. (1981). Citation analysis. *Library Trends*, 30, 83–106. 14, 15, 68, 89

Sonnenwald, D. H. (2008). Scientific collaboration. *Annual Review of Information Science and Technology*, 41, 643–681. DOI: 10.1002/aris.2007.1440410121. 37, 73

Spärck Jones, K. (1999). Automatic summarizing: Factors and directions. In I. Mani and M.T. Maybury (Eds.), *Advances in automatic text summarization* (pp. 2–12). Cambridge, MA: MIT Press. DOI: 10.1016/j.ipm.2007.03.009. 9

Sternitzke, C. (2009). Patents and publications as sources of novel and inventive knowledge. *Scientometrics* 79(3), 551–561. DOI: 10.1007/s11192-007-2041-0. 10

Stokes, T. D. and Hartley, J. A. (1989). Coauthorship, social structure and influence within specialties. *Social Studies of Science*, 19, 101–125. DOI: 10.1177/030631289019001003. 68

Strotmann, A., and Bleier, A. (2013). Author name co-mention analysis: Testing a poor man's author co-citation analysis method. *Proceedings of the 14th International Society for Scientometrics and Informetrics Conference*, July 2013, Vienna, Austria. 41, 90

Strotmann, A., and Bubela, T. (2010). Does commercialization impact academic collaboration? The usefulness of sensitive science and technology indicators. *Eleventh International Conference on Science and Technology Indicators*, Leiden, the Netherlands, 9–11 September 2010. 112

Strotmann, A., and Zhao, D. (2008). Bibliometric maps for aggregated visual browsing in digital libraries. *Proceedings of The SIGIR 2008 Workshop on Aggregated Search*, July 24, 2008, Singapore. 9

Strotmann, A., and Zhao, D. (2012). Author name disambiguation: What difference does it make in author-based citation analysis? *Journal of the American Society for Information Science and Technology*, 63(9), 1820–1833. DOI: 10.1002/asi.22695. 55, 94, 106, 107, 114, 115, 129, 138, 139, 141

Strotmann, A., Zhao, D., and Bubela, T. (2009a). A multi-database approach to field delineation. *Proceedings of the 12th International Conference of the International Society for Scientometrics and Informetrics* (pp. 631–635), July 14–17, 2009, Rio de Janeiro, Brazil.

Strotmann, A., Zhao, D., and Bubela, T. (2009b). Author name disambiguation for collaboration network analysis and visualization. *Proceedings of The American Society for Information Science and Technology 2009 Annual Meeting*, November 6–11, 2009, Vancouver, BC, Canada. DOI: 10.1002/meet.2009.1450460218. 37, 113, 115

Strotmann, A., Zhao, D., and Bubela, T. (2010). Combining commercial and Open Access citation databases to delimit highly interdisciplinary research fields for citation analysis studies. *Journal of Informetrics*, 4(2), 194–200. DOI: 10.1016/j.joi.2009.12.001. 66, 84, 89, 112, 114

Strotmann, A., Zhao, D., and Mathiak, B. (2013). Was the 2012 Nobel Prize in medicine awarded for a Kuhnian paradigm shift? *Proceedings of the 13th International Symposium on Information Science* (pp. 192–197), March 19-22, 2013, Potsdam, Germany. 62

Strotmann, A., Sawitzki, F., Mayr, P. (2012). How to build your own citation index: First-hand experience with Web of Science, Scopus, and CSA reference data. Oral presentation at the *2nd Global TechMining Conference*, Montréal, Quebec, Canada, Sept. 05, 2012 (Satellite conference of Science and Technology Indicators (STI) 2012). DOI: 10.13140/2.1.2908.3528. 115

Strotmann, A., Sawitzki, F., Mayr, P. (2013). Toward a semantic citation index for the German social sciences. Oral presentation at *Bibliometrie 2012: Bibliometric Standards in the Sciences, Social Sciences, and Humanities: Current State and Future Trends*. Regensburg, Germany, Sept. 18–22, 2012. 115

Sullivan, D., Koester, D., White, D. H., and Kern, R. (1980). Understanding rapid theoretical change in particle physics: A month-by-month co-citation analysis. *Scientometrics*, 2, 309–319. DOI: 10.1007/BF02016351. 13

Sullivan, D., White, H. D., and Barboni, E. J. (1977). Co-citation analyses of science: An evaluation. *Social Studies of Science*, 7, 223–240. DOI: 10.1177/030631277700700205. 5, 13

Suomela, B. P., and Andrade, M. A. (2005). Ranking the whole MEDLINE database according to a large training set using text indexing. *BMC Bioinformatics*, 6, 75, DOI: 10.1186/1471-2105-6-75. 84, 85

Swanson, D. R. (1986). Undiscovered public knowledge. *Library Quarterly*, 56(2), 103-118. 2

Tarrant, D., Carr, L., and Payne, T. (2008). Releasing the power of digital metadata: Examining large networks of co-related publications. At *Joint Conference on Digital Libraries*, June 16–19, 2008, Pittsburgh, PA, USA. DOI: 10.1007/978-3-540-87599-4_18. 96

Testa, J. (2012). The Thomson Reuters journal selection process. Web of Knowledge. Retrieved from http://wokinfo.com/essays/journal-selection-process/. 69

Teufel, S., Siddharthan, A., and Tidhar, D. (2006). Automatic classification of citation function. *Proceedings of the 2006 Conference on Empirical Methods in Natural Language Processing* (pp. 103–110), Stroudsburg, PA, USA. Association for Computational Linguistics. DOI: 10.3115/1610075.1610091.

THE Methodology: The essential elements in our world-leading formula. (2013). *THE World University Rankings*. Retrieved from http://www.timeshighereducation.co.uk/world-university-rankings/2012-13/world-ranking/methodology. 4, 65

The Open Citation Project [Website]. (2009). Retrieved from http://opcit.eprints.org.

Thelwall, M., Vaughan, L., and Björneborn, L. (2005). Webometrics. *Annual Review of Information Science and Technology*, 39, 81–135. DOI: 10.1002/aris.1440390110. 47

Torvik, V. I. and Smalheiser, N. R. (2009). Author name disambiguation in MEDLINE. *ACM Transactions on Knowledge Discovery from Data*, 3(3) DOI: 10.1145/1552303.1552304. DOI: 10.1145/1552303.1552304. 107, 113

Torvik, V. I., Weeber, M., Swanson, D. R., and Smalheiser, N. R. (2005). A probabilistic similarity metric for Medline records: A model for author name disambiguation. *Journal of the American Society for Information Science and Technology*, 56(2), 140–158. DOI: 10.1002/asi.20105.

Trancy, K. E. (1980). Norms of inquiry: Rationality, consistency requirements and normative conflict. In R. Hilpinen (ed.), *Rationality in science* (pp. 191–202). Dordrecht: Reidel. DOI: 10.1007/978-94-009-9032-6_13. 12

Tseng, Y.-H., and Tsay, M.-Y. (2013). Journal clustering of library and information science for subfield delineation using the bibliometric analysis toolkit: CATAR. *Scientometrics*, 95(2), 503–528. DOI: 10.1007/s11192-013-0964-1. 62

United States Patent and Trademark Office [Website]. (2010). Retrieved from http://patft.uspto.gov/.

Van de Sompel, H., and Beit-Arie, O. (2001). Open linking in the scholarly information environment using the OpenURL framework. *D-Lib Magazine*, 7(3). Retrieved from http://www.dlib.org/dlib/march01/vandesompel/03vandesompel.html. DOI: 10.1045/march2001-vandesompel. 8

Van der Veer Martens, B., and Goodrum, A. A. (2006). The diffusion of theories: A functional approach. *Journal of the American Society for Information Science and Technology*, 57(3), 330–341. DOI: 10.1002/asi.20285. 7

Van Eck, N.J., Waltman, L., Dekker, R., and Van den Berg, J. (2010). A comparison of two techniques for bibliometric mapping: Multidimensional scaling and VOS. *Journal of the American Society for Information Science and Technology*, 61(12), 2405–2416. DOI: 10.1002/asi.21421. 124, 126, 127

Van Eck, N. J., Waltman, L., Van Berg, J. D. (2005). A novel algorithm for visualizing concept associations. *Proceedings of the 16th International Workshop on Database and Expert Systems Applications* (DEXA'05) (pp. 405–409), August 22-26, 2005, Copenhagen, Denmark. DOI: 10.1109/DEXA.2005.23. 47

Van Hooydonk, G. (1997). Fractional counting of multiauthored publications: consequences for the impact of authors. *Journal of the American Society for Information Science*, 48, 944–945. DOI: 10.1002/(SICI)1097-4571(199710)48:10<944::AID-ASI8>3.3.CO;2-K.

Van Leeuwen, T. N., Moed, H. F., Tijssen, R. J. W., Visser, M. S., and van Raan, A. F. J. (2001). Language biases in the coverage of the Science Citation Index and its consequences for international comparisons of national research performance. *Scientometrics*, 51(1), 335–346. DOI: 10.1023/A:1010549719484. 17, 71

Van Raan, A. F. J. (1996). Advanced bibliometric methods as quantitative core of peer review based evaluation and foresight exercises. *Scientometrics*, 36, 397–420. DOI: 10.1007/BF02129602. 61

Virgo, J. A. (1977). A statistical procedure for evaluating the importance of scientific papers. *The Library Quarterly*, 47, 415–430. DOI: 10.1086/620723. 13

Von Neumann, J., and Morgenstern, O. (1944). *A theory of games and economic behavior*. Princeton: Princeton University Press. 6

Wagner, C.S., and Leydesdorff, L. (2005). Network structure, self-organization, and the growth of international collaboration in science. *Research policy* 34 (10), 1608–1618. DOI: 10.1016/j.respol.2005.08.002. 47

Waltman, L., Calero-Medina, C., Kosten, J., Noyons, E. C. M., Tijssen, R. J. W., van Eck, N. J., van Leeuwen, T. N., van Raan, A. F. J., Visser, M. S., and Wouters, P. (2012). The Leiden Ranking 2011/2012: Data collection, indicators, and interpretation. *Journal of the American Society for Information Science and Technology*, 63(12), 2419–2432. DOI: 10.1002/asi.22708.

What does Scopus cover? (2013). *SciVerse*. Retrieved from http://www.info.sciverse.com/scopus/scopus-in-detail/facts.

White, H. D. (1983). A cocitation map of the social indicators movement. *Journal of the American Society for Information Science*, 34, 307–312. DOI: 10.1002/asi.4630340502. 5, 13

White, H. D. (1990). Author co-citation analysis: Overview and defense. In C. L. Borgman (ed.), *Scholarly communication and bibliometrics* (pp. 84–106). Newbury Park, CA: Sage. 6, 12, 13, 14, 15, 27, 49, 52, 68

White, H. D. (2001). Authors as citers over time. *Journal of the American Society for Information Science and Technology*, 52(2), 87–108. DOI: 10.1002/1097-4571(2000)9999:9999<::AID-ASI1542>3.0.CO;2-T. 29

White, H. D. (2003a). Author cocitation analysis and Pearson's r. *Journal of the American Society for Information Science and Technology*, 54, 1250–1259. DOI: 10.1002/asi.10325. 46

White, H. D. (2003b). Pathfinder networks and author cocitation analysis: A remapping of paradigmatic information scientists. *Journal of the American Society for Information Science and Technology*, 54(5), 423–434. DOI: 10.1002/asi.10228.

White, H. D. (2004a). Replies and a correction. *Journal of the American Society for Information Science and Technology*, 55(9), 843–844. DOI: 10.1002/asi.20032. 46

White, H. D. (2004b). Reward, persuasion, and the Sokal Hoax: A study in citation identities. *Scientometrics*, 60(1), 93–120. DOI: 10.1023/B:SCIE.0000027313.91401.9b.

White, H. D. (2010a). *Citation analysis. Encyclopedia of Library and Information Science*, 3d. ed. New York: Taylor and Francis. 1012–1026. 12, 14, 18, 29

White, H. D. (2010b). *Information Science: A Bibliometric Overview. Encyclopedia of Library and Information Science*, 3d. ed. New York: Taylor and Francis. 18

White, H. D. (2011). *Scientific and scholarly networks. In The Sage Handbook of Social Network Analysis*. London: Sage Publications. 271–285. 18

White, H. D., and Griffith, B. C. (1981). Author cocitation: A literature measure of intellectual structure. *Journal of the American Society for Information Science*, 32, 163–171. DOI: 10.1002/asi.4630320302. 5, 13, 33, 35, 41, 44, 47, 123, 124, 130

White, H. D., and Griffith, B. C. (1982). Authors as markers of intellectual space: Co-citation in studies of science, technology and society. *Journal of Documentation*, 38, 255–272. DOI: 10.1108/eb026731. 41, 42, 51, 130, 131

White, H. D., and McCain, K. W. (1989). Bibliometrics. *Annual Review of Information Science and Technology*, 24: 119–186. 14, 15, 23, 24, 26, 56

White, H. D., and McCain, K. W. (1998). Visualizing a discipline: An author co-citation analysis of information science, 1972-1995. *Journal of the American Society for Information Science*, 49, 327–355. DOI: 10.1002/(SICI)1097-4571(19980401)49:4<327::AID-ASI4>3.0.CO;2-4. 40, 41, 42, 43, 51, 52, 53, 54, 55, 62, 70, 108, 124, 125, 130, 131

White, H. D., Buzydlowski, J., and Lin, X. (2000). Co-cited author maps as interfaces to digital libraries: Designing pathfinder networks in the humanities. *IEEE International Conference on Information Visualization* (pp. 25–30), July 18–22, 2000, London, England. DOI: 10.1109/IV.2000.859732. 2

White, H. D., Lin, X., Buzydlowski, J. W., and Chen, C. M. (2004). User-controlled mapping of scientific literatures. *Proceedings of the National Academy of Sciences of the United States of America*, 101(Supplement 1), 5297–5302. DOI: 10.1073/pnas.0307630100. 33, 47

White, H. D., Wellman, B., and Nazer, N. (2004). Does citation reflect social structure? Longitudinal evidence from the "Globenet" interdisciplinary research group. *Journal of the American Society for Information Science and Technology*, 55(2), 111–126. DOI: 10.1002/asi.10369.

Wilkinson, D. M., and Huberman, B. A. (2004). A method for finding communities of related genes. *Proceedings of the National Academy of Sciences of the United States of America* 101(Suppl. 1), 5241–5248. DOI: 10.1073/pnas.0307740100. 47

Winstanley, M. (1976). Who knows their DNA. *New Society*, 36(707), 192–193.

Youngen, G. (1997). Citation patterns of the physics preprint literature with special emphasis on the preprints available electronically, found at http://www.physics.uiuc.edu/library/preprint.html, 2000. DOI:10.5062/F4XP72XZ. 97

Zhang, G., Ding, Y., and Milojević, S. (2013). Citation content analysis (CCA): A framework for syntactic and semantic analysis of citation content. *Journal of the American Society for Information Science and Technology*, 64(7), 1490–1503. DOI: 10.1002/asi.22850. 18

Zhang, Y., Pan, Y., and Hong, X. (2011). A brief statistical analysis of stomatology papers published in international journals by researchers from the mainland of China, based on Thomson Reuters' Journal Citation Reports for 2009. *International Journal of Oral Science*, 3(1), 1-6. DOI: 10.4248/IJOS11003. 71

Zhao, D. (1990). Citation analysis of agriculture research fields in China. Master's thesis, Peking University, China. 100

Zhao, D. (1992). Citation network analysis and its methods and technical procedures. *Journal of the Chinese Society for Scientific and Technical Information*, 11(5), 381–388. 100

Zhao, D. (1993). Co-citation analysis: An effective method of studying the structure and characteristics of literatures and disciplines. *Journal of Information*, 12(2), 36–42. 100

Zhao, D. (2003). A comparative citation analysis study of Web-based and print journal-based scholarly communication in the XML research field (Doctoral dissertation, Florida State University). Retrieved from http://etd.lib.fsu.edu/theses/available/etd-09232003-012028/unrestricted/DangzhiZhao_dissertation_summer03.pdf. 21, 96, 97, 98, 100

Zhao, D. (2005a). Challenges of scholarly publications on the web to the evaluation of science: A comparison of author visibility on the web and in print journals. *Information Processing and Management*, 41(6), 1403–1418. DOI: 10.1016/j.ipm.2005.03.013. 66, 73, 96, 97

Zhao, D. (2005b). Going beyond counting first authors in author co-citation analysis. Sparking Synergies: Bringing Research and Practice Together. *Proceedings of the American Society for Information Science and Technology 2005 Annual Meeting* (pp. 635–653), October 28-November 2, 2005, Charlotte, NC, USA. DOI: 10.1002/meet.14504201210. 36

Zhao, D. (2006a). Towards all-author co-citation analysis. *Information Processing and Management*, 42, 1578–1591. DOI: 10.1016/j.ipm.2006.03.022. 36, 42, 66, 96, 97, 131

Zhao, D. (2006b). Dispelling the myths behind straight citation counts. Information realities: Shaping the digital future for all. *Proceedings of the American Society for Information Science and Technology 2006 Annual Meeting*, November 3–8, 2006, Austin, TX, USA. DOI: 10.1002/meet.14504301194. 29

Zhao, D. (2009). Mapping library and information science: Does field delineation matter? Paper presented at the *American Society for Information Science and Technology 2009 Annual Meeting*, Vancouver, British Columbia, Canada. DOI: 10.1002/meet.2009.1450460279. 7, 17, 64

Zhao, D. (2010). Characteristics and impact of grant-funded research: A case study of the library and information science field. *Scientometrics*, 84(2), 293–306. DOI: 10.1007/s11192-010-0191-y. 79

Zhao, D., and Logan, E. (2002). Citation analysis of scientific publications on the Web: A case study in XML research area. *Scientometrics*, 54, 449–472. DOI: 10.1023/A:1016090601710. 15, 73

Zhao, D., and Strotmann, A. (2004). Towards a problem solving environment for scholarly communication research. *Proceedings of Canadian Association for Information Science 2004 Annual Conference*, June 3–5, 2004, Winnipeg, Manitoba, Canada. 98

Zhao, D., and Strotmann, A. (2007). All-author vs. first-author co-citation analysis of the Information Science field using Scopus. *Proceedings of the American Society for Information Science and Technology 2007 Annual Meeting*, October 19–24, 2007, Milwaukee, Wisconsin, USA. DOI: 10.1002/meet.1450440262. 36

Zhao, D., and Strotmann, A. (2008a). Information science during the first decade of the web: An enriched author co-citation analysis. *Journal of the American Society for Information Science and Technology*, 59(6), 916–937. DOI: 10.1002/asi.20799. 5, 17, 23, 25, 26, 36, 42, 44, 47, 48, 49, 50, 53, 56, 62, 125, 126, 129, 131, 136, 139, 141

Zhao, D., and Strotmann, A. (2008b). Evolution of research activities and intellectual influences in Information Science 1996–2005: Introducing author bibliographic coupling analysis. *Journal of the American Society for Information Science and Technology*, 59(13), 2070–2086. DOI: 10.1002/asi.20910. 17, 23, 25, 26, 27, 38, 39, 44, 47, 49, 53, 54, 62, 70, 92, 129, 136, 139, 141

Zhao, D., and Strotmann, A. (2008c). Comparing all-author and first-author co-citation analyses of information science. *Journal of Informetrics*, 2(3), 229–239. DOI: 10.1016/j.joi.2008.05.004. 17, 25, 26, 30, 44, 45, 47, 129, 136

Zhao, D., and Strotmann, A. (2011a). Counting first, last, or all authors in citation analysis: A comprehensive comparison in the highly collaborative stem cell research field. *Journal of the American Society for Information Science and Technology*, 62(4), 654–676. DOI: 10.1002/asi.21495. 30, 36, 45, 49, 61, 63, 66, 73, 84, 89, 129

Zhao, D., and Strotmann, A. (2011b). Intellectual structure of stem cell research: A comprehensive author co-citation analysis of a highly collaborative and multidisciplinary field. *Scientometrics*, 87(1), 115–131. DOI: 10.1007/s11192-010-0317-2. 25, 26, 30, 49, 61, 63, 66, 73, 84, 129

Zhao, D., and Strotmann, A. (2014a). The knowledge base and research front of Information science 2006-2010: An author co-citation and bibliographic coupling analysis. *Journal of the Association for Information Science and Technology*, 65(5), 996–1006. 17, 18, 19, 23, 25, 26, 38, 48, 49, 52, 58, 62, 65, 92, 128, 129, 130, 138, 141

Zhao, D., and Strotmann, A. (2014b). In-text author citation analysis: Feasibility, benefits and limitations. *Journal of the Association for Information Science and Technology*, 65(11), 2348–2358. DOI: 10.1002/asi.23107. 15, 66, 89, 92

Zhu, X., Turney, P., Lemire, D., and Vellino, A. (2014). Measuring academic influence: Not all citations are equal. *Journal of the Association for Information Science and Technology*. Early view (DOI: 10.1002/asi.23179). 15, 91

Zitt, M. (2006). Scientometric indicators: A few challenges. Retrieved from http://eprints.rclis.org/6306/.

Zitt, M., and Bassecoulard, E. (2006). Delineating complex scientific fields by an hybrid lexical-citation method: An application to nanosciences. *Information Processing and Management* 42(6), 1513–1531. DOI: 10.1016/j.ipm/2006.03/016. 8, 61, 63, 64, 84

Author Biographies

Dangzhi Zhao is Associate Professor in the School of Library and Information Studies at the University of Alberta, Canada. Dangzhi earned her Ph.D. from the School of Library and Information Studies at The Florida State University, U.S., and her M.S. and B.S. from the Department of Library and Information Science at Peking University, China.

Her research and teaching interests are in the areas of information systems, bibliometrics, scholarly communication, and knowledge network analysis and visualization as well as their application in information retrieval and digital libraries.

Andreas Strotmann studied Mathematics, Physics, and Linguistics at the University of Cologne, where he also spent many years as a staff scientist supporting computational applications in the sciences and the humanities, including in mathematics, physics, biology, linguistics, education, and publishing. He earned his doctorate in Computer and Information Science from The Florida State University. He has worked as a researcher at the University of Cologne, the University of Alberta, and the GESIS Leibniz Institute for the Social Sciences. For the past decade, he has been working closely with Dangzhi Zhao on improving scientometric methodology.

Printed in the United States
by Baker & Taylor Publisher Services